THE
EVERYTHING.
MARIJUANA
BOOK

As a cannabis grower of thirty-five years, I have enjoyed writing this book. It made me think through many things that have long been on an intuitive level, and having to explain what I do has been a learning experience for me, too. I hope this book will be of use to the first time grower of cannabis. It is easy to feel intimidated about growing for the first time, especially with the wealth of detailed technical information that other growers are willing to throw at you.

Learning to grow is a lifelong experience and experiment; no one knows it all, and all growers are always learning. Start simply, ask questions, read, observe, research, and experience. You will learn, and your plants will grow. Eventually you will develop your own style and feel confidence in your garden knowledge, and your plants will grow even better. The most important step to being a grower is to start.

I also hope that you will be moved to question cannabis prohibition in the United States, and to support the growing movement toward legalization.

Sincerely,

Alicia Williamson

Welcome to the EVERYTHING® Series!

These handy, accessible books give you all you need to tackle a difficult project, gain a new hobby, comprehend a fascinating topic, prepare for an exam, or even brush up on something you learned back in school but have since forgotten.

You can choose to read an *Everything®* book from cover to cover or just pick out the information you want from our four useful boxes: e-questions, e-facts, e-alerts, and e-ssentials.

We give you everything you need to know on the subject, but throw in a lot of fun stuff along the way, too.

We now have more than 400 *Everything®* books in print, spanning such wide-ranging categories as weddings, pregnancy, cooking, music instruction, foreign language, crafts, pets, New Age, and so much more. When you're done reading them all, you can finally say you know *Everything®*!

QUESTION

Answers to
common questions

FACT

Important snippets
of information

ALERT

Urgent
warnings

ESSENTIAL

Quick
handy tips

PUBLISHER Karen Cooper

DIRECTOR OF ACQUISITIONS AND INNOVATION Paula Munier

MANAGING EDITOR, EVERYTHING® SERIES Lisa Laing

COPY CHIEF Casey Ebert

ASSISTANT PRODUCTION EDITOR Jacob Erickson

ACQUISITIONS EDITOR Katrina Schroeder

ASSOCIATE DEVELOPMENT EDITOR Hillary Thompson

EDITORIAL ASSISTANT Ross Weisman

EVERYTHING® SERIES COVER DESIGNER Erin Alexander

LAYOUT DESIGNERS Colleen Cunningham, Elisabeth Lariviere, Ashley Vierra, Denise Wallace

Visit the entire Everything® series at *www.everything.com*

THE EVERYTHING® MARIJUANA BOOK

Your complete cannabis resource, including history, growing instructions, and preparation

Alicia Williamson

Avon, Massachusetts

This book is dedicated to Fleep—
you're the one who started all this.

An Everything® Series Book.
Everything® and everything.com® are registered trademarks of F+W Media, Inc.

Published by Adams Media, a division of F+W Media, Inc.
57 Littlefield Street, Avon, MA 02322 U.S.A.
www.adamsmedia.com

ISBN 10: 1-4405-0687-6
ISBN 13: 978-1-4405-0687-1
eISBN 10: 1-4405-0688-4
eISBN 13: 978-1-4405-0688-8

Printed in the United States of America.

10 9 8 7 6 5 4 3 2 1

Library of Congress Cataloging-in-Publication Data
is available from the publisher.

Certain sections of this book deal with activities that would be in violation of various federal, state, and local laws if actually carried out. We do not advocate the breaking of any law. The authors, Adams Media, and F+W Media, Inc. do not accept liability for any injury, loss, legal consequence, or incidental or consequential damage incurred by reliance on the information or advice provided in this book. The information in this book is for entertainment purposes only.

The excerpts on pages 24–25 are from the essay "Mainstreaming Cannabis." Essay copyright © 2009 by Alicia Williamson. Essay originally published in *Citadel of the Spirit: Oregon's Sesquicentennial Anthology*, edited by Matt Love. Copyright © 2009 by Matt Love. Used with permission.

This publication is designed to provide accurate and authoritative information with regard to the subject matter covered. It is sold with the understanding that the publisher is not engaged in rendering legal, accounting, or other professional advice. If legal advice or other expert assistance is required, the services of a competent professional person should be sought.
—From a *Declaration of Principles* jointly adopted by a Committee of the American Bar Association and a Committee of Publishers and Associations

Many of the designations used by manufacturers and sellers to distinguish their products are claimed as trademarks. Where those designations appear in this book and Adams Media was aware of a trademark claim, the designations have been printed with initial capital letters.

This book is available at quantity discounts for bulk purchases.
For information, please call 1-800-289-0963.

Contents

Acknowledgments

I would like to acknowledge the contributions to this book made by Richard Bayer, MD. His medical cannabis expertise, wonderful capsule research, and recipe were invaluable.

I would also like to acknowledge Robert Connell Clarke. I first received a copy of his *Marijuana Botany* in 1981. His book opened my eyes to the world of cannabis breeding in an entirely new and exciting way, and for that I am very grateful.

And, finally, I would like to thank my dear husband, Richard Volkman, for doing all the farm chores for the last three months, and making me grilled cheese sandwiches to eat in front of my computer while I wrote.

The Top 10 Steps to Good Cannabis

1. Start with the best possible genetics and keep track of your propagation. If you produce something spectacular, you will want to know how you did it! Name the plants individually. Not only is it fun to do, but it's also a great memory aid for you, the plant breeder.

2. Always remember that this is an herb you will be putting into your body, either by eating or inhaling. Grow organically, and treat the plant with love and respect. You will notice the difference.

3. Take the time to observe your plants every day. You will be surprised by how much you can learn by watching and noticing details like color, size, and different responses to water or feedings. Make certain to take notes for review.

4. Start out with a small garden. Your first few gardens will be a learning experience, so keep it a fun one. You will be able to enjoy a larger garden with more confidence once you have a sense of what you are doing and a feel for the plants' life cycle and characteristics.

5. Grow what you personally like, but try out different strains. You will be putting quite a bit of work into your garden, but the end result should be quite individual and please you or a patient you grow for.

6. Learn about properly curing cannabis. The length of time required and the complex chemical changes in the plant will surprise you. Most commercial cannabis is not cured at all. It has been dried and is smokable, but it is not cured.

7. Read about cannabis. This is one of the most fascinating and complex plants you can grow, so the more you learn, the more interested you will become, and the better your plants will grow.

8. Always store your cannabis as carefully as you would any food or medicine. Periodic checks are ideal, and storage conditions are important to preserve the quality of the herb. You should also carefully think through your storage plan to avoid inadvertent consumption by children or pets.

9. Keep a light and happy heart while you work on your plants. Cannabis seems to respond to its caretaker's moods far more than any other plant. The plants will benefit, and you will, too.

10. Consider the ramifications of prohibition and why this plant has to be grown indoors in such an expensive process. The best and happiest place for plants is outdoors. Get involved in your local legalization movements and make sure you vote!

Introduction

THIS IS ACTUALLY A fairly simple book about a very complex subject. Cannabis is a plant, a political movement, a legal issue, an agricultural crop, a medical drug, and a recreational intoxicant all rolled into one.

All persons planning to grow cannabis should understand its history; no other plant has been so widely and unfairly maligned. The legal implications of using or propagating an illicit substance are important to grasp before you jump lightly into what American culture seems so confused about. Is using cannabis harmless and amusing? Has everyone tried it? How many use it daily? Is it a threat to national security and part of a plot to destroy the very fiber of our nation?

States like California and Oregon have had medical cannabis use for well over ten years, and the sky has not fallen. The government has not been overthrown, people still go to work, and the streets are not full of stoned teenagers; the dire predictions made by anti-cannabis advocates have not come true. The average American is ready to acknowledge that all the horror stories about cannabis are just that, stories.

And what about the money? What drives this war on cannabis? Could it be that there is a large financial incentive to keep cannabis illegal? The black market certainly has one. Prohibition has kept the price artificially high. Law enforcement has one, too. Billions of American tax dollars are spent on eradicating cannabis and prosecuting and incarcerating cannabis users and growers. The War on Drugs has become a war on the American people by their own government.

As legalization of cannabis in the United States finally appears to be closer to reality than it has ever been, growers and users of cannabis are becoming more outspoken and more organized in their efforts to end cannabis prohibition throughout the country. All of these activists deserve our thanks; secretly growing and using cannabis has its practical points, but until there is legalization, all cannabis lovers are at risk of being punished for growing or using a natural plant.

Lastly, the information contained in this book is the accumulation of many years of personal experience. Please keep in mind that others will have more to add and that new research will provide updated knowledge. The world medical community continues to explore and expand our understanding of how truly valuable cannabis is to humans, and horticulturists continue to find new ways to improve our ability to grow it.

Enjoy.

CHAPTER 1

What Is Cannabis?

Cannabis hemp is one of the most useful, beautiful, and botanically interesting plants that humans grow and use. It is hardy; grows on an annual and sustainable basis; actually improves agricultural soils; requires very little chemical assistance in order to grow bountifully and pest-free; and generously provides cultivators with fuel, fiber, medicine, food, and recreational pleasure. Cannabis can grow outdoors in every part of the United States. Unfortunately, cannabis is illegal to grow or possess in all forms in many, if not most, places in the United States.

An Overview

Before the twentieth century demonization and resulting criminalization of cannabis in the United States, Americans relied on cannabis grown in the U.S. for clothing, rope, fuel, nontoxic medicine, and as an intoxicant.

FACT

Hemp has a proud place in American history. The original Declaration of Independence was drafted on hemp paper. The first flag hand-sewn by Betsy Ross was made of cloth from American hemp. The original Levi's jeans were made of durable hemp, as were early American military uniforms. In 1850 there were more than 8,300 hemp farms in the United States. Source: *The Emperor Wears No Clothes* by Jack Herer.

Now many Americans use cannabis hemp products without even knowing they are doing so. These products usually come in the form of beautiful and durable fabrics and hemp food products legally imported from Canada or Europe. Cannabis hemp is a legal agricultural crop in Canada, whose government acknowledges that the hemp variation of cannabis is an extremely valuable agricultural crop. Hemp has no value at all to a recreational user since the psychoactive ingredient in recreational cannabis is found in very low amounts in its agricultural version.

American farmers are prohibited from growing hemp, and years of legal battles against the American federal government's restrictions on any sort of hemp propagation and production have yet to change that. The products created from industrial hemp outside of the United States can be legally imported, but the cultivation of the actual hemp to create the products remains illegal within U.S. borders.

Current Legal Battles

The legal struggles to propagate hemp continue today. Several states have legalized growing hemp, but agriculturists in those states haven't been able to take advantage of these new laws thanks to resistance from the federal Drug Enforcement Agency (DEA). The federal government itself typically drags its feet, makes counterarguments, and engages in diversionary arguments about the evils of marijuana whenever the topic arises. No legal hemp crop has been planted in any of the American states.

North Dakota fully legalized agricultural hemp propagation and cultivation in 2007, but not a seed has been germinated, planted, grown, or harvested as of the writing of this book. This is somewhat surprising since the legal efforts are funded by large North Dakota agricultural interests and not solely by the small, eccentric, alternative-type farmers you typically think of when discussing this product. Hemp production outside this country is big business, and American farmers would like to claim a portion of the world market share by growing and selling hemp.

Legalization versus Prohibition

Since California legalized the medical use of cannabis in 1996, multiple states have followed suit. This has created a confusing patchwork of legal zones in which some states practice zero tolerance while others have passed legalized medical use laws. For example, the medical cannabis patient who legally possesses the drug in Oregon will be considered a criminal as soon as he crosses state lines into Utah. No other medicine is treated with such a fragmented legal structure in this country. Imagine how complicated this can make things, especially for a patient on a medical cannabis regimen who travels out of state for treatment. In many states, medical cannabis users must also wrestle with providing their own medicine or with finding a grower to provide it for them for free. Why for free? Because reimbursement for cannabis is illegal. No other legal drug is treated or regulated this way.

What is so special about cannabis that people continue to battle for the freedom to possess and use it, despite severe penalties that are sometimes more far-reaching than punishments for almost any other crime?

Why is cannabis perceived as so evil and dangerous to the well-being of American citizens that the DEA and state and county law enforcement spends billions of American tax dollars to investigate, indict, prosecute, and incarcerate peaceful users and growers of what is, after all, an herb? According to the Federal Bureau of Investigation, a cannabis user is arrested every thirty-eight seconds in the United States.

Cannabis and American Society

How has the prohibition of cannabis affected the American way of life? The ramifications of these laws have certainly not been positive. Prohibition has caused untold harm to individuals' lives through arrests, forfeitures, incarceration, loss of custody of their children, denial of social benefits, the stigma of a felony, and coerced treatment for their perceived addiction to cannabis. Prohibition has deeply tarnished the public perception of law enforcement as citizens and taxpayers start to recognize the self-serving and self-perpetuating nature of the War on Drugs. Prohibition of cannabis has caused billions of tax dollars to be spent enforcing these laws, and is the direct reason for the loss of valuable medical and industrial research in the United States. Cannabis itself has been extremely beneficial to many people over the years, continuing to provide medicine, durable fiber, and for many users, if not most, cannabis provides a much safer and more pleasurable intoxicant alternative to alcohol.

The unreasonableness of cannabis prohibition is its own greatest weakness. Americans today seem to tolerate a certain amount of illogical thinking and outright lying by the United States Government, but the war on cannabis is so unnecessary and unwarranted that the false structure of prohibition is rapidly breaking down. The Obama Administration has finally acknowledged a state's right to make its own laws regarding cannabis propagation, use, and possession.

Despite the last sixty years and immense amounts of government resources and force used against cannabis, its users, and growers, it remains in the U.S. and is more prevalent and of better quality than ever before. Prohibition continues to fail while remaining a misguided waste of time, energy, and dollars.

Cannabis's Many Benefits

Why would people risk their freedom for a plant? Many take the risk to use it recreationally, but many also risk to propagate it lovingly; sometimes at great financial expense. It can be explained in part by the high profits to be made due to prohibition, but long time growers of cannabis love and name their plants almost like pets or children. It is not just the end product that engages, but the living plant itself. Why? Unless you have grown cannabis, this fascination is hard to explain, but in part it has to do with how complex and responsive the plant is to the grower. The sheer beauty and variety of the genus, and the potential for mind-altering qualities are key attributes that humans seek out and breed for.

Medical users see cannabis as a beneficial, nontoxic gift from nature. Not only does cannabis provide symptom relief for a broad spectrum of illnesses, but ongoing research in Europe is proving that cannabis actually has curative and preventative medical benefits as well. Unlike many government-approved pharmaceuticals, even those freely available as over the counter drugs, cannabis has no potential for liver damage, or any negative physical side effects at all. Why would a government deny its citizens access to one of the least harmful natural substances known to mankind?

No other plant cultivated by humans has such a baffling, long, and contentious political and legal history. Many of the mysteries and benefits of cannabis are just now starting to be revealed; an end to prohibition would accelerate our knowledge and help us understand just how valuable the plant can be in many scientific areas. Early data from European scientists with more access to cannabis for research purposes have shown that cannabis has the potential to cure cancer and not just manage symptoms. Researchers at the Project on Cellular and Molecular Biology and Gene Therapy, located in Madrid, Spain, in conjunction with a long list of universities and hospitals that participated in the project, reported: "Ongoing research is determining whether cannabinoid ligands may be effective agents in the treatment of, for example, pain and inflammation, neurodegenerative disorders such as multiple sclerosis and Parkinson's disease, and the wasting and emesis associated with AIDS and cancer chemotherapy. In addition, cannabinoids may be potential antitumoral agents owing to their ability to induce the regression of various types of tumors, including lung adenocarcinoma, glioma, and thyroid epithelioma in animal models."

And, said in conclusion:

"In any event, the present report, together with the implication of CB_2- or CB_2-like receptors in the control of peripheral pain and inflammation, opens the attractive possibility of finding cannabinoid-based therapeutic strategies for diseases of the skin and other tissues devoid of nondesired CB_1-mediated psychotropic side effects." Source: *The Journal of Clinical Investigation*, Research Article: *Inhibition of skin tumor growth and angiogenesis in vivo by activation of cannabinoid receptors*

Many such studies exist in scientific literature, and are ongoing as scientists explore the potential in cannabis.

The moderate long-term use of cannabis is associated with a reduced risk of head and neck cancer, according to the results of a population-based control study. The authors reported: "After adjusting for potential confounders (including smoking and alcohol drinking), ten to twenty years of marijuana use was associated with a significantly reduced risk of head and neck squamous cell carcinoma." Source: August 2009 *Cancer Prevention Research*.

Medical research centers in the United States could benefit from access to cannabis for research, and various universities have filed suits against the DEA to allow cannabis for research purposes. To date, though, cannabis is still deemed "too dangerous" for serious scientists to have access.

Botanical Definition

Cannabis, frequently referred to as marijuana, is an exceptionally beautiful tall herb. Even amongst botanists, cannabis confounds one set description. Most today agree that the plant's genus is *Cannabis* and at least three distinct species (*sativa*, *indica*, and *ruderalis*) exist. According to an alternative classification, however, the genus has only one highly variable species, *Cannabis sativa*, with two subspecies, *indica* and *ruderalis*.

Cannabis as an ornamental plant alone is striking: the elegant leaf structures and sheer size of the plant are impressive. The aromatic qualities of the flowers are intense and very distinctive; sativas are more likely to have a pleasing sweet, flower-like scent, while indicas can be so musky and strong that the common term for their scent is "skunk."

For clarity, the herb referred to herein will generally be pure sativa, a pure indica, or a hybrid cross of the two. Ruderalis has very little THC content, but flowers in a very short cycle; its only possible use is in the hands of a skilled breeder to introduce the short cycle trait to a line. Hemp is also considered to be cannabis, but it is produced for fuel and fiber and lacks high tetrahydrocannabinol (THC) content, and is therefore differentiated from the medical or recreational types and their propagation, as described later in this book.

Cannabis Varieties and Their Properties

Musicians and artists have known for centuries that ingesting cannabis can unleash their creative sides. Physicians knew and respected its medicinal qualities, and people in general (sensation-seeking creatures that we are) have always appreciated its properties as an intoxicant.

Early humans valued cannabis and carried it for propagation to varying corners of the world. A strong and adaptable annual plant, cannabis could be quickly bred to adjust to different climates and varying growing seasons.

FACT

In 1533, King Henry VIII issued a royal proclamation that imposed a fine on any farmer that refused to participate in hemp production. The proclamation commanded a quarter acre of hemp production per sixty acres of arable land. Large amounts of hemp were needed for the navy to rig a Tudor man-of-war (it is estimated eighty tons were required to provide enough hemp for the sails and lines for one of England's massive war ships). Elizabeth I later increased this fine. The decree was finally repealed in 1593.

Due to the wonderful variety of strains within species, cannabis breeders today can work to emphasize desirable characteristics for whatever use they wish. These characteristics can vary depending on a user's needs. New greenhouse technologies allow indoor growers to fix hybrid strains in five generations of twelve weeks each. In other words, cannabis qualities can be manipulated now on a greatly accelerated timeframe, allowing hybridizers to move ever quicker toward their ideal strain. Hybridizing sativas and indicas can produce many variations on the observable effects of cannabis. Typically, breeders of medical cannabis tend to weight the genetics toward indicas, while breeders of high-end recreational cannabis aim for the more psychoactive properties.

A Precise Science

Propagators of cannabis do not just throw random seeds into the ground, any more than a vineyard owner would throw a few grape pips on the soil and call the output high-quality. The usual practice entails a careful analysis of different strains or types and their unique qualities before beginning to grow.

Growers breed and grow for very specific purposes in the twenty-first century. In general, indicas are more medical in their effects: they relax muscle spasms, induce restful sleep, stimulate appetite, and tend to create a calm, relaxed state of mind that users sometimes refer to as being "stoned." Sativas are more cerebral, or psychoactive, and produce what is commonly known as a "high" that has more potential for connecting with the user's creative energies. Sativas are also used medically, but the more common medical use for sativas is generally for conditions such as depression and anxiety.

Experimentation for Patient Relief

A good cross of sativa and indica can create a strain that can change the lives of patients with a chronic illness. For example, exchanging an opiate like morphine for a hybrid cannabis strain that relieves muscle spasms and eases depression will generally make for a much happier quality of life. One benefit of the adaptable nature of cannabis is that a propagator can work with a patient's feedback and linebreed a strain that is very specific to the individual patient's symptom relief.

Some patients have what they call "daytime" strains that provide pain relief but allow the patient to remain alert and functional, and then a "nighttime" strain that is more relaxing and helps with sleep. All cannabis is not alike; a certain amount of experimentation and dialogue between propagator and patient are usually required to match the right cannabis to the patient's needs.

All this experimentation and the patient's control over types and dosages may sound risky, and it's true that cannabis is a drug. But, animal tests have proven that extremely high doses of the active ingredients in cannabis (cannabinoids) are needed to have lethal effect. The ratio of the amount of cannabinoids necessary to intoxicate versus the amount required to make a dose lethal is 1 to 40,000. To achieve a lethal overdose, you would have to consume 40,000 times more cannabis than you needed to achieve intoxication. To help put this in perspective, note that the ratio for alcohol varies between 1 to 4 and 1 to 10.

Even if you were for some reason determined to overdose, you would be hard pressed to afford or assemble that much cannabis, let alone to try to consume it. Unlike the mortality track record for FDA approved prescription and over the counter pharmaceuticals, no one has ever died from an overdose of cannabis.

THC and Its Effects

Probably everyone has heard the initials THC in discussions of cannabis and its relationship to psychoactive properties. Although THC is very important (it is estimated that 70 to 100 percent of the marijuana high results from THC), as with anything to do with cannabis, the intoxicant effect is more complex than originally thought. Part of how THC works has to do with how it reacts with other chemical properties in the plant.

THC is a shorthand way to say "delta 9-trans-tetrahydrocannabinol." It is regarded as the main psychotomimetic, or intoxicating, ingredient of cannabis. It occurs in all cannabis to some degree, in concentrations that vary from trace amounts in commercial hemp to 30 percent in very potent recreational strains. THC and other cannabinoids are produced significantly in only one place on the cannabis plant: inside the heads of the trichomes, or the resin glands found on the flowers and the small leaves near the flowers called sugar leaves. The sugar leaf is so named because it usually has enough trichomes to sparkle like sugar crystals, and effects users who ingest it, either by smoking or eating the prepared leaf.

Some cannabis is considered more potent than others, regardless of how much THC is present in the plant. The reasons for this are not fully known, partly because current research suggests that cannabis has far more distinctly different cannabinoids than originally suspected. Some have been identified, but not all. This lack of knowledge about cannabinoid interactions is mostly due to cannabis's ill-deserved illicit status. Too few clinical studies with known combinations of multiple cannabinoids have been undertaken with human subjects, although Europe has been making great strides in this direction.

Other Cannabinoids and Their Properties

Currently, there are sixty-six identified cannabinoids, the class of compounds known to exist only in the cannabis plant. Although American research into the effects of cannabinoids is significantly impacted by the lack of legal availability of cannabis, a few of these compounds have been more widely studied than others.

ESSENTIAL

Unlocking the pharmacological secrets of cannabis relies on scientific understanding of the active ingredients of a chemically distinct family of interrelated molecules. Of the known cannabinoids, there are twelve categorical types: Cannabigerol (CBG), Cannabichomene (CBC), Cannabidiol (CBD), D9-Tetrahydrocannabinol (D9-THC), D8-Tetrahydrocannabinol (D8-THC), Cannabicycol (CBL), Cannabielsoin (CBE), Cannabinol (CBN), Cannabinodiol (CBND), Cannabitriol (CBT), Miscellaneous Types, and Other Cannabinoids.

CBN, or cannabinol, is produced by the oxidation degradation of THC. It is suspected of increasing the power of certain aspects of what recreational users call the high, but probably is more desirable in high quantities only for medical use where it can help treat sleep disorders. Recreational users are more likely to use cannabis for euphoric effect, and cannabis with high CBN is generally reported to make the user more drowsy than high.

THC and cannabidiol (CBD) are the two most abundant naturally occurring cannabinoids in marijuana. CBD has sedative, analgesic, and antibiotic properties, and can induce a psychoactive effect by interacting with THC. Different blends of cannabinoids account for the varying psychoactive effects produced by distinct strains of cannabis. In general, cannabis users now use the term "potency" to describe the sum effects of the cannabinoids and the overall effects induced, not just THC levels.

Cannabinoids and Medical Uses

Although using cannabis to treat the symptoms (including nausea and pain) of disease is fairly well entrenched in the public consciousness, scientists are currently investigating cannabinoids' capacity to moderate autoimmune disorders like multiple sclerosis and rheumatoid arthritis, as well as neurological diseases like Lou Gehrig's Disease and Alzheimer's.

According to studies published in *The Lancet Oncology* and *Endocrinology* regarding the anti-cancer benefits of cannabis, cannabinoids can reduce the spread of specific cancer cells, among others. These are significant and exciting applications for cannabinoids that more American researchers would like to study. An example of how scientists are frustrated in their requests for access to study cannabis has been the experience of Ethan Russo, MD. Beginning in 1997, Russo, a leading cannabinoid researcher, submitted three protocols for research on cannabis for treating migraines. According to a 1999 letter from Russo to the DEA, Public Health Service denied Russo's protocol despite its being approved by the FDA and Russo's institutional review board earlier that year. In the hearing, the DEA said that Russo was not registered by the administration to conduct cannabis research.

Another researcher, Lyle E. Craker, PhD, a professor of plant and soil sciences at the University of Massachusetts-Amherst, applied directly to DEA in 2001 to be a private cultivator of cannabis for medicinal research. Craker's research interest is directed toward the control of mechanisms regulating essential oil synthesis and composition of several herbs. His interest is in the effect of light and environmental stress on physiology and biochemistry of herbs and other plants, especially as related to increasing production and quality of plant extracts. His action was based on the Controlled Substances Act's (CSA) provision that the DEA shall register manufacturers of Schedule I controlled substances if it is in the public interest and in accordance with international treaties. When the DEA had not responded after three years, Craker sued the administration for the lengthy delay. On February 12, 2007, DEA Administrative Law Judge Mary Ellen Bittner recommended that the application be granted. On Jan. 7, 2009, DEA Deputy Administrator Michele Leonhart issued a final ruling rejecting Craker's petition.

More than 17,000 papers on the subject have been published in worldwide scientific literature, but unfortunately the United States DEA remains adamant in its stance that cannabis has "no accepted medical use."

Terpenes and Their Functions

Terpenes are a large and varied class of hydrocarbons, produced primarily by plants, like conifers, and insects, though the latter is rare. The name terpene is derived from the word turpentine, which smells like conifer trees. Aromatic kitchen herbs like rosemary contain a particular terpene profile that gives them a distinctive flavor and aroma, as does the herb cannabis.

FACT

The Green House Seed Company has started a breeding revolution by providing customers and anyone interested with terpenes profiles of the resin of all its strains. The 2008–2009 seed catalogue contains an example of this analysis, and the Green House Seed Company website has the updated profiles for all strains.

Terpenes function as smell and taste molecules and are the major components of plant resin. The most prevalent terpene in cannabis sativa is known as Myrcene. It is also present in high amounts in mangos, hops, lemon grass, and flowering plants like verbena and mercia. The complexity and variety of cannabis plants allows for great variety in how the terpenes express themselves; cannabis breeders have an almost endless palette of aroma and tastes to breed from and elaborate on.

The Importance of Trichomes

Trichomes are tiny outgrowths of resin that form on the flower and sugar leaves of the cannabis plant. Although the plant is primarily using this resin to protect itself and its seeds from the environmental dangers, it is also this resin that contains the euphoric properties so attractive to humans.

The trichome's adhesive resin forms a protective layer against destructive insects, prevents seed desiccation, and inhibits some types of fungal disease. Trichomes also help the plant by acting as a sunscreen that protects against UV-B light, and help the plant stay cooler in the hot sun. Some claim that the resin makes cannabis less palatable to animals. This may be true for some types of mammals, but hungry deer, elk, wild pigs, goats, and some-times dogs all enjoy eating cannabis and will do so at every opportunity.

Trichomes can come in as many shapes and sizes as there are strains of cannabis. Heavy trichome production is not necessarily an indication of a potent plant; the resins may not hold the THC and other cannabinoids needed for psychoactive effect.

ALERT

The trichome's THC level and cannabinoid ratios can change depending on environmental conditions. Although the genetics of the plant may be superior, part of the quality will be determined by environmental conditions. These include light, temperatures, humidity levels, and nutrition.

Growers, particularly outdoor growers, use trichomes as indicators of when to harvest their cannabis. Trichomes are very small, so they must be monitored daily, using a jeweler's loupe, near harvest time. The most desired coloration of the resin will initially be almost clear or only slightly amber. THC levels peak and begin to degrade soon after this coloring is achieved. If growers wait much longer to harvest the plant, the trichomes will darken and the psychoactive effect will be weaker, so cultivators must time their harvest very carefully while watching the trichomes.

For survival of the cannabis plant overall, perhaps the most beneficial aspect of trichomes has been their role in the seduction of humans. People have valued and propagated cannabis worldwide for centuries primarily for its recreational use, with medical or industrial purposes taking a back seat. Humans continue to breed many variations into cannabis and spread different strains all over the planet, both activities that will guarantee the widespread survival of this wonderful and versatile plant.

CHAPTER 2

A Brief Political History of Cannabis in the United States

Cannabis is not heroin. It is a non-addictive, benign, and frequently beneficial herb. No one has ever overdosed on cannabis, either by eating or smoking it. In our modern times, the most common social perception is that cannabis can make the user friendly, calm, apt to laugh, and probably craving chocolate. So where does the fear come into it? Why the draconian laws prohibiting a plant?

How Cannabis Became Illegal

"The motion picture you are about to witness may startle you. It would not have been possible, otherwise, to sufficiently emphasize the frightful toll of the new drug menace which is destroying the youth of America in alarmingly increasing numbers.

Marihuana is that drug—a violent narcotic—an unspeakable scourge—The Real Public Enemy Number One! Its first effect is sudden, violent, uncontrollable laughter; then come dangerous hallucinations—space expands—time slows down, almost stands still . . . fixed ideas come next, conjuring up monstrous extravagances—followed by emotional disturbances, the total inability to direct thoughts, the loss of all power to resist physical emotions . . . leading finally to acts of shocking violence . . . ending often in incurable insanity." (Introductory crawl from *Reefer Madness*, 1936 anti-cannabis propaganda film)

Now that you've read the above, and have hopefully stopped laughing, you should know that the year 1936 is significant; why would a versatile and widely used plant suddenly become so maligned, and eventually prohibited in the United States? Beginning in 1935, and meeting in secret, the Treasury Department had drafted new tax laws; the significant one in this story being an "occupational excise tax upon dealers, and a transfer tax upon dealings in marijuana." A "marihuana" tax bill was introduced to the House Ways and Means Committee on April 14, 1937.

The Legal Years

Americans relied heavily on cannabis beginning as early as the 1680s. They were so dependent on the plant that, in 1762, Virginia imposed penalties upon farmers who chose not to grow hemp. Early Americans used cannabis hemp for rope, cloth, paper, food, animal fodder, and medicine.

Cannabis extracts and tinctures were widely used in medicines for both humans and livestock. Unfortunately, medical research into the properties of cannabis slowed, if not completely stopped, with the invention of the hypodermic syringe in the 1850s. Syringes allowed soluble drugs to be injected for fast pain relief and medicine delivery. Hemp products are insoluble in water, and therefore not easily administered by injection, so they fell out of favor.

The nineteenth century industrial revolution set the stage for large-scale utilization of hemp. Prior to late nineteenth and early twentieth century industrial innovations, hemp still lacked efficient harvesting and processing machines needed for mass production.

In 1916, United States Department of Agriculture Bulletin 404 announced that such machines were now in development, and predicted that hemp would become the United States' largest agricultural industry. One acre of cannabis hemp, in annual rotation over a twenty-year period, would produce as much pulp for paper as 4.1 acres of trees cut over the same twenty-year period.

FACT

If the hemp pulp paper process of 1916 were in use today, it could replace 40–70 percent of all pulp paper, including corrugated boxes, computer printout paper, and paper bags.

The Bulletin also reported that the amount of sulfur-based chemicals needed to complete the hemp pulping process would be only one quarter the amount of chemicals needed for the tree pulping process. The wood pulping process uses chlorine bleach (causing dioxin contamination of rivers), while hemp pulping employs the safer hydrogen peroxide in the bleaching process. Sounds like a win-win, doesn't it?

By 1938, *Popular Mechanics* and *Mechanical Engineering* magazines were on the cannabis bandwagon, projecting billions in income using hemp for pulp paper. As early as 1916, hemp pulp technology for papermaking had already been invented by scientists employed by the U.S. Department of Agriculture.

In early 1937, cannabis was still legal to grow. In the same year, DuPont patented processes for making plastics from oil and coal, as well as a new sulfate/sulfite process for making paper from wood pulp. At the time, DuPont's chief financial backer was Andrew Mellon of the Mellon Bank of Pittsburgh, an extremely rich and powerful man who also served as President Herbert Hoover's Secretary of the Treasury.

In the mid-1930s, the new mechanical hemp fiber machines were available and on their way to becoming an affordable reality. DuPont, the timber barons who owned thousands of acres of trees, and wood paper pulp manufacturers like the Hearst Paper Manufacturing Division seemingly woke up to the fact that large-scale commercial production of hemp was a threat to their riches.

The Prohibitionists

William Randolph Hearst began an almost nonstop campaign against cannabis, greatly aided by both his tremendous wealth and his ownership of a chain of newspapers. Headlines published in his newspapers and tied to Harry J. Anslinger portrayed African Americans and Mexicans as vicious marijuana smoking criminals.

ALERT

If hemp had not been made illegal, 80 percent of DuPont's business would never have materialized, preventing the great majority of the pollution that has poisoned our Northwestern and Southeastern rivers.

According to Hearst-owned newspapers, jazz music and "marihuana" supposedly led persons of color to "disrespect" whites (disrespect could apparently include looking a white person in the eye or even laughing at him), and to rape white women. Hearst's headlines also changed the American perception of a plant called "cannabis hemp." What was thought of as a useful and benign plant became a strange, foreign substance called "marihuana" that was worthy of the public's fear.

In 1931, Mellon, in his capacity as Secretary of the Treasury, appointed Anslinger to head up the Federal Bureau of Narcotics (which later became the United States' current Drug Enforcement Administration). This was a cozy family arrangement since Anslinger had married Mellon's niece, Martha Denniston, in 1917. Prior to 1931, Anslinger had been the Assistant U.S. Commissioner for Prohibition.

In 1937, Anslinger testified before Congress saying, "Marijuana is the most violence-causing drug in the history of mankind." Anslinger would rule the bureau for the next thirty-one years.

The Swindle

Now that the players were in place, the stage was set to continue the demonization of cannabis and proceed with the eradication of hemp. Secret meetings on this subject began in 1935, and the Treasury Department drafted new tax laws; the most significant being an "occupational excise tax upon dealers, and a transfer tax upon dealings in marijuana." A "marihuana" tax bill was introduced to the House Ways and Means Committee on April 14, 1937.

FACT

In 1937, William G. Woodward, MD, a physician and an attorney for the American Medical Association, testified on behalf of the AMA against the prohibition of cannabis. He protested, "We cannot understand . . . why this [marijuana] bill should have been prepared in secret for two years." He and the AMA were quickly denounced by Anslinger and the entire congressional committee. Later in the hearing it was asked, "Did anyone consult with the AMA and get their opinion?" Representative Vinson replied, "Yes, we have . . . and they are in complete agreement." Source: *The Marijuana Conviction*, University of Virginia Press.

Importers, manufacturers, sellers, and distributors were required to register with the Secretary of the Treasury and pay the occupational tax. Transfers were taxed at $1 an ounce; $100 an ounce if the dealer was unregistered. The new tax doubled the price of the legal "raw drug" cannabis, which at the time sold for $1 an ounce.

Ways and Means Chairman Robert L. Doughton, a key DuPont ally, quickly rubber-stamped the secret Treasury bill, and despite objections from the American Medical Association (one of which dealt with the secret preparation of the bill), it was sent through Congress to the President for signature.

Almost no one in America (other than a few rich industrialists, their friends, and their friends in the government) knew that cannabis hemp was being outlawed by taxation. The use of the word "marihuana" for cannabis hemp was rather clever since proponents of cannabis might have testified before the committee, but no one was really alerted to stand up for a strange Mexican drug called "marihuana." The American Medical

Association became aware of the bill very late in the process; its sole representative was treated derisively by the committee when he testified positively about cannabis.

The bill passed and became law in December of 1937. Anslinger assiduously fanned the flames of marijuana mania, and while he never managed to get a federal ban on cannabis (this was achieved by the Controlled Substances Act, called the CSA, of 1970), by 1937 anti-cannabis laws of some type existed in every state of the union.

The Struggle

In 1938, New York Mayor Fiorello LaGuardia appointed a scientific committee to study marijuana use in New York City. The committee included pharmacologists, public health experts, and psychiatrists, as well as the director of the Division of Psychiatry of the Department of Hospitals. The committee presented its findings in 1944.

Despite the tax act proponents and the Hearst newspaper empire's lurid claims about cannabis, the committee found "no proof that major crime was associated with marijuana or that it caused aggressive or antisocial behavior; marihuana was not sexually over stimulating and did not change personality; there was no evidence of acquired tolerance." "The Marihuana Problem in the City of New York" is commonly known as "The LaGuardia Report."

Although cannabis was removed from the United States Pharmacopoeia and National Formulary in 1941, *The American Journal of Psychiatry* published "The Psychiatric Aspects of Marijuana Intoxication" in 1942. This study noted "habituation to cannabis is not as strong as habituation to tobacco or alcohol."

In December of the same year, an editorial in *The Journal of the American Medical Association* (JAMA) mentioned the possible therapeutic benefits of using cannabis to treat appetite loss, depression, and even opiate addiction.

This enraged Bureau of Narcotics Director Harry Anslinger, who denounced the LaGuardia report in a scathing letter that JAMA published in 1943. More pressure on the JAMA followed, this time coming from the Narcotics Commission of the League of Nations.

By 1945, the JAMA fell into line with the Federal Bureau of Narcotics, and, in a Journal editorial, dismissed the LaGuardia report as built on a "thoroughly unscientific foundation."

ESSENTIAL

"It is important to note that neither the ingestion of marihuana nor the smoking of marihuana cigarettes affects the basic outlook of the individual except in a very few instances and to a very slight degree. In general the subjects who are withdrawn and introversive stay that way, those who are outgoing remain so, and so on. Where changes occur the shift is so slight as to be negligible. In other words reactions which are natively alien to the individual cannot be induced by the ingestion or smoking of the drug." Source: Summary from "The LaGuardia Report"

Parts of the editorial almost seem written by Anslinger. In reference to the LaGuardia report's finding ". . . that the use of this narcotic does not lead to physical, mental or moral degeneration and that permanent deleterious effects from its continued use were not observed," the JAMA editorial asserts, "This statement has already done great damage to the cause of law enforcement. Public officials will do well to disregard this unscientific, uncritical study, and continue to regard marihuana as a menace wherever it is purveyed."

For sixty-three years the JAMA opinion has bolstered the position of federal law enforcement and helped the DEA squash attempts to reschedule cannabis. There is a catch-22 here that prevents further examination of the issue. No studies on the medical benefits of cannabis exist, yet the Schedule I designation prevents scientists and researchers legal access to cannabis for study.

Legalization Movements in the United States

Just as cannabis has a variety of uses—medical, industrial, and recreational—there are proponents for the legalization of all three. As the movement to regain access has gained traction, each specialized area continues to petition the DEA.

Medical

The most visible and well-supported efforts are in the medical cannabis arena. Compassionate use, or providing access to drugs prior to FDA approval, is perhaps the most understandable to a non–cannabis user.

In November 2009, the AMA urged the federal government to reconsider its classification of cannabis. The oldest national doctors' group has said cannabis should be classified as a medicine and made available for more cannabinoid drug development research and clinical trials. Thanks to the reputations of the people involved in this effort, this was a major setback for cannabis prohibitionists. In addition, the AMA's previously negative position had provided the dominant medical opinion. The DEA has rejected every effort to reschedule cannabis, despite the growing number of states allowing the medical use of cannabis. The following is from the DEA 2010 website, and defines Schedule 1 (where cannabis is listed as "marijuana"). For comparative reasons, included are the definitions for Schedule II drugs:

SCHEDULE I
- The drug or other substance has a high potential for abuse.
- The drug or other substance has no currently accepted medical use in treatment in the United States.
- There is a lack of accepted safety for use of the drug or other substance under medical supervision.
- Examples of Schedule I substances include heroin, lysergic acid diethylamide (LSD), marijuana, and methaqualone.

SCHEDULE II
- The drug or other substance has a high potential for abuse.
- The drug or other substance has a currently accepted medical use in treatment in the United States or a currently accepted medical use with severe restrictions.
- Abuse of the drug or other substance may lead to severe psychological or physical dependence.
- Examples of Schedule II substances include morphine, phencyclidine (PCP), cocaine, methadone, and methamphetamine.

Note that the DEA considers cannabis (marijuana) to be a "drug or other substance [that] has no currently accepted medical use in treatment in the United States." This is a case of the federal law enforcement's opinion overriding the 250,000-member American Medical Association, despite the overwhelming evidence that cannabis does have proven medical benefits and is currently approved for medical possession and use by fourteen states of the Union.

The DEA has blocked universities and medical centers from studying cannabis, despite numerous applications for access to cannabis for study. By doing so, the DEA is able to maintain a stance that cannabis "has no currently accepted medical use." Since qualified medical studies would prove this to be completely untrue, the DEA denies researchers access to the plant.

It is also interesting to note that, for more than forty years, the University of Mississippi has had an exclusive contract with the National Institute on Drug Abuse (NIDA) to produce cannabis. The cannabis grown under federal contract is for patients who receive free federal cannabis as part of an Investigational New Drug program started in 1978. The first Bush Administration closed the program to all new applicants in 1992 after being flooded with applications from suffering AIDS patients.

FACT

The U.S. Department of Health and Human Services updated its medical marijuana policy on December 1, 1999. The IND program would not be reopened. The program remains in operation only for the six surviving previously approved patients.

Medical cannabis may be available for research soon, however. After lobbying by Americans for Safe Access, a pro-medical cannabis group, sixteen members of Congress sent a letter to Attorney General Eric Holder urging the DEA to act "swiftly to amend or withdraw" an order that significantly curtails medical marijuana research in the United States.

Just seven months after the DEA again rejected a judge's recommendation that a university be granted a license to grow research cannabis, a 2009 federal "Request for Proposals" has been issued for the production and distribution of cannabis.

States' Rights

Oregon was the first American state to decriminalize the possession of marijuana. Under Governor Tom McCall in 1973, the sentence for possession of less than an ounce became akin to receiving a traffic ticket.

In 1979, the Oregon Legislature passed a law requiring state police to turn over cannabis seized in drug raids for distribution to people suffering from glaucoma or undergoing chemotherapy. This was later repealed, as it proved unworkable.

Francis L. Young, an administrative law judge with the DEA, declared in 1988 "in its natural form, (cannabis) is one of the safest therapeutically active substances known."

Despite this earlier progress, on July 3, 1997, Oregon Governor John Kitzhaber signed House Bill 3643 to recriminalize the possession of less than one ounce of marijuana. Kitzhaber explained:

The difficult question raised by this legislation . . . is the delicate balance between the public safety of our society at large and the civil liberties of it's individual citizens . . . I am willing to give this legislation the benefit of the doubt, but I will direct the Criminal Justice Commission to closely monitor how it is being implemented and what effect it is having . . . . If . . . the measure proves to be ineffective—or if it is used for such purposes as harassment rather than for legitimate law enforcement objectives—then it should be repealed and we should return to current law.

To a staunch believer in the Fourth Amendment, the rest of the Governor's statement was less than reassuring:

Furthermore, the fact that most cases under this new law will still be treated as violations rather than as misdemeanors, leads me to believe that this measure has less to do with the possession of marijuana as it does with expanding the powers of search and seizure.

The Governor admitted that he was unsure of his actions when he signed the measure:

I have taken this action after much deliberation and with a good deal of reluctance. On one hand, at a time when juvenile drug use is a growing problem, it is important to reinforce our message to young people that the possession of drugs is against the law. On the other hand, based on discussions with law enforcement officials, it is estimated that approximately 80 percent of the cases will continue to be treated as violations. Thus, while a major symbolic change in our law, I believe that the individual impact of this legislation will be marginal.

The Governor's belief that expanded powers of search and seizure would have only "marginal impact on individuals" allowed him to sign the bill into Oregon law.

Legalizing Medical Marijuana

Only a year after Oregon Governor John Kitzhaber signed House Bill 3643, law enforcement's expanded search and seizure powers received a major setback from Oregon voters. This blow came when 1998's Ballot Measure 67, known as the Oregon Medical Marijuana Act, passed by a margin of 54.6 percent to 45.4 percent.

Although Federal prohibitions still apply and are frequently enforced, the following states have legally approved cannabis for medical use by their citizens. Each state has different laws; some allow only an "affirmative defense" for medical need, while others go much further and even mandate dispensary programs for patient access. The list includes the year these laws passed.

- Alaska (1999)
- California (1996)
- Colorado (2001)
- Hawaii (2000)
- Maine (1999)
- Michigan (2003)
- Montana (2004)
- Nevada (2000)
- New Jersey (2010)

- New Mexico (2007)
- Oregon (1998)
- Rhode Island (2006)
- Vermont (2004)
- Washington (1998)
- District of Columbia (1998)

State by state, Americans are voting for access to medical cannabis. More conservative areas of the country are finally proposing new laws as the public wakes up to the idea that cannabis is actually a relatively benign and useful herbal source of medicine. Educational efforts by pro-cannabis groups are showing Americans the enormous costs associated with prohibition, and the self-perpetuating nature of the War on Drugs.

Medical use states received some acknowledgment from the federal government in October 2009 when Attorney General Eric Holder announced formal guidelines for federal prosecutors in states that have enacted laws authorizing the use of cannabis for medical purposes. Those guidelines were contained in the following memo from Deputy Attorney General David W. Ogden, which was sent to United States Attorneys

October 19, 2009

MEMORANDUM FOR SELECTED UNITED STATES ATTORNEYS

FROM: David W. Ogden, Deputy Attorney General

SUBJECT: Investigations and Prosecutions in States Authorizing the Medical Use of Marijuana

This memorandum provides clarification and guidance to federal prosecutors in States that have enacted laws authorizing the medical use of marijuana . . .

The Department of Justice is . . . committed to making efficient and rational use of its limited investigative and prosecutorial resources . . .

The prosecution of significant traffickers of illegal drugs, including marijuana, and the disruption of illegal drug manufacturing and trafficking networks continues to be a core priority in the Department's efforts against narcotics and dangerous drugs, and the Department's investigative and prosecutorial resources should be directed toward these objectives. As a general matter, pursuit of these priorities should not focus federal resources in your States on individuals whose actions are in clear and unambiguous compliance with existing state laws providing for the medical use of marijuana. For example, prosecution of individuals with cancer or other serious illnesses who use marijuana as part of a recommended treatment regimen consistent with applicable state law, or those caregivers in clear and unambiguous compliance with existing state law who provide such individuals with marijuana, is unlikely to be an efficient use of limited federal resources . . .

Of course, no State can authorize violations of federal law . . . . Accordingly, in prosecutions under the Controlled Substances Act, federal prosecutors are not expected to charge, prove, or otherwise establish any state law violations. Indeed, this memorandum does not alter in any way the Department's authority to enforce federal law, including laws prohibiting the manufacture, production, distribution, possession, or use of marijuana on federal property. This guidance regarding resource allocation does not "legalize" marijuana or provide a legal defense to a violation of federal law, nor is it intended to create any privileges, benefits, or rights, substantive or procedural, enforceable by any individual, party or witness in any administrative, civil, or criminal matter. Nor does clear and unambiguous compliance with state law . . . create a legal defense to a violation of the Controlled Substances Act. Rather, this memorandum is intended solely as a guide to the exercise of investigative and prosecutorial discretion.

Finally, nothing herein precludes investigation or prosecution where there is a reasonable basis to believe that compliance with state law is being invoked as a pretext for the production or distribution of marijuana for purposes not authorized by state law . . .

cc: All United States Attorneys

Source: The United States Department of Justice (*www.justice.gov/opa/documents/medical-marijuana.pdf*)

In 2010, Pennsylvania became another state moving toward legal access for patients. Senator Daylin Leach sponsored the bill, saying:

It's long past time we move beyond the misinformation and ancient wives tales and allow people to have the medicine that will make them feel better. Medical Marijuana has been proven repeatedly to help people who are desperately ill. It is nothing more than gratuitous cruelty to deny it to them.

Federal Prohibitions

Although cannabis acceptance is gaining momentum on a state by state basis, federal prohibition remains a huge roadblock for medical and recreational users as well as industrial applications for legally grown American hemp. Despite increasing petitions from all three segments of the cannabis movement (medical, recreational, and industrial), the fed has so far stayed adamant that cannabis will not be legalized any time soon. This impasse may come to a head if California's current move to legalize recreational use and sales is approved by voters in 2010.

ESSENTIAL

Industrial hemp production became legal under North Dakota state law as of January 1, 2007, making it the first U.S. state to do so. But, as the State Agriculture Department began issuing licenses, it cautioned farmers that they could not actually grow hemp until approved by the federal government.

Hemp for Farmers

There is also no differentiation by the DEA between hemp grown for fiber and cannabis grown for medicine or recreational use. Instead, the DEA continues to deny farmers the right to grow cannabis hemp. Long-term lawsuits continue to move through the country's courts; in these cases the DEA maintains that growing hemp will allow recreational use of cannabis to proliferate. Even though commercial hemp has a very low THC content (the mood elevating component in cannabis), the DEA vehemently contends that growing rope is a front for dope!

Many American farmers see hemp as a valuable crop they are forbidden to grow for fiber and edible seed. Despite legal importation of Canadian and European hemp products, the DEA will not allow American farmers licensing for hemp production.

Although medical cannabis is frequently viewed as the forefront of the legalization movement, sixteen states have passed pro-hemp legislation to date, and eight states (Hawaii, Kentucky, Maine, Maryland, Montana, North Dakota, Vermont, and West Virginia) have removed barriers to its production or research.

FACT

Police arrested an estimated 872,720 persons for cannabis violations in 2007, the highest annual total ever recorded in the United States, according to statistics compiled by the Federal Bureau of Investigation. Of those charged with cannabis violations, approximately 89 percent, or 775,137 Americans, were charged with possession only. An American is now arrested for violating cannabis laws every thirty-eight seconds. Source: Uniform Crime Reports, Federal Bureau of Investigation.

In several bills passed since 1999, the North Dakota legislature has approved industrial hemp cultivation, and state Attorney General Wayne Stenehjem approved implementing rules crafted by the Agriculture Department. Although the Agriculture Commissioner has been a leading proponent of the potential new cash crop, he warned farmers:

"Our rules clearly state [that] persons who hold licenses to grow industrial hemp must also obtain permission from the U.S. Drug Enforcement Agency (DEA). It will be up to the DEA to allow producers to compete with other countries for the profits from this potentially valuable crop."

In order to allay fears that citizens would somehow want to smoke some rope, rigid controls have been placed on North Dakota's licensed industrial hemp farmers, including: criminal background checks, identification of fields by satellite tracking, minimum acreage requirements, seed certification, and mandatory laboratory tests. The chain of custody for viable hemp seed must also be fully documented.

The DEA doesn't seem to care about these safeguards because, to the agency, hemp contains traces of THC and thus falls under the purview of the Controlled Substances Act. In a recent interview, a DEA spokesperson made the agency's position clear: "There is no differentiation between hemp and marijuana. The regulations for hemp are the same as they are for marijuana."

North Dakota farmers have yet to plant a single seed.

Recreational

Despite seventy-three years of criminal prohibition, cannabis remains the third most popular recreational drug in the United States. According to the 2009 report from the U.S. Department of Health and Human Services, over one hundred million Americans have used cannabis at least once, including three presidents, the mayor of New York City, and various Olympic gold medalists. Currently, there are an estimated twenty-five million regular consumers of recreational cannabis.

FACT

Prohibition provides young people with easier access to marijuana than alcohol. (CASA, 2009). Alcohol purchases require identification and that the user be of a minimum age. Black market cannabis providers do not require ID or have any pre-purchase requirement other than cash.

According to FBI statistics, 304,284 citizens have been arrested for cannabis crimes in the first five months of 2010. The majority of these Americans are otherwise law-abiding citizens who work, have families, and are contributing members of their communities. It is plain to see that they are not criminals, and therefore should not be treated as such.

Cannabis prohibition has many indirect costs to taxpayers, without even considering the enormous annual expenditures on enforcement, prosecution, and incarceration. Every citizen arrested for cannabis obtains a criminal record upon booking. These people are likely to lose their employment, property, and possibly custody of their children, all of which would ensure additional burdens upon the taxpayer.

Prohibition also puts control of cannabis production and distribution into the hands of drug cartels, street gangs, and black market dealers (who frequently have other, less benign, substances for sale as well).

A June 2005 report by Dr. Jeffrey Miron, visiting professor of economics at Harvard University, determined that, if the current "non-system" of cannabis prohibition were replaced with taxation and regulation (similar to that used for alcohol), the American taxpayer would benefit from combined savings and tax revenues of between $10 billion and $14 billion per year.

More than 530 distinguished economists endorsed the report—they signed an open letter to President George W. Bush asking for "an open and honest debate about marijuana prohibition."

ESSENTIAL

The Marijuana Policy Project in Washington, D.C. provides some interesting examples of what all those tax dollars could be doing. They report that $14 billion in annual combined savings and revenues would cover the costs of securing all of the "loose nukes" in the former Soviet Union in less than three years. One year's savings could also be used to cover the full cost of anti-terrorism port security measures required by the Maritime Transportation Security Act of 2002. The Coast Guard has estimated these costs, covering 3,150 port facilities and 9,200 vessels, at $7.3 billion total.

Chief among the endorsing economists were three Nobel Laureates in economics: Dr. Milton Friedman of the Hoover Institute, Dr. George Akerlof of the University of California at Berkeley, and Dr. Vernon Smith of George Mason University.

Dr. Miron's paper, "The Budgetary Implications of Marijuana Prohibition," concluded that replacing cannabis prohibition with a system of legal regulation would save approximately $7.7 billion in government expenditures on prohibition enforcement: $2.4 billion at the federal level, and $5.3 billion at the state and local levels.

The paper further indicated that revenue from taxation of cannabis sales would range from $2.4 billion per year, if taxed like ordinary consumer goods, to $6.2 billion if cannabis were taxed like alcohol or tobacco.

The Future

A 2010 California initiative known as the Regulate, Control and Tax Cannabis Act would allow anyone over age twenty-one to possess one ounce of marijuana and grow plants in an area no larger than twenty-five square feet.

Soon, California voters may make their state the first to regulate, control, and tax cannabis. The California State Board of Equalization estimates the "Green Rush" will net California an estimated $1.3 billion in new revenue.

Legalization will also free up state law enforcement to concentrate on destructive crimes against citizens, including murders, burglaries, robberies, sexual assaults, child abuse, and drunk driving.

It's not a stretch to say that California may be the first state to legalize cannabis. Nationally, pro-cannabis activists are watching carefully; if the Golden State becomes successfully Green, other revenue-strapped states are certain to follow suit.

CHAPTER 3

Your Legal Rights

If you are reading this book, it's probable that you have used cannabis, plan to use cannabis, or know someone who does. You also might be planning to grow your own. If any of this applies to you, it is important to know the laws about cannabis use, possession, and propagation that will come into play. It is also very important to know your rights as an American citizen. Recent polls have shown most Americans think cannabis should be legalized, taxed, and regulated like alcohol, but the government has yet to catch up to public sentiment.

Risks of Recreational Use

If your circle of acquaintances is made up of light recreational users who are also well off professionals, you may have a misguided perception that cannabis is already "legal" in some way. Perhaps because mainstream broadcast television hosts receive applause and supportive laughter for showing a bouquet of cannabis flowers in an attractive glass bong as a potential Mother's Day gift idea. No one is frightened by this like they would have been in the past and, in fact, most seem to like the concept. Talk show hosts like Montel Williams talk openly about the benefits of cannabis and their own use without any loss in popularity.

After all, "Reefer Madness" is a joke and a myth, right? As cannabis legalization activists like to say, "It's all fun and games until somebody gets arrested!" If that someone is you, the punitive nature of law enforcement and the justice system will amaze you. Remember, cannabis currently remains a Schedule 1 drug, and a crime under Federal law in *all* states.

It is true that decriminalization has occurred in some states, but this is a somewhat vague term. Typically decriminalization means an offender will see no prison time and avoid a felony criminal record for first-time possession of a small amount for personal consumption. Depending on the state where you live, the conduct is treated like a minor traffic violation or misdemeanor.

Alaska is currently the most lenient state, allowing citizens to possess one ounce or less, as long as it is in their residence. There is no fine, ticket, or misdemeanor associated with such possession. Possession of less than twenty-five plants is also protected under the Alaska Constitution's right to privacy (see *Ravin v. Alaska*). From there, penalties jump severely; possession of twenty-five or more marijuana plants is considered "Misconduct involving a controlled substance in the fourth degree" and punishable by a fine of up to $50,000 or five years in prison.

Any sort of propagation or manufacture of cannabis is generally a felony in most states. Some are slightly more lenient if you have only a few plants; Maine, for example, considers five plants or less to be a Class E misdemeanor. You would still be subject to a possible six months in jail and a $1,000 fine, but would avoid the felony record. Note that, in some states, being a felon strips you of your right to vote, the right to own or use firearms (consider this if you enjoy hunting), and, in some medical cannabis states, the right to be a licensed grower for patients.

Punishment for Students

Another penalty to consider is a 1998 Congressional amendment to the Higher Education Act (HEA), Section 484, subsection R, which delays or denies federal student financial aid eligibility to applicants with any misdemeanor or felony drug conviction. Applicants with a single possession conviction lose eligibility for one year from conviction date; those with a second possession conviction or one sales conviction lose eligibility for two years; and three possession convictions or two sales convictions cost an applicant eligibility indefinitely. In early 2006, the law became limited to offenses committed while a student is enrolled in college and receiving federal Title IV aid.

This can apply to federal student aid programs such as Pell Grants, Work-Study Programs, Perkins Loans, Supplemental Educational Opportunity Grants, and others covered under the HEA. It also applies to the Hope Scholarship Credit, which allows for income tax deductions for people paying college tuition and fees; this law specifically prevents students who were convicted of a drug offense during the tax year in question from taking advantage of this credit, or if their parents are paying the bills, they lose the deduction for that tax year.

ALERT

An excellent and constantly updated resource for current laws in your particular state can be found online at *www.norml.org*, the website for The National Organization for Reform of Marijuana Laws (NORML). It's recommended that you familiarize yourself with these laws; depending on the attitude of your particular law enforcement encounter, a gram or two can make a big difference between a felony and a misdemeanor.

In many ways, misdemeanors are treated the same way as felonies. The law makes no distinction between the possession of cannabis or any other illegal controlled substance. A misdemeanor marijuana conviction denies student aid to any person, but this penalty does not apply to other convictions, including drunk-driving offenses or violent crimes. A student can regain eligibility, however, by completing a rehabilitation program that includes random drug tests.

Punishment for the Disadvantaged

Another area of public assistance that discriminates against the cannabis user in a surprising way is food stamps. Many states, Texas being one, require recipients of food stamps to undergo drug testing. The Texas law is relatively new and states:

Prospective applicants convicted of certain offenses as described in Section 1, Subsection (b) of the bill for a five-year period before applying for food stamp privileges must submit to drug testing. If the test gives a positive reading for controlled substances and prescription drugs that the applicant does not have a prescription for, the applicant is deemed ineligible for food stamp privileges.

The ineligibility will last for a period of one year, after which the applicant may then reapply. He or she will then be required to submit to additional monthly drug tests. Monthly drug tests will also be required of eligible applicants while they are enjoying the benefits of the food stamp program.

It is interesting to note that you can receive food stamps if you have committed a violent crime, but not if you have been convicted of possessing or using cannabis or other drugs.

The 1998 Anti-Drug Abuse Act requires public housing agencies to use leases that allow tenants to be evicted if the tenant, tenant's family member, or a guest engages in drug-related crimes. It is not necessary for the crime to be committed in the housing, and this penalty can apply even if the above people are arrested and not convicted.

In a neat twist, the Act could have applied to both President George W. Bush and his brother, Florida Governor Jeb Bush. Both were occupying public housing (the White House and the governor's mansion), when Jeb's daughter, Noelle Bush, was arrested for fraudulently obtaining a prescription for Xanax, a prescription anti-anxiety drug. This is a drug-related felony punishable by up to five years in prison. Ms. Bush was instead placed in a private drug rehabilitation facility where she was later caught with cocaine in her possession. She was not arrested, although police said they had to log sworn statements that she had been in possession.

In a statement dripping with hypocrisy, Governor Bush said, "This is a private issue, as it relates to my daughter and myself and my wife. The road to recovery is a rocky one for a lot of people who have this kind of problem."

For the rich and powerful, drug-related offenses are a private issue. They are a problem to recover from, not a crime that must be prosecuted and punished twice.

Punishment for Pets

While it is true that many grow sites are guarded by large dogs, many in law enforcement have no problem gunning down your family pet, even if your Yorkie or Corgi poses no threat to them. In a 2010 raid in Missouri, one that was documented on video, two family pets were shot in front of a seven-year-old child. After all of this traumatizing violence, the raid only netted a small misdemeanor amount of personal use cannabis. The SWAT team (using an out of date warrant) broke into the home in the middle of the night, fired seven rounds into the dogs (a pit bull and a Corgi that were both trying to escape the loud noises and bright lights), and arrested the parents on the cannabis misdemeanor and for child endangerment.

Just to review, smoking cannabis equals "child endangerment," but a SWAT team storming a home in the dark, guns drawn, and then firing bullets into the family pets as a child looks on equals "necessary police procedures to ensure everyone's safety." Keep in mind that someone in the United States is arrested for cannabis every thirty-eight seconds. This could have been your home, or your sister's, or your neighbor's.

Possession of Cannabis

One would think that no sensible policeman, district attorney, or judge would get excited about the possession of recreational cannabis, especially in small amounts. In truth, they are not embarrassed to prosecute you; this is part of the law and their revenue stream.

Prohibitionists constantly point to the numbers of Americans being treated for their "addiction" to cannabis. They feel that these numbers validate their argument that cannabis is an addictive and dangerous drug.

There may come a time when you may well agree to be enrolled in a program. In most cases, this will be because your attorney, or maybe the public defender, will advise you to not fight the system, but to participate in treatment and accept a Delayed Entry of Judgment (DEJ). If you complete your treatment for your addiction to cannabis, and do not re-violate, your case will not go to sentencing.

So now you are forced to participate in urine testing and classes that purport to teach you "Why Marijuana Is Bad." These classes are not cheap, and you will be footing the bill for them. It is not necessarily advisable to be a smart aleck in class; these people will also have your urine for testing.

Do I Have Any Rights at All?

Let's say you have considered the risks and still want to grow a small amount for your personal, recreational use. Many people do this; prohibition has made purchasing cannabis extremely prohibitive in cost. Bear strongly in mind that recreational possession and use, not to mention propagation, of cannabis is illegal.

You do have the protection of the Fourth Amendment to the Constitution of the United States. Many people forget this, especially when, deep down, they feel that they are not doing anything wrong. As an American citizen you have the protection of the Fourth Amendment, which reads:

The right of the people to be secure in their persons, houses, papers, and effects, against unreasonable searches and seizures, shall not be violated, and no Warrants shall issue, but upon probable cause, supported by Oath or affirmation, and particularly describing the place to be searched, and the persons or things to be seized.

In other words, do not ever agree to let law enforcement search your home without a warrant!

Knock and Talks

Law enforcement is especially fond of what are called "knock and talks." The knock and talk approach is used exclusively to enter private residences in the absence of probable cause. Vague suspicions, or even neighborhood prejudices, could ultimately determine which locations are singled out for investigation. How you look and dress (the shirt emblazoned with a big cannabis leaf is a definite giveaway) can trigger one of these unpleasant encounters. Innocent people can be arrested in the event that a guest, neighbor, or former tenant left something illegal on their property.

Law enforcement will ask if they can come into your house "just to talk." Many people feel uncomfortable saying no. Law enforcement may use this discomfort as a ploy, imply that your behavior is suspicious, and say that, if you have nothing to hide, you should comply. You are well within your rights to refuse entry without a warrant. You may simply decline the search and tell the officers that you will gladly cooperate if they return with a warrant. Another option is not to answer the door at all, which prevents the police from claiming that they saw or smelled something illegal when you opened the door for them. The following are some exceptions allowed by law:

- **Consent searches.** If the police ask your permission to search your home or other property, and you agree, then the search is considered consensual and they do not need a warrant. Do not agree! The fact that you refuse to consent does not give the officer grounds to obtain a warrant or further detain you.
- **Searches made in connection with an arrest.** When a person is placed under arrest, the police may search the person and the immediate surroundings for weapons that might be used to harm the officer. An officer may only reach into your pockets if he pats something that feels like a weapon.
- **Emergency exception.** If the police have a reasonable fear for their safety or for that of the public (i.e., believes there is imminent danger), they do not need a warrant.
- **The plain view doctrine.** A police officer does not need to obtain a warrant to search and seize contraband that is "in plain view." Simple as it sounds, always be aware of how visible your plants or cannabis are. If they can see it through a window, they are in plain view.

Traffic Stops

A traffic stop is normally just that. If there is no basis to suspect that you are armed and dangerous or involved in criminal activity, the officer cannot search you or your car. If the officer does see something suspicious, then the law allows the officer to do a pat-down search of you and of the passenger compartment of your car. The police officer can also feel the outside of any purses, bags, or other containers in the car that could hold a weapon.

ALERT

Do not to post incriminating pictures of yourself on Facebook. Police search the web these days, so think about what you post and keep an eye out for other people incriminating you as well. Remember what happened to Olympic Gold Medalist Michael Phelps?

Some police will base their suspicions on your appearance. Perhaps your vehicle has bumper stickers from a Grateful Dead concert, for example, or other items that identify you as a "certain type," possibly one that uses or possesses marijuana. Many people do not realize that they can refuse a search, but, if you allow the officer to search you or your car, by giving your consent, then the search will normally be considered valid. This will hold true even if there were no solid reasons behind the officer's request.

You should know that laws in many states authorize police officers to arrest drivers for minor traffic offenses. If a police officer does choose to arrest a driver, then a search can take place legally. Be sure to learn the laws for your state, and any state you may be traveling in.

Be Smart!

Remember that you are vulnerable when it comes to transporting cannabis product or cannabis plants. Avoid attracting attention by wild driving, or any vehicle issues like expired tags, broken taillights, a cracked windshield, or bald tires. Any of these can cause a routine traffic stop that may lead to trouble.

Make sure to wear your seat belt and make others in the vehicle wear theirs, and don't use your cell phone while driving. Many short trips to deliver plants or product have ended unhappily because of inattention to detail.

This should go without saying, but never volunteer information to the police! Always exercise the right to remain silent. Whether you have been arrested or not, anything you say to law enforcement can be used as evidence against you. You have the right to have an attorney present during questioning, but your right to remain silent should always be exercised. In a lot of cases, thinking you can explain something to a friendly appearing police officer will result in his testifying against you later. Never physically resist the police, even when they try to provoke you. Politely assert your rights, request an attorney, and then be quiet.

FACT

"No person shall be held to answer for a capital, or otherwise infamous crime, unless on a presentment or indictment of a Grand Jury, except in cases arising in the land or naval forces, or in the Militia, when in actual service in time of War or public danger; nor shall any person be subject for the same offence to be twice put in jeopardy of life or limb; nor shall be compelled in any criminal case to be a witness against himself, nor be deprived of life, liberty, or property, without due process of law; nor shall private property be taken for public use, without just compensation." —The Fifth Amendment of the United States Constitution

Until cannabis is legalized for personal cultivation and recreational use, the risks to possess, grow, and transport cannabis are very real. All recreational cannabis users are urged to register to vote, and use their voices to help stop this war on the United States' own citizens.

Medical Use States

Since 1996, a growing number of states have passed medical use cannabis laws. Unfortunately, these are state laws, not federal, where cannabis remains an illicit substance, regardless of state law.

Where does this leave the medical consumer who lives in a medical use state and possesses the proper legal paperwork for possession and propagation? Eric Holder, the Obama Administration's Attorney General, issued guidelines for federal law enforcement and prosecutors in a 2009 memo that reads, in part:

> . . . *pursuit of these priorities should not focus federal resources in your States on individuals whose actions are in clear and unambiguous compliance with existing state laws providing for the medical use of marijuana. For example, prosecution of individuals with cancer or other serious illnesses who use marijuana as part of a recommended treatment regimen consistent with applicable state law, or those caregivers in clear and unambiguous compliance with existing state law who provide such individuals with marijuana, is unlikely to be an efficient use of limited federal resources.*

The key phrase is "clear and unambiguous compliance with existing state law." A medical cannabis card is not a get out of jail free card. It is incumbent upon the patient, caregiver, and grower to know the laws and limitations in their particular states, just as receiving a driver's license requires you to know the laws of driving. "I didn't know" is never a defense.

Affirmative Defense

Many people who qualify for medical cannabis choose not to register in their state; fearing they will be put on a list that may identify them to law enforcement. Some states allow unregistered patients what is called an "affirmative defense" should they be arrested and brought to trial.

In general terms (and this varies from state to state), an affirmative defense provides for patients who fail to register with the state, but who possess medical cannabis in amounts compliant with state law, to raise an affirmative defense at trial that their possession is medically necessary. In a few states, registered patients who possess more than their state laws allow may also use this defense. The affirmative defense is not relevant to a federal cannabis charge, meaning a federal judge will refuse to acknowledge it and the defense cannot even be mentioned at trial. However, if your trial is on the state level, and the laws of your state allow for the affirmative defense, it may be available to you. Note that the amount you possess must comply with your state's medical cannabis laws. In some states, cardholders are precluded from using this defense for possessing more than the legal limit; always be certain to stay informed about your state laws.

Some patients rely on the thought that the affirmative defense is available to them, but this is partly wishful thinking. By the time you are asserting your affirmative defense, you have already been arrested, arraigned, and are on your way to plea bargain or trial. These are very, very expensive activities, let alone stressful. Think of it this way: you have a right to own a Rolls Royce, but can you afford one? The affirmative defense is similar. In states where it is allowed, you have a right to mount this rarely successful defense, but can you bear the costs?

Medical Use Programs

Medical use states also vary in who administers their medical cannabis programs; the best ones are properly under the umbrella of the health and human services divisions. The worst ones are for some reason under the control of law enforcement, despite being medical programs. Treatment with any kind of drug is best managed between a patient and their doctor and not by police, whose training is in enforcement, not medicine.

FACT

Despite a popular law enforcement myth that only a few "pot doctors" sign recommendations for patients, even a smaller state like Oregon has had more than 2,300 licensed physicians sign the required annual recommendations for their patients' Oregon Medical Marijuana Program cards. Source: DHS/OMMP for the State of Oregon.

Some states allow patients to appoint a caregiver to grow cannabis for them. Oregon even provides patients the opportunity to appoint a caregiver and what is called a "person responsible for a marijuana grow site;" in other words, a grower. These individuals are usually (again, depending on your state's law) required to pass a criminal background check, but once registered they receive legal protection to possess, propagate, and transport (but not use) cannabis within their state under medical cannabis laws. This is only protection from state laws and only if the cardholder is in compliance with every aspect of the law. Different states that require patients to provide their own medicine have different limits on the number of patients a caregiver or grower can provide for; contact your program for the exact numbers, as these can change with every legislative session.

ALERT

Please note that, to law enforcement, a "plant" can be a tiny cutting in soil that has not even had time to grow roots. Some state laws regarding medical cannabis define what a plant is and what a seedling is. Be sure to check the legal definition in your state. The eighteen seedlings (under twelve inches in any direction, non-flowering) and six plants allowed in Oregon would be illegal in Nevada. The latter's state law says that patients "may cultivate no more than seven marijuana plants, of which no more than three may be mature." The definition of the word mature is not provided, leaving a large hole in understanding for both patients and law enforcement.

The argument has been made that all cannabis use is medical to some degree. Be that as it may, many persons with chronic, painful illnesses are now able to use cannabis legally. Anyone who uses cannabis to manage a health condition should investigate the status of medical cannabis in his state. Contact nonprofit medical cannabis groups in your area for more information on the state of cannabis where you live, or check online at the National NORML website. There is a significant stress relief factor in knowing that you are not breaking state laws when you medicate or propagate and, that peace of mind is good for your health!

Dispensaries

Some state medical cannabis laws allow for dispensaries: not-for-profit outlets where patients can purchase their medicine. These have proliferated where legal, as medical cannabis is not found in pharmacies. The most talked about and studied has been the California dispensary system and jokes about the "Green Rush" and the Wild, Wild West have been common. The most frequently heard complaints have come from the idea of these dispensaries profiting from cannabis, as well as the lack of any real regulation. Dispensaries can range from the most sterling examples of compassion and volunteerism, to flagrant displays of greed and disregard for inspected product sources. One early problem for dispensaries was that pricing cannabis on a compassionate and realistic scale (as opposed to black market pricing) resulted in dispensary purchases being sold on the street at high markup.

Another ongoing problem is security. Dispensaries must protect themselves like pharmacies or banks. Prohibition has artificially inflated the black market price of cannabis to ridiculous levels, and this makes a dispensary an attractive target to thieves.

California is currently being watched closely to see if it becomes the first state to regulate and tax recreational cannabis. The economic implications are large and far reaching; if successful, expect more states to rapidly follow suit. Should this occur, it is to be expected that dispensaries will remain, but as smaller, industry-niche operations for specialty items sold specifically for medical users.

Different States, Different Approaches

Oregon recently had a ballot measure approved to go before voters that will allow for dispensaries. Following the current differences between the California and Oregon medical cannabis programs (Oregon has a statewide patient registry similar to the DMV, California has no statewide official registry for patients; it varies from county to county), the Oregon proposal would have in place far more controls, particularly over the supply sources for dispensary cannabis. All cannabis sold would be required to be produced by licensed growers who, like the dispensaries, would need to keep accurate sales and production records that would be subject to inspection by the Department of Human Services. Currently in California, dispensaries do not have regulated supply sources.

In New Jersey, the state Department of Health is now required to establish regulations for the licensed production and distribution of medical cannabis to authorized patients. The program is not anticipated to be up and running until sometime in 2011.

According to the Associated Press, "The delay allows health officials to write regulations. It also may give politicians time to consider a different model for the program." Republican Governor Chris Christie requested lawmakers postpone implementing the law, which was signed in January by his predecessor, Democrat Governor Jon Corzine.

Governor Christie has also suggested that lawmakers consider amending the law by limiting the production of medical cannabis to a single supply source, Rutgers University, and by restricting the drug's distribution to authorized hospitals.

As of December 2009, Congress has finally allowed DC to implement the District of Columbia's 1998 medical marijuana law. The bill states: "Removing Special Restrictions on the District of Columbia . . . allows the District to implement a referendum on use of marijuana for medical purposes as has been done in other states."

FACT

Section 7 of the bill allows: "Residents of the District of Columbia may organize and operate not-for-profit corporations for the purpose of cultivating, purchasing, and distributing marijuana exclusively for the medical use of medical patients . . . . The Director of DCRA shall issue such corporations exemptions from the sales tax, use tax, income tax, and other taxes of the District of Columbia in the same manner as other nonprofit corporations."

Maine voters approved a medical cannabis dispensaries measure in November of 2009, allowing for the state to license nonprofit facilities to distribute medical cannabis to qualified patients. The vote marked the first time that citizens ever approved a statewide ballot proposal authorizing the creation of dispensaries. In June of 2009, Rhode Island enacted a similar measure.

State by state, as voters approve medical cannabis use, each state must determine how to solve the issue of supplying patients with quality, affordable medicine. The questions of how best to distribute cannabis and the source for the cannabis itself are ongoing.

CHAPTER 4

Indoors or Outdoors— Where to Grow?

Understanding what your plants need is probably the most important part of deciding where to grow them. The other part to consider is what you need and actually want to do. A small outdoor grow takes about the same effort as a small, personal use vegetable garden. If your goal is only a few ounces for the year, a tiny container garden on your deck might suffice. If you are supplying medical cannabis patients, you will need to evaluate their needs and compare those needs to how much you can realistically expect to produce for them. Indoor and outdoor grows both have their place in this scenario, but seriously thinking about a few questions will help you determine which is better for your situation.

Where Do You Live?

The first thing to think about is where you live. Many states have punitive laws about growing cannabis, and you are well advised to educate yourself as to the statutes in your locality.

If you are lucky, you live in a medical cannabis state and can obtain legal permission to grow cannabis, at least on the state level. Otherwise, with very few exceptions, almost every state's laws consider growing or manufacturing recreational cannabis (even small amounts for your own personal use) to be a felony.

Only you can assess the risk you are willing to take; reviewing Chapter 3 might be helpful in understanding and evaluating that risk. Very few people realize how serious law enforcement can be about what is, after all, only a plant.

Legalities aside, your climate and seasonal growing conditions are determined by your geographic location. These factors will impact how well different strains of cannabis will grow outdoors. If you are planning on indoor growing, you can of course dictate climate conditions and manipulate light, thus controlling where the plants think they are growing. This control gives the indoor grower more choice as it pertains to different strains. The indoor grower must also balance his choices, since each strain will not have an individual vegetative or flowering room. Instead, they will have to keep to a medium range that is acceptable to all the strains growing together.

Because the risk of a complete crop failure increases when all of the plants are genetically similar, it is not advisable to have only one strain growing at a time. Similar plants will be uniformly susceptible to a single malady, so you could lose everything should the unfortunate occur. If a particular strain is, for example, found to be mold-prone, particularly tasty to mites, or contracts a plant-killing virus, you could lose your whole crop. If your crop has genetic diversity, there is a far greater chance that some strains will be resistant to whatever plague might choose to visit you. Also, if you harvest a crop of genetically identical plants, you will get easily bored using exactly the same cannabis day in and day out.

Medical Cannabis States

Do you live in a state that currently has medical cannabis laws? Although cannabis remains illegal, and a Schedule I drug under United States federal law, fourteen states (as of the writing of this book) have passed medical marijuana laws.

Since 1996, the states that have passed medical marijuana laws are Alaska, California, Colorado, Hawaii, Maine, Michigan, Montana, Nevada, New Jersey, New Mexico, Oregon, Rhode Island, Vermont, and Washington.

In almost all of these states, the patient is required to produce his own cannabis or to designate an individual to produce it for his. Some states, like California, have dispensary programs, but mostly patients are on their own and, like most recreational users, must turn to the black market if they lack a grower.

Another real benefit of living in a medical cannabis state is your increased access to different strains and to knowledgeable people. Medical cannabis patients can network openly, and, depending upon their state's particular statute, can usually freely exchange medicine and plants.

City, Suburb, Rural?

City and suburban growers are mostly forced to grow indoors because to do otherwise means they are usually raising plants for cannabis thieves, commonly known as "rippers." This name is particularly apt, as not only are they ripping you off, but the smash and grab tactics commonly used involve the literal ripping of the plants from the earth or the plants being torn apart. Few things are more heartbreaking (in the context of cannabis growing) than to lose your beautiful plants or to see them torn and maimed.

FACT

Growing good cannabis is like owning a beloved and well cared for pet when you think about it. You interact with the plants at least once a day, and usually far more frequently. You feed and water them on schedule, groom them regularly, protect them, and pamper them because they please you. You worry because you value them. When you produce a superb individual, you breed or clone it.

The black market value of cannabis is so high, rippers are known to rent airplanes and search out grows from the air. The last thing you want is to have strangers targeting your home and your grow. With that warning in mind, however, a smaller amount of cannabis plants can be intermixed with a "regular" garden and will frequently escape detection. Aerial searchers are also more prone to look in rural areas for bigger grows, while the suburban or city grower is more likely to be overlooked by taller buildings and the plants spotted, or to have someone smell their plants. Rooftop grows are also becoming more common; they are usually far more secure than growing on a deck or in a backyard.

Rural grow sites are clearly better for outdoor growing. In many cases, grows are discovered by passersby smelling the cannabis and doing a little investigating. Acreage and proper placement of the crop eliminate this danger, and inter-mixing the cannabis with a summer vegetable garden will help keep the plants from aerial spotting. In the country, deer and livestock predations make high fencing common for non–cannabis gardens, so casual observers would have no reason to suspect a cannabis crop is also being grown.

ALERT

If you are lucky enough to live in a state that has a medical marijuana law, it is imperative, as a prospective grower, to do your research. It is extremely foolish to ignore statutes that, if followed, will provide you with very real protection from state and local law enforcement agencies.

How Much Do You Want to Grow?

The second variable to consider is how much you want to grow. Usually, the quick answer is as much as possible! There are two kinds of serious answers to this question, as it can be taken in two different ways.

Growing Like a Gardener

One, how much do you WANT to grow? Do you already garden and think, "I can grow a great tomato plant, why would cannabis be any more difficult?" Do you look at friends' cannabis gardens and feel attracted to the plants themselves: their beauty, aroma, and personalities? If you answered "yes," then you actually WANT to grow cannabis. This desire will help you grow healthy, productive plants.

If you already feel like growing will be an added chore or boring labor, it is possible that you just do not have a feel for the enjoyment of gardening, no matter what you are growing. Or you might feel intimidated as to how difficult it might be. In the end, only you can decide. You could try growing a smallish amount once and confirm that your real interest lies in being a consumer, not a producer, of cannabis. Or, despite your initial reservations, you might find yourself captivated and fascinated and become a life-long grower.

Growing for Supply

Once you've established that you want to grow cannabis, the next question to tackle is just how MUCH do you want to grow? Is your purpose in growing to supply yourself or a friend or relative with medical cannabis? If so, you'll need to sit down and figure out how many ounces a month are medically needed. Bear in mind that tinctures and medibles use far more than ingestion by smoking.

ESSENTIAL

As a first-time grower, make your calculations based on a yield of four to six ounces per plant. Once you know what you are doing, it is not unreasonable to expect a pound to a pound and a half per plant yields, but it is always better to be pleasantly surprised by a higher yield than to come up short. This particularly applies if you are growing medical cannabis for patients who rely on you for their medicine.

If you plan to grow indoors at home, the sheer space limitations of your house may make your garden size decision for you; it is not advisable to crowd indoor plants since doing so will substantially reduce yields. Crowding, particularly during the flowering stage, also leads to problems with mold and mites. The space you use for your inside garden needs to be away from general family activities, and in a room you can lock without appearing suspicious. Even if you are growing legally, there is no reason to (and many reasons to not to) let anyone not directly concerned know about your grow.

You also have to think about and plan for home security. Growing the plants inside your home can keep them safer from thieves, but the downside is that indoor plants put you at greater risk for a personal confrontation with a criminal or criminals.

You must also factor in the legal restrictions on plant numbers that pertain to your particular state since some states limit the number of patients for whom a grower can legally grow. This number is important to know and abide by, as unpleasant interactions with law enforcement can literally ruin your life.

Consider a Co-Op

Another possibility for a first time grower is to think about a co-operative grow. This provides an opportunity to share information and strains, as well as space and expenses. If you can join a co-operative with a master grower already in place, you will be able to learn in a hands-on environment. A co-op is just what the name suggests, a place for growers to help each other produce the best crop they can. If one grower has the land, others can provide labor and supplies, or share in costs for water, minerals, and other costs of production. Another benefit comes from sharing the security duties; you may not enjoy being constantly tied to your crop until harvest. A partner or partners in a crop can help each other, and of course help with the harvesting and cleaning the final crop.

Consider What the Plants Need

Think carefully about the space requirements that large, healthy cannabis plants will need, especially outdoors. With a little effort on your part, these girls will get rather large, so figure on at least six feet in height for sativas and, depending on your climate, possibly considerably more. Indicas tend to be shorter and bushier. Planting too closely can lead to poor air circulation and mold, so figure to give each female plant at least six feet in diameter space. Smaller plantings of low growing herbs can be scattered in between; this makes it much harder to discern cannabis from the air.

The plants will need good sunlight, and lots of it, so your in-every-other-way perfect spot that unfortunately is shaded for two-thirds of the day simply won't work. The plants will need water, and in quantities far greater than you will want to carry; there should be convenient access to good, clean water. The plants will need protection, mainly from other humans. Ideally, the grow site will be somewhere you can easily monitor it day and night; this usually means right near your house, unless you plan to sleep outside for the last month before harvest. Be advised, that can get old really fast.

The other thing to consider when selecting a location is that the actual distance from your house to the crop can be a factor if you are robbed and file a claim with your homeowner's insurance. It is worth checking your policy, as it has become more common for insurance to pay damages to legal medical cannabis growers when their plants are stolen. Sometimes there are restrictions on how far insured items can be from your actual house: something on the back forty, even though still on your property, probably would not be covered.

Indoor plants are usually grown in more crowded conditions, especially during their vegetative stage, but investing in fans for good air circulation and dehumidifiers for moisture control will help keep the plants from molding. And, with the ability to control their growth by controlling light, you can have shorter plants as well as a much shorter grow cycle than required for an outdoor crop.

Consider Your Budget

One very important factor to consider as you plan is: What kind of budget are you working with?

Indoor Costs

Indoor growing can be particularly hard on the pockets. A small indoor grow can run to $400 per month very easily, and that is just for ongoing electricity costs. The initial purchase of building materials for vegetative and flowering rooms (each of which requires a different light cycle and different lights), fans, dehumidifiers, filters, ballasts, grow lights, and light bulbs (which wear out and need replacing when they do), containers, and soil can be prohibitive. Other ongoing expenses include renewing the soil mixture for each crop, different mineral additives, and water bills.

Outdoor Costs

Outdoor growing has the advantage of using the sun for free. Other than that bonus from nature, you must factor in the start up costs of fencing, improving your soil, water, mineral additives, and a drying area for after harvest.

Fencing needs to be high and made from stout materials. It has three functions: to screen your garden from casual observers, to keep out livestock and wild browsers like deer, and to keep out rippers. The rippers are the most problematic, as heavy gauge wire can be breached with bolt cutters, they are intelligent enough to avoid or short out electric fencing, and they have no problem climbing over a board fence once they know there is something worthwhile on the other side. For optimizing ripper protection, use a combination of all three: high board fence to minimize visibility, electric wire on the inside of the fence top to discourage climbers, and heavy gauge wire or stock panels around the plants.

ALERT

Both indoor and outdoor grows are safer with security systems. From a large dog to expensive and sophisticated alarmed motion systems, it's a good idea to invest in something to protect your crop. Your budget will usually decide just how elaborate a security system you can put in place.

Soil improvement can involve digging out compacted clay soils and replacing it with a mixture of your own compost and a sandy loam, or with expensive, bagged organic soils. It all depends on the initial condition of your site's soil. Your soil will improve the more years you use a site, but it will always need mulches, new compost, and minerals each time you renew your garden.

Outdoor Money-Saving Ideas

If expenses are a major concern, plan ahead and improve your soil by mulching and composting with free materials. Leaves are abundant in the fall and are an excellent choice for improving soil. Mulch your areas in the fall and till in the composted leaves in the spring. Rain-spoiled hay is usually available for free or very cheaply in the country and is an excellent mulch for fall that will add tilth to your poor soil.

Investigate local livestock owners about the availability of manures; goats, chickens, horses, and cows are all great producers, and usually you can get wonderful nitrogen-rich compost makings for free. This is especially true when the livestock owner is what is referred to as a gentleman farmer. They do not really farm in the sense that their livestock is their livelihood, but they keep some animals and have manure. If their acreage is small, they are usually delighted to give you as much manure as you want to load and haul away.

Once you are drying the crop, consider the expense for a dedicated building or drying room, purchasing fans and dehumidifiers, and the accompanying electrical bills to power them.

Choosing the Right Strains

Once you have decided where to grow (indoors, outdoors, or a mixture of both), you will need to think about what strains of cannabis will give you the optimum chance of success. Cannabis breeders have spent years modifying plant characteristics, so where the strains are typically grown can give you your first clue as to what might optimize your growing success.

Outdoor

Outdoor plants need an environment to which they are genetically acclimated; tall, long growing pure sativas that do well in the California mountains of Mendocino and Humboldt counties will take too long to mature to be grown in the shorter growing seasons of the north. A hybrid cross that introduces an indica, like the classic Northern Lights, will do much better somewhere like the Pacific Northwest. This is where the importance of provenance and knowing the growing characteristics of a strain (i.e. quick finish, typical plant structure, and mold resistance) are extremely helpful.

Sativa type. Note the rangy structure and narrow leaves.

It is interesting to note that the same strain, started indoors and then moved to an outside grow, will look very different from the original mother plant grown from seed outdoors. This would be an example of how the genotype will express differently in different environments, and how early the adaptation starts. An indoors to outdoors plant usually seems to be very bush-like, while the 100 percent outdoor grown plant will have a more tree-like appearance with a thick trunk and longer axials. Due to the outdoor cycle's long growing period, and the chances of rain soaking the plant near harvest time, the tree-like structure is more suited to an outdoor grow. Its air circulation is better than a super bushy, dense structure that is more prone to molds if the leaves get wet. The indoor grower has less concern as he can control where he waters. Cannabis should generally be watered at the base, not by overhead sprinkling.

Indoor

Generally, indoor plants that have been hybridized for that purpose have had the height bred out of them; the goal is short, productive, mold- and pest-resistant plants. The grower has the option of starting the flowering cycle by light trigger and limiting vegetative growth, but the overall form and lanki-ness of pure sativas do not lend themselves well to indoor grows. Pure indi-cas or sativa/indica hybrids will generally perform much better, and lead to happier results for the grower.

Indica type. Note the rounded chubby leaves and stocky nature of the plant.

In conclusion, most new growers are better off starting small. Growing cannabis is an expensive proposition, both indoors and outdoors, and it is best to start out slowly and see if you really have the time and money required. Your first growing experience will tell you whether or not you enjoy the process, and will help you test out how viable and secure your envisioned grow site truly is.

FACT

Most medical cannabis states have or are beginning to have Cannabis Cups, or awards for new strains. Check with your local medical cannabis organizations for such events; usually the award-winning new strains will be available by clones or cuttings that are distributed by the sponsoring organization.

Growing cannabis is somewhat comparable to owning a horse. If you have never done so before, check out the experience in stages. Instead of investing in thousands of dollars worth of equipment, fencing, and full-time care of a large and expensive animal, most sensible persons start out with riding lessons, move on to leasing a horse, and then decide if they really want to make a commitment to actual horse ownership.

If nothing else, your experiments in growing will make you a wiser consumer, with a better understanding of how and why one grower's cannabis is better than another's.

There is no shame in deciding that you are not cut out to be a grower; appreciative consumers are always needed for any product, and are, in return, appreciated by the grower who grows for the love of it.

CHAPTER 5

The Importance of Recordkeeping

There are many benefits to keeping accurate records of your cannabis crop. Licensed medical growers in medical cannabis states can keep their records clearly and without fear, but the illegal propagator in other states should remember that these records can and will be used as evidence against you. It is not wise to keep your records on your computer, and you'd be well served to devise a coded system. Do not leave your grow records lying around; keep them locked up as with anything of value.

Why Keep Records?

If you are growing cannabis for the first time or if you're doing it only for yourself, you might ask "Why keep records at all?" Growing, and growing well, is a continual learning experience. If you grow once a year, it is especially easy to forget details of parentage, start dates, temperature variations—any of the minutia of the garden.

ESSENTIAL

If you keep detailed notes, you will train yourself to note things like temperature and humidity levels, the date of the last frost day for your area, if plants are always smaller in a certain area of your grow site, where the sun moves to during the outdoor cycle, and many, many things that will help you understand your plants and their performance.

Recordkeeping becomes even more important if you are a medical cannabis grower. You need to monitor which strains work for which patients as well as note the feedback patients give you on new hybrids or strains. This is different from recreational use; it is not whether or not they "like" the cannabis, but rather whether the strain worked to alleviate their symptoms. If you have patients who have trouble articulating their experiences with different strains, it is helpful to know how to ask the right questions.

If you are a seed breeder, detailed records are essential; otherwise you are breeding blind. This works, of course, but can leave you not knowing how you produced something spectacular, and searching, perhaps in vain, to reproduce it. And, last but not least, records of your expenses are very helpful, especially when you can be reimbursed for them. People who have never grown cannabis, or gardened in any way at all, have a naïve idea that growing outdoors is free. They forget about water bills, fencing costs, minerals, soils, alarm systems, and other expenses for a serious garden. Throwing some seeds onto unimproved ground and hoping for the best might be free, but you would have very little, if anything, to show for it.

What to Record

In general, you want to record: the source of your genetics, be it seeds or clones; the dates of propagation, breeding, harvesting, curing, and clipping; success or failure of breedings; final product weights; descriptions of product performance, and of course a daily log of temperature, feedings, waterings, and transplantings organized by date. Even if you only have a few plants, these types of notations will make your life much easier. You will be able to diagnose plant behaviors much more quickly and confidently if you have easily accessible, accurate records of when you watered and fed, or rainfall and temperature changes. Your notes will be invaluable for reviewing and improving your general garden and breeding techniques, as well as different curing and storage methods.

When to Record

The first entries for your grow book should include whatever information you have about the seed or clones you are starting from. This could, for example, be a detailed profile of a certified strain you purchased or were lucky enough to have given to you.

QUESTION

How long do cannabis strains last?
Many American growers can trace their strain origins back for more than thirty years. Think about pedigrees for thoroughbred racehorses that go back for 200 years. Studying these pedigrees can provide real insight into performance breeding. The same applies to breeding cannabis, which, after all, is also about performance.

In another scenario, you might not be sure what you have, but you might have more information than you initially think. Sources can be as nebulous as "Pete says this is really good smoke, he bought it in Portland and found some seeds," or "Corky's crop, 2009, indica hybrid." This information, though not ideal, is actually a reasonable beginning for the profile you will build about each plant you cultivate. All strains started somewhere.

For example, let's say you know Pete and often share cannabis with him, so therefore you will know if his appraisal is based on recreational or medical effects. You will know what he typically uses as far as the quality of what he thinks is "really good smoke," another nugget of information.

Pete may have told you all he knows about the origin of the seeds under discussion, but it is still worth writing down this information. His purchase in Portland allows to you make an educated guess that the plant was grown on the West Coast, most likely in Oregon. The seeds found in the finished product would indicate it was most likely grown outdoors and was therefore vulnerable to random, windborne pollination. The geographic location would give a strong chance that the seeds are from an indica hybrid; these are more viable than pure sativa types in Northern Oregon's shortish outdoor growing season.

Your initial note on this plant profile would still be "Pete says really good smoke, he bought it in Portland and found some seeds," but you might add "possibly indica" and record the date you received the seed. If Pete can remember it, put the date he found the seed so you can have some approximation of the seed's age. If, for example, you got the seed in 2006 and are trying to germinate it in 2010, you would know that less of the seed is likely to germinate (having passed the three year optimum mark), and therefore you'll need to soak more seeds from the beginning. Then you would note how many actually germinate and how soon.

ESSENTIAL

Your grow book should be divided into two parts: the day to day garden journal where you note temperature, humidity, general activities like scheduled feedings (how much and what), waterings, transplant dates, damage to plants (lost a branch or attacks by insects), rainfall, if outdoors; and notes about the genetics, general appearance, and performance of each of the individual plants.

Once you have seedlings, you will note their type of leaf formation and whether or not that formation is typical of a sativa or an indica. Until your seedlings sex, you should group them under an easy to remember name that also gives information, like Pete's Portland Pot. The strain source, should

Pete's recommendation prove to be true and you end up propagating and creating a strain from his seeds, will always be "PPP 2006." The same applies to Corky's clones; should you propagate them, the source will be "CC 2009."

Creating Strain Profiles

An important part of your grow book will be a profile of each strain group. If you are using clones, you should use the same name for each plant of an identified strain since they are genetically identical. Some growers number each plant within the strain group, i.e. White Widow 1, White Widow 2, and then track their individual performance that way. This will give you valuable information about which spots are best in your outdoor grow space, or perhaps areas in your indoor grow rooms that need the lighting or ventilation adjusted. The plants are going to act with variation and your notes will help you figure out why.

Hybrids and Naming Plants

If you have bred from seed and created hybrids, the best way to keep good records is to name each plant. Each is unique, unlike the clones, and so ideally their names will reflect what you know about the origins. If we go back to Pete's seeds, let's say you have germinated and raised ten seedlings to the point of sexing. You now have six females and four males. If you want the pollen, pick the strongest, healthiest male and isolate him. There is no need to name him (he is still PPP), but the year changes to the current grow; therefore "PPP Male 2010" is sufficient for knowing your pollen source. The other males can be destroyed. You will note in your book that they were terminated as opposed to being casualties.

Now you have six females. The easiest thing to do is give them all "P" names, so you would end up with Petra, Penelope, Persephone, Paulette, Primrose, and Prunella. Each generation from these females can be named in a way that gives you an easy way to recall their genetics without looking at your notes. Plants designated by numbers are much harder to recall.

Think of it this way; if a few years down the road you have a plant named "Whippersnapper," it would be far easier to remember that her mother was "Prunewhip," whose mother was "Prunella," whose source seed was Pete's Portland Pot, than to remember a sequence of numbers. Of course, you will have your grow book for reference, so the system you use is really more a matter of personal preference.

The naming system is most useful for the smaller grower. Growers who grow in big, commercial quantities may be forced to use a database type numbering system. It would be very difficult to come up with individual names for hundreds of plants at a time. In that instance, only the perfected strain would receive a name. These are frequently cheerful and appealing, like "Bubble Berry," or descriptive in some way, like "Afghan Skunk."

How Should You Record?

As discussed above, your grow book will have two sections, three if you are growing for medical as well as recreational users. The medical section will record which strains are to be used for what symptoms as you receive feedback from the patients.

The Daily Log

The first section will be a daily log of all your activities with the plants, from procuring clones or starting seeds, to weather conditions and feedings. This can be written like a journal, and provides a record of that particular grow. Even though your plants will be labeled, it is still helpful to make a placement map of each plant, depending upon the size of your grow. Obviously, if you only have three plants you will know exactly which plant is where.

Some samples of this sort of entry would be:

- **4/15:** Received three (3) White Widow clones. 4" in height, healthy. Dipped and in isolation.
- **6/10:** Transplanted six (6) Nancy B. Green X Sparkle Toes to 2 gallons. Light rain. 71°F.
- **7/23:** NBG X ST starting to sex. Two (2) females so far. 86°F. Watered all.
- **9/26:** Starting to rain. Too muggy out. 76°F. Watch for mold. Nancy Toes brought in this morning, checked for mold, and hung in big drying shed. Started fans today.

Mostly, you will keep a daily journal, but the examples are to show how simple and brief the information can be. The weather and temperature information is incredibly valuable to the outdoor grower; you will be able to see patterns for your particular micro-climate and to plan your grow's scheduling more accurately each successive year. Every year will of course have some variations, but keeping these sorts of notes will help you notice indicators that will eventually explain differences in the plants' behaviors.

Strain and Plant Profiles

The second section of your grow journal will be a profile of each strain, and if growing from seed, each plant itself. Note as much of the genetics information as you can, as well as the date the seed tailed, the date of planting, the date the seedling came up, characteristics of the phenotype, dates bred and to which male, the date harvested, the date clipped, the final product weight, and performance evaluations. Note some details about the taste, aroma, and psychoactive effect. If you bred the plant, note the appearance and number of seeds produced by the breeding.

ALERT

If you are a grower in a nonmedical state or are an unregistered grower, it is very important to remember that your grow book can and will be used as evidence in legal proceedings. It will be exhibited to prove that you have indeed grown cannabis. In this instance, it is better to use a coded system. Whether registered or not, always keep your grow book in a safe place; it is an invaluable record for the breeder.

If you grow for patients, it is important to keep a profile for each patient, including what strains work for their illnesses. Ask your patients to rate each strain according to taste and aroma, as medicine should be palatable. Cannabis is so complex that its effects can depend on the properties of the specific strain. Ask detailed questions as to the timing of pain or nausea relief, or relief for a specific symptom such as muscle spasms. Have them rate the symptom relief on a scale of one to ten, and ask how long the effect lasts. Some strains will not relieve certain symptoms at all, so these are important questions to have answered since you want to find the best possible strains for your patients.

The other thing to be aware of is that some strains may relieve symptoms but will cause the patient to be very drowsy. These are useful as a sleeping aid, but listen to your patients' feedback; they also need strains that provide symptom relief while letting the patient stay alert and functional. These plants are often called daytime strains. Typically, these will be some sort of indica/sativa hybrid. Eventually you will be able to provide your patients with a good range of medicine that helps them manage their symptoms, but it takes a dialogue and some experimentation. Taking good notes will help you to identify what works for which patient a lot faster.

ESSENTIAL

It is generally not a good idea to keep these records on your computer. A good old-fashioned hardbound blank book works very well, and can be carried around the grow site with you as you make your notes. Otherwise, you will be noting things and then having to transcribe them into a computer file. Laptops can end up damaged by water or dirt if you try to carry them around in the grow environment. In legal terms, it takes some doing to permanently delete records off a computer, so law enforcement can use computer records you long thought lost in the ether against you.

At the end of the day, the simple recording of your plants' lifecycle will make you a much better grower. The more you note, the more you notice; you will be training your eye to spot problems well before they are out of control. The outdoor grower will become much more able to evaluate plant sites and place plants for the best growth; the indoor grower will notice nuances of grow room performance that lead to more productive light placements or better feeding schedules. The plants will benefit greatly and will thank you by being beautiful, healthy, and productive.

CHAPTER 6

Choosing Seeds or Clones

An individual cannabis plant has its own genetically determined unique characteristics, or genotype. The grower propagates selectively in order to replicate desirable characteristics; in the cannabis plant these can include psychoactive effect, medical effect (i.e. spasm relief), aroma, taste, size, and flower type. The genotype can be influenced environmentally, and is ultimately expressed visibly as what is called the phenotype. If you have two genetically identical plants and grow one in shade, it might appear very long and tall. Grow its clone in full sunlight and you'll have a more compact, bushy looking plant. This is important to remember when working with clones or seedlings. To ensure a successful result, start with the best individuals you can procure and provide the correct environment.

What Are Clones and Seedlings?

Young cannabis plants start out life in one of two ways—either propagated by taking a cutting or by germinating a cannabis seed. The term "seedling" also has legal meaning in some medical cannabis states where licensed growers are allowed so many "seedlings" versus a specific number of "mature" plants. The definition of "seedling" varies, but if defined is usually any cannabis plant under 12 inches in height or width, and non-flowering.

Clones

Clones, or rooted cuttings from a female or mother plant, have many advantages. The *genotype* is a known entity. You will already know that the clone is female, and that the plant possesses characteristics of value to the grower. There are no surprises since it is genetically identical to the mother plant you took the cutting from. There is no need to wait for the young plant to display sexual differentiation; it can go immediately into a fast track growing mode. This is particularly helpful when the outdoor grower is working with a short growing season, as it sidesteps the waiting time for sexual differentiation needed for seed-propagated starts.

If you are providing medical cannabis to patients, it is important to remember that clones are valuable in assuring that the patients get strains that actually help with their medical condition(s). A strain that is not effective in controlling a particular symptom is useless to the patient, and can have an adverse impact on her treatment regimen. Most medical cannabis patients have experimented with different strains until they found the ones that work best for their condition; genetic uniformity is essential if you are to supply cannabis as medicine.

Seedlings

Seedlings come from (of course) seed. From seed propagation also has advantages. If stored properly, cannabis seed remains viable for years. Unlike a clone, which immediately needs soil, light, water, and care, the seed will wait for you. This is a convenience, even if you plan to just buy seed and not breed for your own. Seed is also a way for a breeder to easily "bank" certain genetics that she might want to re-introduce at a later point in developing a strain. Trying to store genetics by repeatedly cloning is time-consuming and takes up far more space.

All seed is created by sexual reproduction. Cannabis makes this interesting, as it is a *dioecious* plant, meaning it requires both a male and a female plant to produce viable seed. Sometimes cannabis will produce hermaphrodites, but this is an undesirable characteristic and these individuals should be eradicated from the breeding program. Hermaphrodites can pollinate themselves and the rest of your crop if you let them, leading to flowers full of seed—perhaps useable, but much lessened in quality.

FACT

Many growers produce crops that are a combination of both clones and seedlings. The clones provide the completely known plants, while the seedlings are an opportunity to produce a genetic sport or "new thing." Most growers are always aiming for an improvement to one or more characteristics supplied by the parent plants.

Seed is more versatile than clones, as you can line breed for specific desirable traits and produce their own individualized hybrid strains. Instead of relying on other breeders, you have more independence from outside sources and can control the genetic direction of the breeding program.

A seedling also has the potential to be a male plant that is needed for pollen and, depending on the growing trends in one's area, may be rather rare. Many growers who work exclusively with clones instead of seed are horrified by male plants, viewing them as a threat to the seedless, or "sinsemilla," production of high-grade cannabis. Despite exaggerated fears of out-of-control pollination, you can easily ensure that your male is isolated and only used for controlled pollination and fertilization of specific females. To a seed breeder, males, particularly those from a prized strain, are very valuable in their own right: no males equals no advancement of the strain.

The Benefits of Starting with Clones

If you are a first-time grower, you should not feel intimidated by the idea of growing from seed, but your first grow will be less complicated if you start out with clones. Doing so will let you leap frog over the initial germinating of seeds and move right to planting. Think of using clones like going to the garden center and buying a healthy young tomato start instead of a packet of seed. This is a perfectly reasonable thing to do, especially if the strains are what you want anyway.

Using clones will help your plant count stay mostly the same from start to finish (barring pests, rippers, and accidental breakage to young clones), the plants will be more or less what you expected in terms of genotype, and there will be no anxiety about accurately sexing the young plants. And, having females, you still have the option of procuring pollen from another grower and breeding some seeds for next season.

How Should I Start Growing?

Let's begin with a garden of clones. Assuming you have organized and prepared your garden area, be it indoor or outdoor, you're probably unsure of where you can get clones. If you live in a medical cannabis state, there is a good possibility that clones or cuttings are available from a local compassion organization or from meetings where patients and their caregivers/growers gather to share concerns and cannabis. This is an opportunity to sample various strains and identify which types of cannabis are locally available.

Many meetings have clone tables where growers can acquire labeled strains for free or for a nominal fee or donation. Be sure to discuss the characteristics of the clones you select. You will need to learn about not only their effects, but also what the propagator has observed as far as their performance during the growing phase. Is the strain a bountiful producer? Does it seem prone to mold? Is it prone to hermaphroditism? Has it typically been grown outdoors or indoors? Ideally, of course, you will already know a grower who will take cuttings and make rooted clones of the various strains you specify.

Note that sometimes you will receive cuttings from a mother plant that have not yet produced roots and made the transition to being a real plant. These will require a little more attention than rooted clones, and expect a little more attrition; not all cuttings are going to root. If you are in the position where you have to get cuttings to root, always start with more than you think you are going to need.

Recordkeeping

Be particular about getting as much information as possible on the strains' genetic origins. If accurate, this information will be incredibly useful to you as you raise the plant. If you plan to breed the plant, knowing something about the parents can help you decide which males will be the most likely to add the characteristics you're looking for to improve performance.

Be aware that there are casual, if not dishonest, people who will present a clone as being a certain strain when in reality it is just something they have labeled with a popular strain's name. Until you have a trusted source for cuttings or clones, or have started breeding or cloning your own plants, always note down the name of the strain with a bit of skepticism. The same applies to casually acquired seeds; they may or may not be what is reported.

This does not necessarily mean that people are deliberately lying to you, it is just that people forget, or things get translated incorrectly from person to person like in the old party game Telephone. Of course, this low-key attitude toward sketchy information only applies to free, as in freely given, seed or clones.

If you are going to buy clones or seed, either know the grower or buy from a well-established seed bank. A reputable high-end seed bank will absolutely guarantee its breeding program and seed provenance beyond question; this is partly why you are paying such a high price for the seed.

What Type?

Cannabis can express itself very differently from strain to strain and even plant to plant.

Knowing the characteristics of the parents will also help you know if you have an outdoor strain or an indoor strain—or one that seems comfortable and obliging no matter where you grow it. A sativa bred to be sixteen feet tall outdoors is going to have a miserable time growing in a low ceilinged basement grow room, whereas a chubby little indica type will be much more productive and easier to handle. A late finishing strain may not do as well in an outdoor grow, especially if your season is short. If you are growing that same strain indoors you can easily manipulate the same strain's finish time by controlling the timing of the light it receives, but you will save yourself some frustration if you have accurate information.

Be very careful to label the clone with strain and date, and write down any other information you've acquired in your grow book. You may think you will remember everything at a later date, but chances are you'll miss important details. Keep in mind that you will be using this information some years down the road if you continue as a cannabis grower. Good record-keeping is essential not only for your own records, but for the credibility of your strains' origins. To serious growers, correct identification of a plant's genetics is essential since the effort and expense of growing high-grade cannabis means you should never operate from guesswork. You want the best possible outcome, not something that is of mediocre quality. The plant should be labeled from cutting to clone to planting and to drying; in other words, at ALL TIMES.

ESSENTIAL

A plastic label marked with indelible pen should be either stuck in the soil at the base of the plant, or affixed with a twist tie to an axial branch. Plants should never be left unlabeled.

Perhaps you have decided to acquire some seeds instead of clones. Perhaps clones are not available to you, or you just like the idea of producing your plants from seeds. Many people have small bags of seeds they've kept over the years, and chances are good these bags aren't labeled. It's not the worst thing in the world if these are your only option. You kept those seeds for a reason, most likely because you enjoyed the cannabis it came from (though you might have cursed at the time if you spent good money for sensemilla [seedless] cannabis), so you're not exactly starting from square one.

If you are on a tight budget, have no seeds of your own, or are shocked by commercially produced seed prices, perhaps a non-growing friend has some seeds. Even if people have no plan to grow themselves, they often keep random seeds from what is, in their opinion, particularly good cannabis. If your friend generally consumes what you consider to be high-end cannabis, he may contribute something rather special. Growers call this sort of seed "randoms" or, sometimes, "unknown soldiers." This is somewhat akin to buying a surprise package or buying an abandoned storage locker at auction: you have no real idea of what you will get, but sometimes you end up with something very nice.

Mail order seeds can be very expensive, though generally are of very good quality and known provenance. Most come from Amsterdam or Canada. If you are especially fond of a popular commercial strain, you can generally acquire it by mail order.

Ideally, however, you will get your seeds from a known source: a breeder/grower you know personally or possibly via a mail order house in Canada or Amsterdam. If you plan to grow outdoors, the locally bred seed from outdoor plants has the advantage of being acclimated to your home growing conditions.

Using Feminized Seed

Some mail order strains are available feminized, or guaranteed to be female plants. Feminized cannabis seeds start with selected female clones that are manipulated to produce male flowers and pollen and bred back to themselves. Feminized seeds are difficult to produce but are purported to deliver all (or 99 percent) female plants. There is a claim that feminized seeds also produce genetically stable plants, a useful tool in a breeding program; however some growers report hermaphroditism as a problem. If you plan to use feminized seeds, it is better to purchase them from a reputable seed bank, as most will guarantee that the seed will produce females.

Seed Storage

To keep seeds viable, store them in a dry, dark, cool place and in dry, airtight glass containers labeled with the source and the year of production. Although it is advisable to use fresh seed when possible, cannabis seeds are very strong and long lasting, unlike small, light types of seeds, like those from lettuce.

Although definitely not a Best Practice (since viability is, of course, affected by aging), growers have been known to germinate seeds as old as twenty years, if not older. Ideally, you will use the seed within three years of production. As the seed ages, a smaller proportion will germinate successfully.

ESSENTIAL

A few growers' reasons for germinating very old seed (as in twenty-plus years) have included: out of interest, just for fun, and no other choice (desperation!). One grower reported amazement at the nostalgic recognition and feeling of re-uniting with the long-ago plant via its daughter. In twenty years, their strains had changed, and it was interesting to re-visit nearer the original source genetics.

As noted above, using old seed is not a Best Practice, but it is sometimes useful if a hybrid strain manifests unwanted characteristics. You can go back a few generations and rework the strain going forward by introducing desired characteristics from another line. It is also comforting to know that you, as the breeder, can revisit a particularly good year by germinating and propagating the siblings of superior plants.

Selecting Seeds

Unless you have paid big money for feminized seed, plan on starting twice as many seeds than the final amount of female plants you hope to raise to fruition. The ratio of males to females is generally 1:1. Since you are dealing with living entities this will most likely vary. If you end up with a few more females than anticipated, either grow them in a container (for more variety), or pass along a nice young plant to a friend, a compassion center, or fellow grower.

Examine your seeds carefully under magnification, looking for the most mature seeds. Remove and dispose of any seeds that are cracked or have holes. Depending on the strains you are working with, the mature seeds will be either very dark brown with lighter brown striping, or a strong green-gray with brown striping. Pale whitish-green seeds with no striping are immature and should be discarded.

Germinating Seed

Seeds require moisture, warmth, and darkness for successful germination. Before you start soaking your seeds, plan ahead so that you can consistently provide all three.

To prepare your seed soaking area, assess how well it meets germination requirements; the area should be dark and warm. You'll want to keep the seeds somewhere between 65 to 80°F, but ideally right at 70°F. Some growers use seed starting mats that maintain an ideal temperature, but a warm closet or kitchen cupboard (on an inside wall) will usually be fine.

A foil-covered cookie sheet makes a good tray for small bowls or jars. If you are starting different strains, make certain your labels are prepared and affixed to each tray or bowl so you can keep track of which seed is from which strain. You will need a convenient light source as you will be checking the seeds frequently for germination, as well as monitoring moisture. You do not want the seeds to dry out.

Labeled plastic bag with seeds.

Some growers use plastic zip-top bags filled with clean water for germination. These work well because you can turn the bag and examine the seeds for activity without actually touching the seeds. Another benefit is that less water is lost to evaporation since the bags are sealed, adding another layer of protection against your seeds drying out. On the other hand, the bags make it more difficult to remove and plant a seed that has cracked and shown a tiny white root tip (usually referred to as having "tailed"), since all the seed will not tail at once.

QUESTION

What is the best tool for selecting seeds?
To select seeds for starting, it's good idea to have a loupe or jeweler's eyeglass (or a hand-held magnifying glass). The loupe will also come in handy when you are sexing plants, as the tiny initial indicators take a keen eye, or at least some magnification, to see clearly.

Many growers use small water glasses or jam jars and float the seeds in clean water. Others use small shallow bowls with squares of paper towel cut to fit. The seeds sit on moistened paper towels and are covered by a thin layer of damp towels on top. The top layer is easily lifted to check the seeds. The paper towel method mimics nature more closely (simulating the damp soil a seed would have fallen to), and is the easiest for removing germinated seeds for planting.

Remember, at this point you will have started your grow book and therefore you should note the date you start soaking your seeds. Knowing your start date will help you considerably, particularly if you are using older seeds that can take longer to germinate. If you are seeing less germination, you will need to evaluate whether or not to start soaking more seeds, and knowing exactly when you started is vital. Fresh seeds generally tail within twenty-four to forty-eight hours, but some, particularly older seeds, can take up to a week or even ten days.

Check your seeds twice a day, but avoid handling them excessively. You are looking for germination, but also need to stay on top of moisture requirements. Do not let the seeds dry out; this almost always kills the seed embryo. If you are using the small bowl method, a chopstick is useful for gently turning or separating seeds from each other so you can look for the tiny white tail. As soon as a seed tails, note the date in your book. This is part of the history of this particular plant.

Preparing the Seed Pots

You can prepare your first little seedling pots while you are waiting for your seeds to germinate. You will need new and clean 4-inch plastic pots, or previously used ones carefully washed with a light bleach solution and then rinsed with clean water. These can be set up on trays and ready to label. An indelible pen can be used to write directly onto the pots as the little seedling will be too tiny to wear a label yet. Some growers use a garden center plastic stick for the information, and just move the stick with the plant as it gets transplanted to bigger containers.

ALERT

An invaluable and inexpensive tool you should keep handy is an infrared laser surface thermometer. These are sold for cooks, but take a lot of worry out of seed starting. You can see instantly if your seeds are staying warm enough, and take steps to correct an environment that is too cold or too warm.

Seed planting will go easier if you have a clear, clean, and well lighted work area, and are able to assemble your materials ahead of time. Germinated seeds are fragile, so plan your time so you can work without hurrying.

The soil mix for seedlings should be light, clump-free, and well drained. Seeds need moisture, but excessive soil wetness can lead to a condition called "damp off." The little taproot becomes infected with a fungal parasite and rots once damp off sets in, and you lose the seedling. A light, sterilized potting soil works very well for this stage of growing.

As soon as the little seed tails, it needs to be planted. Do not wait or fool around; this is why you are checking the seeds at least twice a day. Leaving a germinated seed floating in water will kill it and you will have wasted your time and your seed.

Planting the Seed

YOU WILL NEED:
- Sterilized potting soil
- Clean 4-inch pots
- A chopstick or pencil marked to ½-inch from tip
- A clean mister bottle with clean water
- Sharpie or other indelible pen

Use a chopstick or pencil that you have measured off and marked at a half inch above the tip (a scratch or pencil line works fine) for making a "drill" (as a seed hole is known). Make sure the potting soil is uniformly damp (if the soil is dry when you fill your pots, give it a good soak, stir with the ever-useful chopstick to make certain there are no dry spots, soak again, and let drain). Make a half-inch drill in the center of each pot, and you are ready to plant some seeds.

ALERT

Seeds that are planted upside down will eventually find their way and turn, but it takes time, and is less than ideal for the plant. Working in good light and paying attention will pay off in the end.

Using your thumb and forefinger, very gently grasp the seed at the opposite end from its tail. The moisture will help the seed stick to your finger, so very little pressure, if any, is needed to hold the seed. Place the seed in the mouth of the drill, tail down (this is the taproot, so planting it in the right direction is helpful to the seedling).

Once the seed is in the drill, gently cover it with damp potting soil and water the drill lightly with a teaspoonful of clean water. Note the planting date in your grow book.

Locating the Pots

Place your trays of pots in a warm, humid environment; 67 to 78°F, and keep moist, not soaking wet.

A mister bottle with clean water is the best way to add moisture to your seedling pots. If you are starting plants or planning on growing indoors, use horticultural lights or a south-facing and well-lit window bay. At this point, a small fan will provide adequate air circulation for the seed trays; the gently moving air will help prevent damp off.

ESSENTIAL

Take your time and use a thermometer to make certain that the germinating area is truly warm (67 to 78°F). Trying to germinate seed in the cold is a complete waste of seed and time.

You will need to wait for your little seedlings to ideally push vigorously from the soil; this should occur within a day or two, so be patient. Sometimes a seed is accidentally planted with its taproot pointing upwards, so it will take longer to find its way. Do not over water, as this can drown your little start; just keep the soil lightly moist by using your mister bottle.

Hardening Off Your Plants

Outdoor growers frequently start indoors under lights and transfer the seedlings after the last frost date. The transfer from indoors to outdoors will require a short period of hardening off in a cold frame to minimize shock in young seedlings or clones.

ALERT

To avoid chilling the plants, always have the open side of the frame on the leeward wind direction. Make certain the window is shut tight on cold days, and always shut at night while covered with a blanket or some other type of insulation.

Making a Cold Frame

A cold frame can be made very simply by placing an old window on top of a low cinderblock square. The seedling pots are not going to stay in it for long, so three to four cinderblocks in height is sufficient. The window is easily propped for ventilation during warm days.

There are also some excellent and inexpensive heavy plastic greenhouses now available. An 8-foot by 8-foot structure can be acquired for under $200, including some pea gravel for the floor. Most have different zippered windows that can be adjusted for ventilation. These work very well for the hardening off phase.

Seedlings in pots (approximately 3-inch to 4-inch plants).

And, of course, if you are starting out with a small experiment in growing and do not want to make cold frames or buy greenhouses, it is perfectly viable to wait until all danger of frost is past. You can then germinate your seeds, plant them in the starter pots, keep them moist, and set them in a secure area outside to pop up and start growing. They will.

CHAPTER 7

Propagation

Why would you want to create seed? There are many advantages to breeding your own strains and propagating by seed. Cannabis is a very complex plant, and different strains have different benefits for each individual who uses them. You will discover that some strains are exactly what you are looking for, while others are not worth the trouble. Breeding for a certain level of psychoactivity, muscle relaxation, or aroma will customize your strains for your optimum benefit, in terms of both palatability and effects. And, as mentioned before, seeds will wait, (those powerful little bundles of DNA), until you release their potential through germination. Once you have created a strain that pleases you, how do you preserve the identical genetics? At this point, cloning, or asexual propagation is easy, fun, and provides an excellent way to share your exact strain with other growers.

Propagation of Fixed Hybrids (or How to Breed for Seed)

Cannabis produces both male and female plants, with an occasional hermaphrodite thrown in just to keep you on your toes. Ideally, you will have both parents for observation and can assess the desirable traits you want to be passed on to the offspring. In general, these include:

- Vigor
- Yield and size
- Hardiness
- Disease resistance

And, specifically:

- Cannabinoid expression
- Taste
- Aroma
- Pain relief

Additionally, ease of manicuring, typical rates of maturation, and color are all of interest to a seed breeder, and some of many traits that can be fixed by line breeding.

ALERT

Accidental pollination will not improve the strain, and may even harm or degenerate the strain by allowing the random selection of undesirable traits. This is, in part, why hermaphrodites are always terminated.

Here again, the importance of good recordkeeping is imperative; only a few parent individuals will approach the ideal. If your strain wanders from where you are trying to go with it, you can review the characteristics of the hybrid generations that came before, and breed back into the strain for improved performance. Trying to guess how you arrived at a certain genetic combination is rarely successful.

Inbreeding, or selecting and crossing individuals that are close to the ideal, can produce strains that are fairly close to uniform in six to seven generations. Inbreeding can also produce recessive or less than desirable traits in some individual plants. These should be removed from the breeding program completely. Inbreeding can also reduce vigor, at which point the breeder goes back a few generations (another advantage of seed) and back-crosses, or, alternatively, introduces another desirable strain into the line.

How to Segregate Male and Female Plants

Your initial little seedlings will be just that, seedlings, with no sexual differen-tiation. Your main concern is to provide them with light, water, and plenty of food for strong roots and healthy vegetative growth. At this point, all of your seedlings can stay together, although you'll want to think through how many males you want and where to put them. They will have to be moved quickly once they provide proof of their sexual determination, or "declare," to use the term preferred by growers.

Site for checking primordia for sexing plants. This is the initial "nub."

The male and female cannabis plants have different flowers that develop from a tiny nub, known as the primordia, located initially on the main stems. Flowering is triggered by a change in light (which is how indoor growers can speed their crop cycles by manipulating the timing of lights). As a general rule (though genotype may cause some variation), figure dropping to twelve hours of daylight will trigger flowering.

ESSENTIAL

Unless you have the eyes of a falcon, examining the primordia is done much more easily with your jeweler's loupe.

The best place to check for flowering is at the top of the plant at the nodes (or intersections) where the plant develops a small leaf spur. The initial primordia will appear behind this spur and will start out looking like a tiny rounded pod. Eventually, the primordia elongates into either a tubular looking female calyx or the more rounded nubbin of the developing male flower. The final proof of sex is the two white hairs or pistils that will appear from the end of the female calyx. These pistils can also appear pinkish or yellowish.

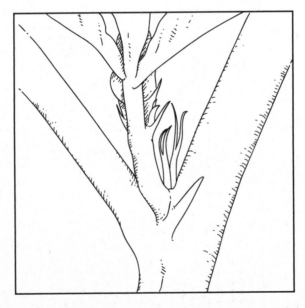

Early female declaration. Note the "hairs" that have come out of elongated nub.

Once your plants have declared, you must remove the males at once. Ideally, you will have already decided which males, or in some cases just one male, to keep for breeding. These males can stay in smaller containers and do not need feeding for vegetative growth. In fact, they barely need watering. All you want is their pollen, and a tiny (relative to how big the females are going to get) male can produce more than enough for breeding purposes.

Early female flower beginning developing.

Cutting male flowers for pollen collection. Note the extreme difference in the early female and the male flowers.

Because all you want from the males is their pollen, space is not as much of an issue as it is with the females that you want to grow big and productive. Make certain the males will be indoors where they can be severely segregated; absolutely no random pollen transfer should be possible.

When and How to Collect Pollen

The male flowers develop into long hanging clusters of little pods full of pollen, and are very pretty to look at. At this point, the male(s) should have been isolated in a spare bathroom, shed, or similar area that is easy to seal off, has light, and is not somewhere the household needs to access (like your main bathroom). Remember, once they start flowering and shedding yellow pollen, you can become a conduit by carrying pollen on your clothing or hands. Keep contact and handling to a minimum, and change your clothing before visiting the girls.

As soon as the male has started the actual release of its bright yellow pollen, go ahead and cut some branches with good pollen clusters that appear ripe and ready to go. These can stand in tall vases of water set on clean glass (a large mirror works fine). The rest of the plant can be terminated and double bagged for later disposal.

Cut male flowers waiting to burst.

How to Store Pollen

The catch, or the pollen that falls off branch, is then scraped off the glass with a sterile razor blade and stored in very clean, dry glass Mason jars that are sealed tightly and then labeled. Do not touch the pollen with your hands.

Make certain only pollen is stored; small parts of the pollen flower or other debris can contain moisture and ruin the delicate pollen with molds. Keep in a cool, dark, dry place until ready to use.

Choosing the Flower to Pollinate

The benefit of selectively breeding by hand is that a female plant can be crossed with one or more male plants, provide seed, and yet retain most of the female as sinsemilla, or seedless cannabis.

ALERT

To avoid cross-contamination, make sure to thoroughly clean your tools and hands in between collecting pollen from different males.

If you are trying more than one cross, make a label for each male so you can identify the breeding later. If you are only working with one male, select a glittery twist tie (the glitter makes them easier to see) for easy marking of the pollinated (or seeder) branch.

Select healthy, well-shaped female flowers on strong axial branches approximately two thirds of the way down the main trunk of the plant. The flower can be bred any time after it shows multiple whitish pistils on the cola, as the female flower is known. Maturing seed will take between two to five weeks, so plan for an outdoor plant to set seed before your rainy season starts. It is possible to harvest the main plant and leave the seed branch(es) out to finish, but leaving it too late can invite mold.

Do not choose your top colas for pollination. Any pollen drift will be downwards on a still day, so lower branches are preferred for seeders.

Pollination Techniques

Pollination is the actual meeting of the pollen with the pistil of the female plant. Germination of the pollen grain requires meeting the ripe pistil and takes approximately ten to twenty minutes after contact. Successful germination results in fertilization (the union of the chromosomes of the parent plants), and is somewhat temperature-dependent. In colder weather, fertilization can sometimes take up to two or even three days.

FACT

In the wild, cannabis is pollinated by wind borne pollen. This, of course, is not going to work out well for the sinsemilla grower, so extreme care must be taken to prevent accidental release of pollen to the females.

Pay attention to the breeze patterns where you grow. If there is always a little breeze in the evenings, you may have to do your pollinating in the still of early morning. Ideally you will pollinate on a still evening, but the lack of wind is most important. Just as with planting seeds, make sure you have time to work slowly and carefully when it comes to pollination. Assemble all your tools ahead of time:

- Labels
- Bags (these should be long, light, narrow paper bags—baguette bags are good)
- Twist ties
- Grafting tape

Review the process before starting. Turn off your cell phone and get rid of other distractions. You want to be extremely focused.

First you want to pick out and label the branches on the females you will pollinate. Pick strong lower branches with healthy colas. Ideally, the female plant should be covered in colas with thick clusters of white pistils and very few brown. Once all the pistils are brown and withered, the reproductive period has passed. Remove most of the large shade leaves from the tips of the chosen branches (this will not hurt the plant).

Second, you will place a very small amount of pollen (1/8 teaspoon is sufficient) in the toe of your bakery bag. Do not shake this around. Pinch the bag shut to contain the pollen until you open it to slip onto the chosen branch. Gently work the bag down the branch and tie off with grafting tape to securely seal the bag to the branch. Gently tap the bag and shake the branch to distribute the pollen as evenly as possible.

ESSENTIAL

There is no need to breed every female you have, but as quirky as nature is, the one plant you do not breed is somehow always one of the best of the crop. Bear this in mind when deciding how many to breed.

Leave the bags in place approximately three to four days, then carefully remove them directly into a plastic trash bag and take the bag far away from the grow site to be destroyed. There is still a small chance that viable pollen can escape, so continue to wash your hands and change your clothes after handling. Keep an eye on the pollinated branches; you should start to see swelling of the calyxes within the week.

Propagation by Cloning

Remember that you will be reproducing an exact replica of the genotype when you create cloned plant. It is important to start with a mother plant or plants of superior quality. You won't be able to improve the strain, so what you start with is what you get.

Also bear in mind that having an entire crop of identical clones can have two negatives: in time you will get bored with the taste and effects and want a change, and more importantly, you set yourself up for more risk of crop failure. The cloned plants are identical, which means they will react to disease and pests in exactly the same way. If the strain you have chosen to reproduce lacks the genetic ability to fight back infections, or is particularly susceptible to molds or mites, you could lose it all.

Picture the large commercial dairy herds that provide most Americans with milk. Although they are not cloned, purebred dairy cattle have a pretty small genetic diversity. The standardized genetics help with consistent levels of milk production and butter fat content, but a virus could take out entire herds, if not the majority of the American dairy industry. A century ago there was much more genetic diversity; each county had its own breeds, adapted to the conditions of the land in their specific area. Now milk cows rarely go outdoors. Their milk production is manipulated by artificial light, and more crowded conditions create an environment more conducive to the spread of disease (not unlike cannabis grown in grow rooms). Based on this factor alone, it is strongly advised to have more than one cloned strain in your crop.

FACT

Even if you are taking cuttings or clones from a local grower, research the strains they provide. Most of the big seed banks have online detailed information on characteristics of different strains. This can help you balance your crop for variety.

Take more cuttings than you are planning to need as some will possibly fail to develop roots, especially while you are on a learning curve. If you are successful in rooting all your cuttings, however, you will have a few extra plants to either give away or grow as back ups.

How to Take a Cutting

Preparation and organization will make this process easier. Be sure to have the time set aside to work calmly and without distraction. Get all your tools ready, and prepare the rooting pots and soil beforehand. Plants will try to heal themselves as rapidly as possible (just like your body will try to stop a bleeding wound), so leaving cuttings hanging around will greatly lessen your chance of successful rooting. Ideally you will take the cutting with the stem itself in water. You will need to recut the stem if you must wait (say, a friend took a cutting and gave it to you), but this is not really the way to go. An air bubble or embolism can be trapped in the hole in the stem as soon as the stem is cut. This will cause the clone to die, as the air bubble blocks fluid flow.

Cloning Essentials

Uniformly successful cloning requires the cut stems to have a high carbohydrate level and low nitrogen concentrations. Make certain the mother plant has good drainage and flush the plant with large amounts of water to leach out nitrogen. Do this for three or four days. The nitrogen levels will fall as the plant uses what is available, and carbohydrate levels will build. Some growers encourage the same process by foliar feeding the mother with clean water; heavy misting daily for four days. If the mother plant is in less than ideal drainage, foliar feeding is safer since heavy soaking of poorly drained soil can cause root rot. The plant will have less nitrogen, growth will slow, and the green of older leaves will become lighter.

The clones will also perform better if the cuttings have high levels of root growth hormones. These hormones concentrate mostly at the base of the plant, so take your cuttings from this area close to the main stem or trunk of the mother plant. This is newer growth with the most hormones. It is possible to take cuttings from the top of a plant, but the lesser amount of root growth hormones will cause these cuttings to root very slowly. Generally, you can expect cuttings from older growth (the plant tops) to take twice as long to be ready to transplant.

The reason for this is that root growth hormones speed up the growth of interim phase undifferentiated cells. Obviously the cutting assumed it would stay on its mother plant and of course not need its own roots. It must now convert to producing root cells if it is to survive and become a separate plant. The undifferentiated phase is part of this conversion while your little cutting figures out what's happening and adjusts accordingly. Cutting to maximize root growth hormones is an important help to your potential clone as it struggles to convert from producing stem cells to producing root cells.

How to Help Your Cutting

Another good way to assist your cutting is to use a rooting hormone. Although these are available in powder and liquid forms, most cloners seem to prefer using a gel application such as Clonex. Gels are much less messy, require no mixing, and efficiently seal cut tissue. Powder forms generally contain talc, which humans should avoid breathing.

If you are organic to the core and want to use a natural hormone booster, try willow water. This very old technique has proven for years to boost rooting activity. Willow water has been shown to promote 20 percent more roots than using plain water. To make willow water, you'll use slim willow branches (approximately 1 inch in diameter), cut into short lengths and stripped of their leaves. Pack them in a clean glass jar, fill the jar with clean water to cover the branches, and soak them for 24 hours. Pour the water into smaller jars and let your cuttings soak for another 24 hours. Then plant them in soil. Clones perform better at rooting with a pH of five to five and a half. It is advisable to test the pH if you are planting the cuttings directly into soil or a soil and compost mix.

The Cutting Procedure

In addition to the chosen mother plant(s), you will need:

- New, sharp, single edge razor blades
- Rooting gel
- Alcohol (for sterilizing, not for drinking)
- Disposable gloves (optional)
- Sharpie pen
- Containers
- Soil or a growing medium, like rooting cubes, well moistened

First, you will need to have decided which females to take cuttings from, and then flushed those mother plants for three days, if necessary. Make certain the mother is at least two months old. Look carefully at the plant and determine how many cuttings you want to take, and how many the plant can give you; a lot depends on the actual size of your mother.

Next, you'll want to spread out your tools and label the containers for the cuttings. It is best to do the labeling first, especially if you are taking cuttings from more than one mother plant during a session.

Make certain the growing medium is well moistened with a drill pre-made in the center of the pot or grow cube. You can use a pencil or your little finger, but prepare the soil to accommodate the stem and two trimmed nodes. The drill, or hole, should stop around a half inch to an inch from the bottom of your container.

Taking cuttings is like a little surgery for your plant; it is very important that everything be quite clean. Wash your hands with soap and hot water, and tools that will touch the cutting should be cleaned with alcohol. Many growers use disposable surgical gloves when they are taking cuttings, but washing your hands well should suffice. Take the clean razor and make an angled cut on the chosen stem. Remember, you will be taking cuttings from the area close to the main stem or trunk and near the base. You want a nice clean cut at a forty-five degree angle, not a straight cut. Take three to four sets of leaves in a cut about four inches in length. Immediately place the cut ends in clean water until you are done taking cuttings.

Making an angled cut on the chosen stem.

Cutting at a forty-five degree angle.

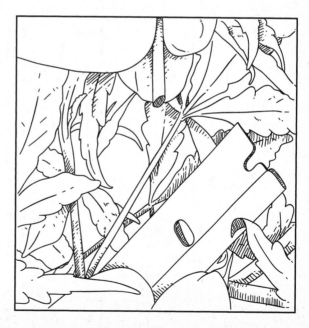

Next, trim off two sets of leaves and growth nodes nearest to the cut end of the stem, leaving the other two sets of leaves intact. Take your rooting gel and generously apply it to the cut end and all the way up to your trimmed nodes. The rooting gel immediately protects the cuttings and gives them what they need to reroot.

ALERT

While it is possible to take cuttings from a flowering female plant, it is much more difficult once the flowering hormones have launched. You will be trying to reverse a powerful force of nature; it can be done, but growers report difficulty and mixed results.

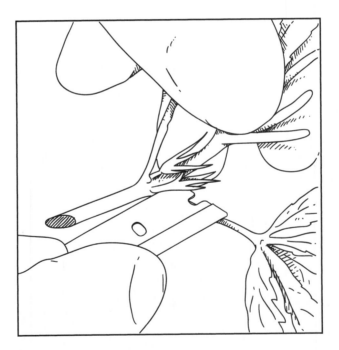

Trimming off two sets of leaves and growth nodes nearest to the cut end of the stem.

Finished cutting.

Rooting a Cutting

Place the cutting gently into the prepared potting soil or rooting cubes. If you are using soil, fill in the drill with a little soil and water. If you are using root cubes, pinch the top of the cube to bring the stem into full contact with the cube.

The cuttings need to be kept at very high humidity (90 to 100 percent) for the first few days, and then the humidity should be gradually reduced to around 80 percent by the third or fourth day. Some growers use small humidity domes because it is essential you keep the cuttings moist at all times. The domes are good labor-saving devices as they cut down on the amount of misting you need to do. The remaining leaves need to be lightly misted with water for the plant to drink; remember that at this point the cutting has no roots at all and therefore needs to foliar drink until it can grow some.

Clones will root in a small greenhouse, but experienced cloners advise giving them eighteen to twenty-four hours of fluorescent light. The little cuttings leaves are doing all the work for the soon-to-be plant, and consequently cannot tolerate intense light. A cool, white light like fluorescent is best.

You can get your clones to root faster if you keep the soil or growing medium slightly warmer than the air temperature. Some growers use a heating mat or raise the clone tray up higher and place a light bulb underneath it for warmth.

ESSENTIAL

Cuttings can be helped along by trimming their starter leaves as they brown off. The cutting should always have some leaves (so it can transpire), but cutting off parts of or the entire dead leaf makes it easier on the little clone.

The clones should look like they are perking up within a few days to a week. They are probably not going to make it if they stay wilted after seven days. Sometimes you will have to cull these nonachievers since leaving them wilting amongst the healthy clones can lead to disease. The cuttings that have rooted successfully should be ready to transplant in one to three weeks. Check to see if there is healthy looking root growth from the grow cube or bottom of the little pot.

Once you have healthy white roots growing at least an inch and a half long from the cube, you can transplant your rooted clone and proceed with vegetative growth. Remember not to shock it by suddenly exposing it to bright and hot light (whether from the sun or grow lights); gradually lower the fluorescent lights to within a few inches of the clones to get them ready for more and hotter light.

CHAPTER 8

Soil and Growing Mediums

The first-time grower may ask, "Why not just used premade potting soils and be done with it?" This is an option, albeit a rather expensive one if you are growing more than a few plants on your deck. Raising healthy plants of any kind requires the grower to provide nutrients and to activate the microbial life in the soil. This is what feeds the plants. The good organic cannabis grower wants to promote a full range of beneficial organisms for healthier soil, which of course leads to healthier, happier, and more productive plants. It is important to have living soil, and the right type of soil for cannabis; it is well known for needing heavy feeding, very slightly acid soil, and good drainage.

What Is the Best Soil Mix for Cannabis?

It is helpful here to think about the nature of cannabis and what the plant needs for optimum growth and flowering. The final goal for the cannabis grower is to produce large, healthy, plants with large, healthy, resin-covered flowers. Without the proper soil mix and proper feeding during the grow, your plants could be stunted, low-producing, and have inferior flowers.

ESSENTIAL

Once your little seedlings are above ground, they are in a phase of vegetative growth. The plant is building healthy roots and making green leaves, size, and height. The right mix at this time will make the difference between stunted, starved little plants, and large, luscious, green, and happy plants. You need large roots to support a large superstructure.

Cannabis is a big feeder and fast grower. Many a novice grower has been astonished by transplanting off-schedule or late, and finding the container completely filled with a dense root ball. This is also why container growers must top feed on schedule; a plant in the ground can reach out and search for more food, but the container-bound plant depends on you to feed it.

The basic requirement of cannabis is nutrient-rich, well-drained soil. A good starter mix is one-third sandy loam for drainage, plus one-third compost you have made, finished off with one-third organic bagged soil like Fox Farm's Ocean Forest Potting Soil. You could just start out with Ocean Forest, as it contains sandy loam already and is an excellent mix for cannabis, but it is very expensive. Using sandy loam is important not only for the drainage, but also for a slightly firmer soil texture; cannabis is less than happy with the typical fluffy structure of many commercial bagged potting soils. Sandy loam can be purchased in bulk at garden centers and by the yard at what are typically called "feed and fuels" in rural areas.

Soil Types

An indoor grower may access soil or compost they have outside, but the outdoor grower has to consider whether or not to plant young plants directly into the ground or in large containers. There are good reasons for both alternatives: containers protect plant roots from burrowing rodents and allow the grower to control exactly what soil the plant has access to, while growing in the ground allows cannabis to really show its ability to get extremely large. The ground-planted cannabis plant is able to spread out its roots and really flourish.

ALERT

Always make certain your young plants have reached a viable size (at least two feet tall) before ground planting. Throwing seeds into the ground is wasteful, and tiny starts are vulnerable to garden pests.

If you plan to grow in the ground in the soil you have existing, you will need to identify your soil type and amend it for optimum cannabis production. The main types of soil include:

Clay

Clay soil is typically composed of 60 percent clay, 20 percent silt, and 20 percent sand. The clay actually has quite a few nutrients for the plant, but it is made up of very fine particles that tend to compact, interfering with the oxygen supply that plant roots require to actually use the nutrients. This compaction also makes your soil like concrete, allowing water to run off the surface and not enter the soil.

Obviously, clay soil is a poor choice for growing almost anything, let alone cannabis. If you plan to ground plant, you must dig out the offending clay and replace it with your own amended soil mix. The bigger the hole, the better, but two to three feet in diameter and three feet deep will accommodate an outdoor plant quite well.

Adobe

Adobe is the mother of all clay soils; dig it out and replace, or rather than struggle with iron-hard adobe, accept that you will be using containers and adjust your growing plans. You can try to amend adobe soil, but it will take years and truckloads of compost materials.

Sandy

Sandy soil can be very difficult to correct; it is on the other end of the spectrum from clay, as it drains too well and the plant loses the nutrients as water carries them away. It also wastes water and makes it difficult to know how much water the plants are actually receiving. A typical sandy soil will be almost 70 percent sand. Start amending your sandy soil immediately with organic materials, but plan on growing your cannabis in containers for the first few years. It takes a lot of work to adjust sandy soils, although with time, lots of organic material, and patience, it can be improved.

Loam

Loam is the Holy Grail of soils. It retains nutrients and water for "self service" access by the plants, and is very easy to work with. Most growers do not wake up one morning and find their soil has turned into loam, but good organic gardening practices can improve a reasonable soil until you do have it. Loam is made up of 40 percent sand, 40 percent silt, and 20 percent clay. In this mix, the plant can access the good nutrients in clay soil because there is sufficient air available. When you are mixing your own soil, strive to match the blend that makes loam so special for plants.

Alternative Mediums for Growing

The so-called "soil-less" or artificial soil mixes are inexpensive and sterile growing mediums used by commercial growers, particularly the people who use hydroponic techniques.

Artificial soils are generally made from perlite, vermiculite, peat moss, sand, and other components like coconut coir and pumice. Since the artificial soil is just a medium, be aware that you will have to supply all the nutrients the plants will need if you plan to use it.

Perlite

Perlite and vermiculite are both widely used in the horticultural industry because they are sterile and free from diseases, provide aeration and drainage, have a fairly neutral pH, are nontoxic, and are relatively inexpensive. Indoor growers use them extensively, while outdoor growers frequently use them to lighten a soil mix.

Peat Moss

Peat moss was once living sphagnum moss from bogs that has partially decomposed. As a soil amendment, peat moss breaks down too fast, compressing the soil and creating an unhealthy lack of air for plant roots. It can be useful when lightened with perlite, but the mining of peat moss is an environmentally unsound practice.

ESSENTIAL

Moisture retention and drainage are a bit different when the grower uses artificial soils as opposed to natural soil. Use a saucer or reservoir under the pots. Ensure that the artificial soil is moist; do not worry if the top is slightly dry. The lower parts where the roots are should be moistened by capillary action from the bottom reservoir.

Scraping off the top layer of living sphagnum moss affects the habitat for many rare plants, insects, and birds. Delicate communities that rely on the bog are disrupted and destroyed during this process. Sphagnum moss can eventually regrow, but the ecosystem it sustained cannot easily renew itself, if it can at all. For this reason, if you consider yourself a friend to the environment, you should consider the implications of using peat moss.

Be aware that peat moss is quite acidic. If you must use this artificial soil, check the pH level by testing the run off water, and adjust as needed.

Is Your Soil Healthy?

Plant roots need air to access food as well as water. A dense, compacted soil like clay may have lots of nutrients, but they remain unavailable to the plant due to lack of air. Good aeration stimulates beneficial bacterial activity, allowing the plant to use more organic matter.

Compacted soil will also speed up moisture loss; in packed soils, water rises rapidly to the surface and is lost through evaporation. This can get frustrating, especially when you are paying a large water bill.

Minerals are also essential for healthy growth in cannabis. Most chemical fertilizers only focus on measuring levels of nitrogen, phosphorus, potassium, and calcium; these primary elements are essential, but used in excess can result in deficiencies in other elements your plants will need. Remember, more is not necessarily better.

The grower must also be alert to the acidity or alkalinity of the soil mix. Cannabis prefers a soil that is not too acid and not too alkaline; a pH of 6.5 is just about perfect. Some growers swear by a slightly lower pH; most estimate that the range for soil-grown cannabis is 6.5 to 7.5.

ESSENTIAL

Acidic soil will lock up nutrients, making them unavailable to your plant for growth and flowering. A high acid content also damages the soil balance by limiting the growth of beneficial soil organisms. This is why you do not plant your cannabis in pure compost: too much organic content can raise the acid level to the point where your plant cannot use the nutrients you provide. Highly alkaline soil can lead to salt accumulation that will limit the roots' ability to take up water.

The soil for your cannabis should be organic and alive. Cannabis is a consumable, like a vegetable, that you will put into your body. If you use organic, live soil, you will see greatly improved plant health and also notice an increase in the quality of your end product.

Why Use Living Soil?

Soil organisms interact with one another, with plants, and with the soil. The combined result is a number of beneficial functions including nutrient cycling, moderated water flow, and pest control. Living soil organisms decompose organic compounds, separate nitrogen and other nutrients, and capture nitrogen from the atmosphere, making it available to the plants. These soil organisms also prey on crop pests.

Soil organic matter is used for the energy and nutrients the plants need. Bacteria, fungi, and other soil dwellers transform and release nutrients for the plants to use. In living soil, the soil directly around plant roots is teeming with bacteria. These bacteria feed on sloughed-off plant cells as well as the proteins and sugars released by roots. The protozoa and beneficial nematodes that eat the bacteria are also concentrated near roots. Complex organic compounds called humus remain after the many soil organisms have used and transformed the original material. Humus is important for improving water and nutrient holding capacities.

This nutrient cycling and disease suppression is a complex process your plants need to flourish. Dead, chemically treated soils cannot supply an environment conducive to good plant health and natural disease controls. It is far better to work with nature and encourage natural controls than to dump in chemical fertilizers that will eventually destroy your soil.

How Do I Encourage Living Soil?

Start with compost. Successful compost building must balance four ingredients: carbon, nitrogen, moisture, and oxygen. Leaves, straw, and cornstalks are high in carbon while manures are good sources of nitrogen. Ideally, use three parts carbon-rich materials like dead leaves, shredded newspaper, straw, or cornstalks to one part nitrogen-rich materials like fresh leaves, manures, vegetable peelings, or fresh grass clippings. Or, even more simply, use one third horse or cow manure layered with two thirds leaves. Sprinkle in some high nitrogen blood meal, keep it moist, and turn it weekly. The more finely shredded your ingredients, the faster they will become finished compost.

Your pile should be at least three cubic feet, if not larger. If you use a composter, inoculate the mix with soil, finished compost, or fresh manure.

You want the pile to get hot and "cook" in the beginning. The heat will kill weed or grass seeds that may be in the manures. Turn the pile once a week and keep it moist. The compost is ready when it is cool and looks like moist chocolate cake. It should smell good, like fresh-turned earth.

Since compost can take nine to twelve months to mature, outdoor cannabis gardeners should build compost piles in the fall. Some growers build a new compost pile over each plant site each fall. They then mix it into their soil in the spring and test the compost to see what amendments, if any, are needed, and if the planting sites are ready and refreshed.

FACT

A pH meter is a long lasting tool that will give you more accurate results than other methods of measuring pH. Unfortunately, the price may be too expensive for first time grower on a budget. These tools use probes and batteries that eventually will need to be replaced, so consider a one-time use pH test kit. If you continue growing, and are continually buying new test kits, a meter can be a good investment.

Organic compost is also available in bags from garden suppliers. There is nothing wrong with using the bagged variety, but the grower who has space for composting will save a great deal of money making his or her own. You will also find that you can be much more generous to your plants when you are able to use compost you made yourself; the bagged varieties can make a budget-conscious grower stingy without wanting to be.

Soil Testing

Every type of plant has a different perfect level of soil acidity/alkalinity, or pH measurement, that allows it to perform to an optimum standard. Cannabis in general prefers soil to be just slightly acidic at 6.5 pH. This is about the same as a tomato plant, so if you have a garden spot where you have successfully grown large and healthy tomatoes, it is probably going to be all right for your cannabis. Soil pH is measured on a scale from 1.0 to 14.0. A pH of 7.0 is pH neutral, while a pH below 7.0 is considered acidic. And pH level higher than 7.0 is considered to be alkaline.

The pH level of your soil will determine how well your plants are able to absorb nutrients. If the pH level is out of the proper range, the growth rate of the plants will slow down or even stop. Your plants will become visibly stressed. It is worthwhile to purchase a meter or test kit since it will allow you to put your young cannabis plants into properly balanced soil from the start and avoid stressing or damaging the plants from too high or low pH levels.

The nitrogen, phosphorus, and potassium (N-P-K for short) levels should be listed if you are using purchased, bagged, pre-mixed soils. If you are mixing your own soil, it is advisable to test your soil for N-P-K using a soil test kit. These are easy to use, and there are reliable kits available that contain separate tests for pH, nitrogen, phosphorus, and potassium.

A single soil test kit will have a certain number of tests that can be done before you have to run out and buy another; some can be used to check pH, nitrogen, phosphorus, and potassium levels ten times. You will probably need to make some amendments once you have tested your soil. Cannabis is extremely forgiving of less than perfect soil conditions, but your goal is to raise healthy, productive plants that produce delicious, resin-covered flowers. If the plants are struggling, you will fall short of this goal.

Soil Amendments

Different organic soil amendments are usually needed when you are starting a grow site. Organics are typically safer than chemical fertilizers because they rarely burn plants, but testing your soil and understanding the different properties of different organic amendments can help you choose wisely. As an added benefit, this understanding will help your budget, too.

Packaged amendments generally list the Big Three of plant needs as follows: nitrogen (N), phosphorus (P), and potassium (K). Always check, though, as extremely high nitrogen can burn plants.

Nitrogen and Manures

The great value of manure is its extended availability of nitrogen, a selling point of particular value in readily leached sandy soils. Nutrient content and rate of availability can vary, depending mostly on manure source or type, how it's applied, and water content. Fresh manure worked in immediately after spreading will retain the most nitrogen.

Generally speaking, poultry manure is highest in nitrogen content, followed by hog, steer, sheep, dairy, and horse manure. Feedlot steer manure tends to have lower nitrogen concentration and lower gradual nitrogen release. Faster nitrogen-release sources, such as poultry manure, require more constant application rates to maintain nitrogen availability.

FACT

If you are growing in containers on a deck you may not have the option of building soils easily. Although they are expensive, there are many good organic boxed products for soil amendments available.

The advantages of adding organic matter content, and the disadvantages of possible weed seed, should be considered in using uncomposted manure. Manures should be composted before directly applying them to growing cannabis plants. Uncomposted manures should be applied in the fall to outdoor grow sites; they will compost and mellow through the winter as the winter rains to leach any salts.

Composted manure can also be used to make a tea to feed your plants during the vegetative stage; there is little chance of burning the plants, so you can be quite generous and feed a manure tea as often as once a week.

Hot or fresh manure should be composted before using. Manures are usually available free from small farmers or horse stables. Some stables will even load your truck for you since manure management and disposal is always a headache for horse owners.

Mushroom Compost for Tilth

Mushroom compost is not made from mushrooms, but rather for them. Mushroom farms make this compost as a growing medium for commercial mushroom crops. Mushroom compost is normally made in a hot composting process with straw, animal manure, and gypsum. The materials frequently come from race tracks, where race horses are bedded on oat or wheat straw. Other nutrients are usually added as well, either while composting or after composting. Many of these additions are organic in nature, such as blood meal or cottonseed meal, but sometimes there are inorganic additives such as urea.

The compost heats up to about 160°F and is turned several times, then steam-pasteurized to kill micro-organisms and any opportunistic wild fungi that might be competition for the mushroom crop. This medium is used for around fourteen weeks; then it is steam sterilized again and sold as spent mushroom compost.

Problems with Mushroom Compost

Sterilization is a problem with mushroom compost because microbiology is vital for disease prevention and supplying nutrients to your plants. Spent mushroom compost lacks these benefits; it is basically dead matter, though it still provides a good substrate and food source for that biology. Steam pasteurizing is not like using fungicides. You can reintroduce micro-organisms by mixing them with your own compost before applying it, or set it outside and let nature start working on it. Always check with the supplier to make certain they have not used pesticides, and smell the compost before you buy it. Start asking questions if it has a distinct chemical smell.

Another problem with mushroom compost is that it tends to have a high salt content. This is not necessarily different from any manure-based compost, so put the compost outside for a while to allow the rain to leach away the salts. You can also speed up the process by watering the pile. Use mushroom compost to improve tilth in clay soils, but avoid using it too heavily year after year because of the high salt content. You will eventually have too much salt, and this will impede the plants' ability to take nutrients from the soil.

You also need to be aware that many mushroom composts contain traces of synthetic fertilizers. This it is yet another reason why this should not be your preferred yearly compost on outdoor grow sites. Do not use mushroom compost as a replacement for good compost, but rather as a cheap soil amendment.

Benefits of Using Mushroom Compost

The one big advantage of using mushroom compost is the price; large amounts are incredibly cheap, especially if you pick it up yourself. The fine texture of mushroom compost also makes it easy to dig and work with. Ideally, you will have a mushroom farm close enough to pick it up yourself and in many cases the farm will load your truck for you. Some farms will give the compost away, but most are now charging a nominal fee for a truckload.

Lime for Acidic Soil Control

A good way to stabilize soil pH is to use dolomite lime, or calcium-magnesium carbonate. Dolomitic lime acts slowly and continuously, so your soil will remain pH-stable for a few months. It has a pH that is neutral (7.0). When added to soil in the correct proportions, it will stabilize soil at a pH near 7.0.

Use fine size dolomite lime, as the plant will take longer to break down and use coarser grades; they can take a year or longer to work. Fine size dolomite lime is readily available at any garden supply center.

For container growing, add one cup of fine dolomite lime to each cubic foot of soil. Mix the dry soil thoroughly with the dolomite lime, water lightly, and then remix. Recheck the pH after two days.

Wood Ash, Oyster Shells, and Eggshells

Small amounts of hardwood ashes or crushed oyster or eggshells will help to raise the soil pH. If you use wood ash, make certain it is from a good hardwood like white oak that you have specifically burned for clean ash. Do not use colored paper or chemical fire starters to start your burn since these can add undesired elements to your clean wood ash.

Eggshells should be organic and finely ground. A good way to ensure a fine grinding is to use a clean coffee grinder. The fine grind will make the shell more quickly available to the plants; it takes much longer to break down big chunks of shell.

Oyster shells are available preground at most garden stores; as with eggshell, a fine grind will make the shell easier for the plants to use more quickly.

Even with gentle amendments like eggshell, you should wait at least a day or two before checking the pH level of your soil. If adjustments still have to be made, use small amounts and keep testing. It is easier to add to soil than to try to remove amendments; like salt in cooking, a bit too much can ruin everything.

Bone Meal

Bone meal is made from animal bones (usually cow bones) that are steamed and then ground. It is an excellent source of phosphorus, which helps with cell division and root growth in plants. Bone meal also contains phosphates, usually amounting to 10 percent of the product.

Bone meal is recommended for its controlled-release form of phosphorus. The nutrients are insoluble in water, and so the plants slowly convert it to a form that they can use. Other sources of organic phosphorus include rock phosphates and colloidal phosphates, but both are more expensive than bone meal and can be hard to find. Cheaper synthetics offer high levels of phosphorus that are more immediately available to plants, but these aren't recommended. Super phosphates are made by treating minerals with acid that can burn your plants and are not considered organic.

Bone meal is available at almost any garden center. It is quite gentle, so you can be fairly generous when you are mixing your soil; two or three handfuls can be added to a wheelbarrow load of soil or later scratched into the surface of your plant container.

Blood Meal

Blood meal is exactly what it sounds like: dried, powdered blood that is used as a fertilizer. Slaughterhouses usually make blood meal as a by-product. Blood meal is a high-nitrogen (approximately 13 percent) organic plant food, so care should be taken not to apply too much since soil bacteria break down the blood proteins rapidly to make ammonia. The plant roots absorb the ammonia to take up nitrogen, which is useful during the vegetative phase of cannabis as it adds lots of leafy growth.

ESSENTIAL

Although it may seem far easier to add chemicals to your soil, organics will pay off in the long run. Chemicals will end up creating dead soil; organics feed the living soil.

Many new growers initially confuse bone and blood meal, but they will only do so once. Unlike bone meal, blood meal is very acidic, should be used sparingly, and should not be applied to young seedlings. Decomposition can be too rapid in warm moist conditions like grow rooms, causing enough ammonia to be released in to damage delicate roots.

Blood meal applications last up to four months, and should be used with caution; use no more than four ounces per square yard during the growing or vegetative phase. Growers sometimes use it as an element in tea for their plants since diluting the meal makes it less likely to burn tender young plants. It can also be used to kick start a compost pile that has mostly high carbon ingredients. Some growers have reported success in using it to repel deer, attributing the effect to the "blood smell." This may or may not work for you; it all depends on how hungry the deer are in your area. Blood meal is available at all garden stores.

Bat Guano

Bat guano, or bat feces, is a natural super fertilizer and a favorite among cannabis growers. It contains many necessary macro- and micro-nutrients, as well as a whole host of beneficial micro-organisms that cannot be provided by chemical fertilizers. It is often very high in nitrogen, but this can depend on whether the guano comes from insect-eating bats or fruit-eating bats. Fruit eaters produce guano that is higher in phosphorus.

Guano generally consists of ammonia, along with uric, phosphoric, oxalic, and carbonic acids, some earth salts, and a high concentration of nitrates. The Big Three nutrients are supplied in these approximate amounts: 9 percent nitrogen, 6 percent phosphorus, and 2 percent potassium.

Unless you have a source for guano, like a convenient bat cave, generally the grower must purchase it from an organic garden supplier. It can be quite expensive, but the benefits are so great that it is worth the money. Many growers stretch their guano dollars by making bat guano tea to feed their plants:

Use 3 tablespoons of bat guano to 1 gallon of water. Premix the tea in a large bucket using warm (but not hot) water. The warm water breaks down the bat pellets much more efficiently than cold and minimizes stirring. Let the tea steep for at least forty-eight hours before feeding to your plants. Although not strictly necessary, an aquarium pump and air stone will dissolve oxygen into the solution and keep the good bacteria alive and thriving. Let it bubble for a day or two before you use it if you use this method.

It is best to feed vegetative plants a cupful of the tea directly after watering because you may flush out all your good bat guano nutrients if you feed before watering. A diluted, non-burning mixture for young plants or seedlings can be made with as little as a tablespoon of guano.

Kelp Meal

Kelp meal (1–0–8) is a dry fertilizer made of iron seaweed that is very high in potassium and trace elements. Kelp meal is an excellent organic source of plant hormones that stimulate plant and root growth. Some cannabis growers use a liquid seaweed (4–2–3) mix for a quick boost that helps foliage and roots develop. Kelp meal is readily available at garden centers or can be ordered online from organic garden suppliers.

Gypsum

While some growers like to use gypsum to break up heavy clay soils, it is a much-preferred idea to use compost and other less intense methods to gradually improve your soil. Gypsum is calcium sulphate, so it adds calcium in a somewhat soluble form. The calcium it provides is exchanged on the soil particle surface for any excess sodium or magnesium present in the soil. Gypsum should only be used when exchangeable calcium is low and there is an excess of magnesium or sodium. Moisture is essential to dissolve the gypsum and then to leach out the magnesium and sodium.

Never use gypsum without testing your soil first. Gypsum should not be applied at all where there is a shallow, saline water table and no subsurface drainage; after the excess sodium and magnesium are leached down to the water table, the soil's own capillary action may bring them back to the plants' root zones. If you feel you must use it, gypsum can be found at garden centers. Be sure to read the directions very carefully.

Worm Castings

Worms are natural soil conditioners. They help soil structure by loosening soil and improving aeration and drainage. An abundance of earthworms is an excellent indication of healthy soil; if your pH is off, the earthworms will leave. Earthworms should be introduced to compost piles, new beds, and containers whenever possible.

Earthworms derive their nutrition from organic matter in your soil, processing decayed plant parts, decomposing remains of animals, and living organisms like nematodes, protozoans, rotifers, bacteria, and fungi. Earthworms produce their own weight in castings every twenty-four hours. They convert many insoluble minerals to a plant-available soluble form during their digestive process, and long-chain molecules such as cellulose are partially broken down by bacteria in the digestive tract. Fresh earthworm casts are several times richer in available nitrogen, available phosphates, and available potash than in the surrounding topsoil. Worm castings also contain many beneficial bacteria and enzymes, making them another favorite of cannabis growers. Most high-end organic potting mixes already contain earthworm castings; check the ingredients when you purchase them, as worm castings are extremely beneficial and useful to your plants.

As with any soil amendments, always read labels when available and pay close attention to dilution instructions. Just because something is organic does not mean it will not harm a plant if used in excess. More is not always better, and can lead to trouble if you dump large amounts of additives into your soil and hope for the best.

That being said, most unimproved soils are not ready for prime time; any efforts you make toward creating a near to perfect soil environment will always be rewarded by the ever-obliging cannabis plant. As this sort of problem-solving eventually becomes familiar to you as a gardener, you will find it exciting to build soil and will therefore evolve your own "perfect" soil mix to suit to your micro-climate and plant strains.

CHAPTER 9

Growing Cannabis in Containers

An outdoor container garden can be grown on a deck or interspersed with other cover/companion plantings within your regular garden. This can be one of the best ways to start off growing cannabis; it allows you to try growing without a large outlay in labor and materials and allows for easy moving of the plants as you learn how the sun moves around your property during the growing season. And, of course, 99 percent of indoor grows are by circumstance container grown.

Things to Consider When Growing in Containers

If you are thinking of a small outdoor grow in containers, the first two things to look at are how close your neighbors are and how accessible your deck or backyard garden is to passersby. Ideally, your grow area will fenced in and have a locking gate.

Light

Another big factor in urban or suburban grows is the presence of artificial light; do your neighbors have nighttime security lights or bright porch lights? Are there streetlights on all night? Cannabis's flowering is triggered by light cycle, be it natural seasonal duration of the sunlight, or by artificial light, so light shining on the plants for twenty-four hours a day can be a problem.

Proximity to Schools

Be sure to check into the laws in your particular state, since many legal medical growers have been dismayed to find out that growing (even indoors) within 1,000 feet of a school is a prohibited activity. This is something far better known ahead of time, as the legal implications can be very troublesome.

Potential Thieves

Even if you are growing legally on your own property, remember that your cannabis will be very attractive to thieves. The best way to protect your plants is to have them blend in with an existing container garden, or mix containers and larger varied plants that are perennial, larger, and growing in the ground.

Remember that many, if not most, people do not see plants as different entities at all; if pushed, they might be able to identify a tomato plant, and then only if it is covered with large red tomatoes. Make this general lack of knowledge work for you. An array of different greens and leaf types (think of how camouflage works) make it much harder for the non-gardener to spot cannabis. Most cannabis thieves are not gardeners; that is why they are out stealing yours!

Container Types

There is a wide variety of useful containers available, so you will need to assess them according to availability, cost, and efficiency. The size of the containers you use for mature cannabis plants will, in part, be determined by how big you can allow the plants to get. If you live in a suburban town-house and are growing a few on your deck, you will want to keep the plants small to avoid detection and theft. Cannabis plants are somewhat like gold-fish: if you keep giving them more space and food, they will mostly grow to fit their space. A ten-foot sativa towering on your balcony will make its presence known to even the most unobservant.

Small Containers

Let's start with the smallest first. Say you plan to grow four plants on your deck. You have access to water, and ideally already have some general plants out there, including herbs and container tomatoes. To simplify, you start with clones, so you know they are females. You have identified the sunniest spot, and have checked that your deck is not overlooked by taller buildings.

ESSENTIAL

Cannabis likes lots of drainage; there is nothing it resents more than having its toes wet and soggy. Most nursery pots lack enough drain holes, so take a drill to the bottom and double the drain holes. Put in a bottom layer of drain rock to improve drainage.

The least expensive way to go is to use recycled nursery pots. These can come from a friend who has recently purchased and planted large shrubs in the ground, or nurseries will frequently give used plastic pots away or sell them for a nominal fee. Ones used for baby trees can be quite large; up to fifteen or twenty gallons in size.

Give recycled pots a thorough cleaning, including wiping them down with a light bleach solution and then rinsing them with clean water. This will help eliminate any harmful fungi or bacteria that may have been in the previous soil.

Go for the five gallon pots since you are keeping your plants small. The taller variety seems to work better than the shorter, fatter version; they both hold five gallons of soil, but the taller pots suit the cannabis growing style a bit better. Of course, if all you can find are the shorter pots, cannabis will accommodate you and adjust itself accordingly.

Wine Barrels

Another, more elegant, solution for containers is recycled oak wine barrels. In the early heyday of cannabis growing in 1970s Mendocino County, wine barrels were cheap. The California wine industry was growing rapidly at this time, and the barrels were not typically reused once wine had been bottled. If purchased directly from the winery, the whole barrels also had the interesting benefit of frequently containing up to a gallon or so of good wine to be salvaged! Now wine barrels are sold as half barrels for $20 and up.

ALERT

It might seem obvious, but be careful and think ahead when using power tools to make drain holes. Drilling through the bottom of a container is simple until you figure out you just drilled through too far and made holes into your (or your landlord's) nice deck. Flip the container over for this activity!

While wine barrels are attractive, breathe well, and have excellent drainage, they are also expensive, hard to clean, and will eventually rot. If you are going to use half barrels, make certain to get your drill out and make multiple drain holes in the bottom. The wine barrels hold more soil, so be prepared for your plants to get quite large. With the right feeding and watering, a sativa cross grown in a half barrel can easily reach eight feet in height.

Plastic Barrels

Less elegant, but much cheaper and lighter to move when empty, are food-grade 30-gallon plastic shipping barrels. Each barrel can be cut in half to yield two containers. The plastic is very tough, but still easy to drill through and cut. If you are lucky enough to live near a port, do some telephoning and find a source for the used barrels. They must be rated food-grade, which means they originally contained something like soy sauce and not motor oil. Used barrels are sold clean and typically the whole barrel will cost somewhere between $8 and $15. The plastic barrels will last for years, unlike the similar-sized half oak barrel.

Sometimes food grade barrels come in bright colors like light blue, but the plastic will hold paint well. It is advisable to paint the outside surface with more natural colors (various greens, light browns; think camouflage again) so the barrels don't stand out too much. If you are planting a mixed garden totally in barrels, this is less of an issue. It's obviously not a good idea to have just the cannabis in bright containers, as it will draw attention specifically to the cannabis. You want the cannabis plants to blend in with your other garden plants.

Again, as with the half wine barrels, the plants will get quite large with so much growing space. Outdoor growers who experience vole or gopher problems with direct ground planting frequently use food grade barrels. The barrels can be half-buried in the ground for less visibility. If you use this option, be sure to make extra drain holes as the barrel will drain more slowly when buried. If voles or gophers are a problem, place a protective screen of chicken wire over the surface of the half-buried barrel to prevent rodents from top burrowing into your container.

Grow Bags

Grow bags are another container solution that can be economically sound for the grower; the main disadvantage is the need to support the bag and plant as the plants get large. Because of this, these are mainly advised for the grower with a greenhouse and larger crop size. Grow bags also come prepacked with peat or compost, so you have less control over your soil mix. Peat-free composts are improving, but most people still find peat bags give the best results.

If you are starting out in coldish spring weather, warm the bags by either storing them inside a heated room for a few days or covering them with black plastic sheeting in the sun. This will take the chill off and warm the compost. Remember, young plants crave warmth.

Preferably wearing gloves, shake the bags hard enough to loosen the compost and prick the bottoms with a knife or a garden fork for drainage before putting them in their planting positions.

One disadvantage of grow bags is their need for support. Set up supports for tall plants against a wall, hammer stakes into the ground around the grow bag, or purchase a self-supporting grow bag frame. You will also need to position your watering aids before planting. Trying to do this later will disturb the plants' roots and slow growth.

Cut pot-sized crosses in the top of the bag between your centered plant spot and sink a 4-inch plastic plant pot into the compost up to its rim in each position. Direct the water and feed into these pots so it will quickly soak down to the bottom of the bag.

ALERT

If you have more than a few bags, it is worth investing in a drip feed watering system with a timer. Cannabis has an enormous appetite for water and will quickly fill the bag with roots, which, unlike soil, do not retain water. Bags can dry out much more rapidly than barrels.

Now that you have the bags set up, cut a cross in the center of the top of the bag the size of the plant's interim pot, peel back the plastic, un-pot the plant, and plant.

Smart Pots Aeration Containers

Smart Pots Aeration Containers are a recent innovation in containers that are being successfully used by many growers. The technology is a super strong black fabric material that warms up quickly in the spring, giving the plants a friendly environment for rapid growth. The porous nature of the fabric has the excellent breathability needed for root development, and allows heat to escape through evaporative cooling when the temperature rises in the summer. The fabric also drains very well, an essential need of cannabis.

Of interest to the outdoor grower is that the fabric base will contour to and establish capillary contact with the soil. Both outdoor and indoor growers will appreciate that the Smart Pots come in many sizes, from small to very large, so you can customize your purchases to fit your growing space without compromising your ideal.

Raised Beds

A larger container the grower might consider, depending on space and privacy considerations, is a large raised bed. The advantages include an abundance of food, good drainage that matches a direct ground planting into improved soil, and the roots are protected from burrowing rodents by the wire bottom of the container. The extra height makes for greater ease in working on the plants, and the grower maintains excellent control over the soil mix.

Four large cannabis plants can be grown in an eight foot by eight foot raised bed. If you have sufficient sunlight and pay attention to feeding and watering, you can normally expect a yield of a pound to a pound and a half from each plant. You will need:

- A roll of chicken wire or similar mesh size metal (heavier gauge is fine)
- 12 heavy (preferably 8 × 8) 8-foot posts. Railroad ties are not recommended as they are soaked with creosote to prevent wood rotting. Unfortunately, creosote is now a known carcinogen, and should therefore not be used when planting consumables. If you do use railroad tie, enclose the inside of the bed with flashing or heavy-duty black plastic so the plants do not come in contact with it.
- ¾-inch drain rock (enough to cover square footage 2 or 3 inches in depth)

Prep Work

You'll first want to mark out your square, planning, as always, for the seasonal movement of the sun. Second, check the soil drainage where you plan to locate the bed. Do a small perk test by digging a few small holes to one foot in depth and fill them with water from your hose. Monitor the soil to see how quickly water drains. If it stands for hours, like it would in a bucket, you have poor drainage and probably compacted clay soil. Use a small garden tiller do a light pass over the square to improve drainage, otherwise do a little aerating with your garden fork.

Assembling Your Raised Bed

Of course, if the soil is already well drained you can proceed to spread the drain rock evenly within the square, and lay your wire bottom out flat. If you are using chicken wire, it will tend to curl back into its roll form as you struggle to spread it out, so have it overlap the outside dimension of the enclosure by two to three inches. Use some heavy rocks or soil sacks to weight the ends until you start stacking your walls. The walls will then hold the wire in place solely by weight.

ESSENTIAL

A good garden fork is an extremely useful tool. If you lack a tiller, you can aerate soil by poking holes with the fork, or by using it to actually lifting the soil gently. Do not turn the soil; this disturbs the beneficial bacteria. You are trying to improve drainage and also allow air to reach compacted earth.

Using a heavier gauge rigid panel type of wire is easier to work with alone, as you can just lay the flat panels down. Make sure the holes are no larger than the ones in chicken wire or voles may burrow upwards through a larger hole.

Stack the sides of the raised container to a minimum of sixteen inches in height. If you want to go higher and have the soil resources to fill the container, go right ahead; the plants will not mind at all. If you prepare the raised bed in the fall you can stack it with manures and then mulch the top with spoiled hay to mellow through the winter. In the spring you can till in all the site-made compost; all winter the nutrients have been bathed with rainfall and composting in your bed. A garden fork is all you will need to work the bed, although some growers have tiny tillers (Honda makes a fairly good one).

The containers you use will depend on your budget and your ingenuity; growers are continually finding new sources for earth-containing cannabis homes. There is no right way or wrong way, as long as you remember drainage is a key factor with containers. You can have the best soil in the world, but without proper drainage it will go sour and become unusable for your plants.

Container Soil

A container grown plant is far more dependent on you for food than a plant that grows in improved soil in the ground. Although they are also fed on schedule, the ground planted cannabis can spread out to seek nutrients. The container plant has a much smaller, rigidly limited environment; they react much more quickly if you forget or delay a feeding.

FACT

Once your little seedlings are up, they are working hard at building healthy roots and making large green leaves for efficient photosynthesizing. Photosynthesis is the process your plants use to combine sunlight, water, and carbon dioxide to produce oxygen and sugar (energy). Your soil mix must provide enough food for the plants to work with.

The right soil mix is essential to producing large, green, happy plants. Cannabis is a fast grower and big feeder so planning ahead isn't just a good idea; it's an essential part of your growing process. With cannabis you can't wait until the plant is frantically signaling you that it needs food or that its drainage is poor.

If you are working with clones, there is no reason to delay putting the plants in their final containers right away. If you are starting from seed and must deal with the sexual differentiation phase, you will not have the space, time, money, or inclination to put each little seedling into a big grow container. Until they declare male or female, you will be monitoring them in three to five gallon containers and feeding them frequently. If you are growing indoors, a three to five gallon container may be the largest your plants will get; remember, cannabis will mostly adjust to the space it has been given. Indoor growers have limited space and do not necessarily want the garden to outgrow its room.

Consider the Soil

The basic requirement for all cannabis is nutrient-rich, well drained soil. If you are not a gardener already, you may want to start out using really good, bagged potting soil. Some gardeners have a point of pride about using their own soil mixes; they also mix their own because they want control over ingredients and amendments. And, of course, there is the question of cost if you buy all your soil bagged. There are various kinds available at garden centers, but do not be swayed by price alone. A cheap mix will be heavy on the perlite (not that perlite is bad, in fact, it is very good for drainage, but it contains no nutrients at all).

It is also important to note that many potting mixes are made to support an average-sized houseplant in a small pot. They are frequently manufactured entirely from wood and bark fiber, composts, and soil conditioners, and have a light, fluffy texture. This texture requires the addition of sandy loam to make cannabis happy. Additionally, these mixes seldom contain enough nutrients to support healthy cannabis growth for more than a few months, if even that long. Their nitrogen (N) is usually too low, phosphorus (P) level is adequate, and the potassium (K) level is usually very high.

Starter Mixes

A good starter mix is one-third sandy loam for drainage, one-third compost you have made, and one-third an organic bagged soil like Fox Farm's Ocean Forest Potting Soil. You could just start out with Ocean Forest as it contains sandy loam already and is an excellent mix for cannabis, but that would be very expensive. If your grow site is small, or cost is no object, a mix of the Ocean Forest is really the way to go. If you plan to mix soil, sandy loam can be purchased in bulk at some garden centers and by the yard at rural feed and fuels.

While you are mixing your soil, you should sift all of the soil through a compost screen; this will remove lumps and bits of wood or other compost components that have not broken down. You can easily make a compost screener by using a two by four board and some strong, metal screening. Make a square the size that will fit over a wheelbarrow and nail the screening to one side of the square. The wooden frame will make a lip to hold soil as you rub it through the screen into your wheelbarrow. The discard materials can be thrown back on your compost pile, or used for mulch around other garden plants. Once you have screened your components, the soil will be easy to mix. It is easiest to screen and mix by the wheelbarrow load; the wheelbarrow makes a convenient mixing bowl and you can make certain all components are blended before filling your containers. You should wear gloves and a mask while you screen and mix, especially if the materials are dry enough to be dusty.

Water in the Soil

Once you have filled your containers with the carefully blended, screened soil mix, you need to gently water the soil and mix lightly to eliminate dry spots. Fill the container to standing water three times, and note the water coming from the drain holes. This should ensure that the soil mix is evenly dampened.

Plant Your Seedlings

Prepare a hole slightly deeper than the pot the seedling currently sits in, scratch in (lightly mix) a small handful of bone meal, unpot, and gently place the seedling in the hole. It is better to transplant when the seedling's soil is slightly dry since wet soil can break apart and take some of the seedling's root system with it. Fill in around the seedling, gently but firmly pressing it into the soil; this will make for good soil contact for the roots and will help the plant transition more easily. Water the seedling and gently press it in place one more time. Ideally, transplanting should be done in early morning or in the evening; plants need a short period of recovery when transplanted, and stress from hot noontime sun can shock the little seedlings.

Fertilizing

Whether you start out with pure high-end bagged soil, like the Fox Farm brand mentioned previously, or create a similar blend on your own, there is really no need to initially feed too much extra if the containers are large. A small handful of bone meal worked into the planting hole will start each young plant off with good root building food, and the plant will draw what it needs from the soil.

A manure tea can be fed once a week after watering; manure teas are so gentle that some growers feed each time they water. If your plants' foliage is a healthy green and growing vigorously, you know they are getting what they need. Stay on the lookout for leaves that begin narrowing or turning yellow; these plants are signaling they need food. Bear in mind that indicas tend to have very dark green leaves while sativas are a paler green like healthy bamboo. Do not mistake a genetic trait for a plant problem. Plants that are hungry for nitrogen will pale; so feed them with manure tea and keep a close watch. If you were correct, the plants should respond within three to four days.

FACT

Some non-purist growers will use MiracleGro or similar commercial preparations early on in the vegetative phase. This can be fine, but once the plants start flowering, switch to an organic bloom-specific product, or you risk impaired taste in your final product.

Figure on using about a gallon of composted manure and four gallons of water to brew manure teas. Some kinds of manure are higher in nitrogen than others (bat guano is one of the highest), so you can adjust your blend slightly as you see how your plants respond.

If you use packaged fertilizers or ones you need to mix before applying, try to use only organics, and know that more is not better. Always read instructions and follow them carefully, or you could burn your plants.

Watering

Remember, rooftops or decks can be much windier than grow sites closer to the ground. Wind dries out plants and soil, so these sites will require closer moisture monitoring. Also, large containers of soil can get extremely heavy when fully watered, either by you or by rain. Plan ahead and make certain your deck or rooftop can safely take the weight of your container garden.

The amount and how you water in container gardening will have a large effect on how well your cannabis plants grow. Cannabis likes to dry out a little bit between waterings, so look for the soil to start to pull away from the rim of the containers. Once you see this, you'll need to water slowly with a gentle stream from your hose. The goal is to have the water gradually permeate the soil mix all over, not to have channels of least resistance where water can run down and out.

ESSENTIAL

A moisture meter is an invaluable aid in checking how much water your plants need. These are readily available at your local garden supply, starting at under $5.

Watering ten large cannabis plants in twenty-gallon containers can take a lot longer than you might think. An egg timer is a useful tool for watering; you can start the water going and come back to check at fifteen minute intervals. The container should fill and drain down three times to ensure that the plant is watered thoroughly. Just damping the top surface of the soil may look good, but the lower part of the container soil will be dry as a bone and leave your plants unhappy and thirsty.

Depending on weather conditions, (extra hot, or windy, or rainy and cool), you will have to vary your watering schedule. Stick a finger into the soil near the plants' roots. Is the soil damp from dew and extremely dry underneath? You need to know the answer to this question before the plants show stress.

During the phase of vegetative growth, it is fine for the outdoor grower to spray the plants leaves off after watering in the evening. This will knock off most unwanted insects and refresh the plants after a long hot day. Do not overhead water cannabis as a general practice; the plants do not like or require it, and you risk burning the leaves if the sun is high and hot.

Container gardening of cannabis is a fun and relatively easy way to start out as a grower, and most indoor growers are forced to use containers. It is a good way to protect plants from bad soils and burrowing animals, and is extremely productive if done correctly.

CHAPTER 10

Growing Cannabis Outdoors

Those who grow cannabis outdoors endure many trials and tribulations that the indoor grower never experiences. To make up for this, the outdoor grower will also enjoy some wonderful moments that the indoor grower misses out on by staying in rigidly controlled grow rooms. For example, the late night garden visit with a glorious full moon overhead is not to be missed. The time you spend outdoors with your plants will bring you much closer to nature, something humans need for a healthy and happy life.

The Advantages of Growing Outdoors

Growing indoors or outdoors and what different people view as easy or fun depends, in part, on each individual's personality; some people love to be outdoors and interacting with nature in a very direct way. Others need the feeling of control and protection for the plants they see in the indoor environment. You have to choose the method that suits your lifestyle, growing space, and approach to growing in general.

Less Expensive

Outdoor growing has the advantage of using the sun, air, wind, and rain for free. The plants can grow larger planted in the ground, and are generally healthier with less trouble and preventative labor than is associated with an inside grow. Soil improvement can take place on site, instead of using only expensive bagged organic soils. A lot depends on the initial condition of your site's soil, but the more years you aerate, mulch, and add compost to a site, the better your soil will become. The garden repays you for your ongoing investment in time and materials each time you renew it.

If money is tight, you can plan ahead and improve your soil by mulching and composting with free materials. Leaves are everywhere in the fall, and are excellent for improving soil. People who live in town bag their fall leaves for pickup by the city. Ask politely if you may take the bagged leaves instead; it saves labor for you, and the city homeowner is going to rake and bag the leaves anyway. Mulch your areas in the fall and till in the composted leaves in the spring. Rain-spoiled hay is usually available for free or very cheaply in rural areas, and will hold down weeds in early spring. The composted hay makes a less-than-optimum soil very tilthy very quickly.

The rural outdoor grower can gather manures for composting without offending the sensibilities of nearby neighbors. Goats, chickens, horses, and cows are usually nearby, and you can get wonderful nitrogen-rich compost makings for free.

Outdoor cultivation requires far less expensive equipment, electrical expertise, and labor. The plants still need to be regularly watered and fed, but most of their development will be accomplished simply by allowing them to grow over spring and summer.

Larger Yields

Outdoor plants generally yield more than ones grown indoors simply because they are able to grow larger. Few indoor setups can accommodate plants as large as those grown outdoors. Assuming that detection isn't a problem, outdoor plants can comfortably grow six to eight feet in height. It is fairly normal for plants of this size to produce a pound to a pound and a half of dried buds. Germinating seeds early in the growing season allows your plants a long vegetative period before flowering is triggered by the shorter days of late summer.

Better Taste

Many people prefer the taste and effect of organically grown cannabis, and insist they can easily differentiate between cannabis grown with soil and sun and cannabis produced with hydroponics and grow lights.

Better for the Environment

The sun produces more light than any amount of metal halides in one grow room put together. In addition, there can be no doubt that growing cannabis by burning fossil fuels is less than Earth-friendly.

ESSENTIAL

It is estimated that it takes a half ton of coal to produce eight ounces of indoor cannabis. A single 1,000 watt grow light during a typical ten week indoor cycle consumes approximately 924 kilowatt hours. One kilogram of coal will make about two kilowatt hours of electricity. Powering that single 1,000 watt light for one grow cycle ends up using almost a half ton of coal or 400 pounds of natural gas.

Indoor growers are frequently forced to spray chemicals for pest control or face losing their crop to spider mites. Not only does this encourage the development of pesticide-resistant pests, but there are health implications for the end users of the cannabis as well. The health issues are even more serious when the cannabis is grown for medical use since patients can be especially sensitive to chemical residues.

Materials

Unlike an indoor grow, outdoor growing only requires a little electricity at the beginning and for a few months at the end of the cycle when the crop is hanging and drying. Little seedlings are generally started indoors; partly to get a jump on the growing season, partly because it is easier to monitor them closely if they are near you, and partly to get them to a size where they are in less danger from natural predators like earwigs, pill bugs, slugs, and birds.

Starting

Starting outdoor plants indoors requires very little other than a warm, clean and well-lighted workspace. They are only going to stay inside for ten days at the most. A seed-warming mat is useful, but not really essential. Grow lights can help your plants along, but new, tender seedlings do fine with cool fluorescents and a side source for warmth. The grower needs seeds or clones; small starting pots; clean, lump-free soil; and clean water.

ESSENTIAL

For optimized ripper protection, a grower can use a combination of all three: a high board fence to minimize visibility, electric wire on the inside of the fence top to discourage climbers, and heavy gauge wire or stock panels around the plants. Add a large and noisy dog, and never leave the crop unguarded.

The Grow Area Outdoors

Some outdoor growers fence their cannabis, while others hide it by using camouflage plantings. As with everything else, both of these systems have advantages and disadvantages. To be effective, fencing needs to be high and made of stout materials. This can get expensive and can alert potential thieves that you have something of value enclosed. Using camouflage is generally less expensive, but can cost the grower their crop if casual trespassers, wildlife, or livestock come across the crop and steal it, or browse it to the ground.

Fencing has three functions: to screen your garden from casual observers; to keep out livestock and wild browsers like deer; and to keep out thieves. Of the three groups, the thieves, or "rippers," are the most difficult to prevent reaching your crop. Heavy gauge wire can be breached with bolt cutters, they are intelligent enough to avoid or short out electric fencing, and have no problem climbing over a board fence once they know there is something to steal on the other side.

Containers

The grower who decides to ground plant will still need containers, especially if they grow from seed and must wait for sexual determination by the plants. It is far easier to control the male plants and pollen if you can simply pick up a container and move them into a closed environment away from your females.

FACT

You may find that it is easier and less expensive to run PVC piping to the grow site instead. Either way, bringing water to the crop is an expense to evaluate when you determine the grow site location.

The containers will also protect the seedlings, allowing them to grow strong and tall enough to be planted in the ground once they reach two to three feet in height. The outdoor grower should plan on needing from three- to ideally five-gallon containers for each of the seedlings' interim phase.

Water

The outdoor grower must determine how to get water to the plants. This is generally achieved by using a water hose. This can mean a simple garden hose or two if you are growing in your backyard, but you'll need to estimate how many hundreds of feet of good quality hosing will cost if you are growing in a rural area and the crop is not near the water source. If you are running long lengths of hosing, remember that you should conceal or lightly bury it; visible hosing going into the brush or too far from a "normal" garden will alert thieves that you are growing cannabis. All they have to do is to follow the hosing right to your crop.

Depending on the water source, an outdoor grower should factor in the costs of watering through a long, hot summer. Cannabis, particularly when grown in the ground, uses a great deal of water, especially during the vegetative phase of growth. If your water has a bill attached to it (as opposed to having a well or spring), somewhere between $100 to $200 per month for the three summer months is a reasonable estimate to water eighteen to twenty plants.

Garden Tools

The outdoor grower's most valuable tool is a stout and well-made garden fork. You will use it for aerating soil, digging, and turning compost. You will also need a good long-handled shovel, a wheelbarrow, and a compost screener. Less essential, but still useful, is a composter, especially if you live in a more urban area. Although a well-made compost pile should never smell, an enclosed composter will keep your activities inoffensive to neighbors. This has a side benefit of making them less likely to come over to your garden uninvited, or to start peeking over the fence.

QUESTION

Should I buy or rent a tiller?
Tillers can be rented by the day; this is sometimes the best solution for the minimal use you will make of such an expensive machine. Also, remember, tillers run on gasoline or diesel, neither of which is inexpensive. If you do purchase or rent a tiller, figure on buying a few gas cans as well; you are going to have transport and store fuel to use it.

Some growers invest in a garden tiller. These can range in size from tiny eggbeaters that are useful for raised beds or starting plant site holes, to riding tractors with big tiller attachments run by hydraulics.

Generally speaking, heavy tilling of grow sites is a less than productive use of good soil. Tearing up the soil layers disturbs the natural process, and can actually worsen clay soils by making compressed clods. However, there are times when a tiller is very useful, especially when starting from unimproved soil or for incorporating tilth-building materials like spoiled hay or mushroom compost.

Soil Amendments

Soil amendments are another expense to factor in to your grow site, and can include potting soils, composts, minerals, and soils by the yard. Depending on the overall size of your crop (as in plant count), soil amendments can cost anywhere from a few hundred to a few thousand dollars. Remember that you will also need fuel and time to procure soil supplies, and large amounts of these items will require a truck. As previously noted, outdoor growers have the advantage of actually being able to build optimum soil. This takes time, however, and a first year crop is going to need good soil immediately.

Drying

Once you are drying the crop, consider the expense for a dedicated building or drying room, purchasing fans and dehumidifiers, and the accompanying electrical bills to power them. You will also need heavy gauge wire and hardware to hang it, or at least racks for hanging the plants, as well as clean glass or plastic for storage after curing is completed.

The Soil

The basic requirement for cannabis is nutrient-rich, well-drained soil. As previously mentioned, a good starter mix is one-third sandy loam for drainage, one-third compost you have made, and one-third an organic bagged soil like Fox Farm's Ocean Forest Potting Soil.

FACT

Gardeners and growers of cannabis are frequently frustrated if they start out with unimproved clay soil; it is important to remember that the clay really does have good nutrients in it, it just requires lightening so the plants can use them.

You could just start out with Ocean Forest, as it contains sandy loam already and is an excellent mix of other essentials, but it is very expensive. Using sandy loam is important for drainage, and also for a slightly firmer soil texture; cannabis is not at its happiest with the typical fluffy structure of many commercial bagged potting soils. Sandy loam can be purchased in bulk at garden centers and by the yard at what are typically called "feed and fuels" in rural areas.

Good organic gardening practices can improve a reasonable soil until your amending efforts achieve ideal soil. Loam is the most desirable and is made up of 40 percent sand, 40 percent silt, and 20 percent clay. In this mix, the plant can access the good nutrients in clay soil because there is sufficient air available. Strive to create a similar blend to loam when you are mixing your own soil. The extra effort will be well rewarded, as loam is exactly what plants need to thrive. Plant roots need air to access food, and while a dense, compacted soil like clay may have lots of nutrients, those nutrients remain unavailable to the plant due to lack of air. Good aeration also stimulates beneficial bacterial activity, allowing the plant to access and use more organic matter.

Soil Considerations

Compacted soil speeds up moisture loss; in hard, packed soils, water rises rapidly to the surface and is lost through evaporation. This can lead to a much larger water bill than you initially anticipated for your grow.

The grower must also be alert to the acidity or alkalinity of the soil mix. Cannabis prefers a soil that is not too acidic and not too alkaline; a pH of 6.5 is just about perfect. Some growers swear by a slightly lower pH, but most estimate the range for soil-grown cannabis is 6.5 to 7.5.

Humus is important for improving water and nutrient-holding capacities. Humus contains complex organic compounds that remain after the many soil organisms have used and transformed the original material.

The Importance of Soil Dwellers

Living soil organisms decompose organic compounds, sequester nitrogen and other nutrients, and fix nitrogen from the atmosphere so it is available to the plants. Soil organisms interact with one another, with plants, and with the soil. The combined result is a number of beneficial functions, including nutrient cycling, moderated water flow, and pest control.

Organic matter in soil is used for the energy and nutrients the plants need. Bacteria, fungi, and other soil dwellers transform and release nutrients for the plants to use. In living soil, the soil directly around plant roots is teeming with bacteria. These bacteria feed on sloughed-off plant cells as well as the proteins and sugars released by roots. The protozoa and beneficial nematodes that eat the bacteria are also concentrated near roots.

This nutrient cycling and disease suppression is very complex, but also very much needed for a healthy garden. Dead, chemically treated soils are bad for the environment, and aren't conducive to good plant health and natural disease controls. The wise outdoor grower will work with nature and encourage natural controls. Using chemical fertilizers may be a quick fix, but the practice will eventually destroy your soil.

Choosing the Right Strains

Cannabis breeders have spent years modifying plant characteristics to optimize quality and production. All this observation and genetic manipulation is available information, either through books or on the web, so learning where strains are typically grown can give you your first clue as to what might optimize your growing success.

The Classics

Some strains remain "classics" and are available for years. Others are improved upon and become harder to find as growers prefer upgraded versions. Cannabis strain development and the ability to procure different strains are somewhat similar to rose breeding and purchasing. Like anything else, there are fads and fashions, sometimes driven by clever marketing and publicity. The Northern Lights, Big Bud, and White Widow strains, for example, are in the "classics" division. These are strains that have survived the test of time and are readily available via online seed sites.

The best seed sites will list their strains like a good garden catalog; they list provenance, typical characteristics of the strain in appearance, preferred growing conditions, and the qualities of the end product, usually both for productivity and effects. This is useful if you plan to breed and fine tune a strain of your own that is ideally suited to your tastes and particular microclimate.

Location Matters

Outdoor plants need an environment to which they are genetically acclimated; pure sativa strains that do well in California or in the southern parts of the United States do not finish as well in the shorter growing seasons northwards. A hybrid cross that introduces an indica like the classic Northern Lights will do much better somewhere like the Pacific Northwest. This is where the importance of provenance and knowing the growing characteristics of a strain (i.e. quick finish, typical plant structure, and mold-resistance) are extremely helpful.

FACT

Today's cannabis breeders are similar to the great heyday of amateur rose breeders in previous generations. Some of the best classic roses were hybridized and created by amateurs and are still very popular.

The northern parts of the United States usually experience quite cold weather, so the outdoor grower in this region should use strains specifically bred for colder climates. These are mostly indica or indica/sativa mixed. Some of these strains are commercially available, like a Northern Lights crossed with Big Bud or White Widow. It is important to have strains that can finish in the shorter northern growing season.

Some areas in the southern part of the United States are in a mild and warm climate, and many strains can be grown outdoors in this region. Pure indica, pure sativa, and indica/sativa hybrids can all be used. Pure sativas particularly like long growing seasons and lots of warmth.

Special Considerations

It is interesting to note that the same strain started indoors and then moved to an outside grow will look very different from the original mother plant grown from seed outdoors. An indoors-to-outdoors plant usually seems to be very bush-like, while the 100 percent outdoor-grown plant will have a more tree-like appearance with a thick trunk and longer axials. This would be an example of how the genotype will express differently in different environments, and how early the adaptation starts.

Due to the outdoor cycle's long growing period and chances of rain soaking the plant near harvest time, a tree-like structure is more suited to an outdoor grow. Its air circulation is better than a super-bushy, dense structure that is more prone to molds if the leaves get watered. The indoor grower has less of a concern as they can control where they water, while the outdoor grower has no control over rainfall. Cannabis should generally be watered at the base, not by overhead sprinkling.

If you are acquiring cloned strains from an indoor grower, and those strains are commercially available as well, it is worthwhile to look online to see how it performs outdoors. The performance by the clones as opposed to the indoor mother plant may not be the same once they are raised outdoors.

An Overview of the Outdoor Growing Cycle

If you are growing outdoors, you must determine when spring really starts in your area. California growers have one of the best climates in the country for growing outdoor cannabis; they can get their seedlings out early and grow massive sativas without fear that the plants will not finish in time. Other parts of the United States have a long, cool, rainy spring season; the more northern the area, the shorter the growing season.

Starting the Cycle

The beginning of the cycle is procuring clones or starting your seeds. These little ones will need to be nurtured until they reach a safe size to be put outdoors. The word "clone" can actually be a little vague. A clone does not have to be the size of a cutting; this is just when growers generally receive them from the propagator. Sometimes a clone arrives as a three- or four-foot tall plant, a happy bonus. The downside is that this larger clone is probably root-bound and will experience difficulties as it tries to adjust to real sunlight. The sun is far more powerful than grow lights, so it will take your plants a little while to adjust.

The Vegetative Phase

The first transplant for seedlings is usually from their little four-inch starter pots to a three- or five-gallon container. This will allow enough room for the plants to grow while they make their sexual determination. Clones are known females, so the grower can put them right into their largest container. If the clones are still tiny and will eventually be planted directly into the ground, they will benefit from an interim transplant until they gain enough size to be safely ground planted.

ESSENTIAL

An excellent source for information on your local microclimate is your local Farm Extension Service. It tracks information like frost dates and rainfall levels.

The plants will be in what is called the vegetative phase of growth; they are working at growing roots, gaining size, and building strong stems and lots of healthy green leaves. Cannabis is light-sensitive and requires a light trigger to begin the phase of flower development so desired by cannabis growers. During the vegetative phase, the plants will need plenty of water and more nitrogen than during the flowering phase.

If the grower plans to make clones from this crop, now is the time to take cuttings. It is possible to clone from a flowering plant, but not advised. It takes the cutting far longer to root, and the new little plant may try to flower right away. An eight-inch flowering plant is really not of much use or desirable in any way.

Transition to Flowering Phase

The plants will grow until daylight shortens to twelve hours. This is what triggers the plants to begin flowering. The days remaining for reproduction are dwindling, and the plants will strive to complete their natural goal of flowering and seeding.

If the grower plans to breed for seed, he will have isolated a male or males of preferred lineage and collected and labeled the pollens. As soon as the female plants show pistils, the grower can pollinate selected branches to create new hybrids and fresh seed for next year. The grower can continue to breed the females until harvest time, but late breedings will not give the plants enough time to produce mature and viable seeds.

As the plants grow flowers, their vegetative growth will slow and then stop. They are concentrated on reproduction, and a large array of healthy, resin-covered flowers is their natural way to catch wind-borne pollen. The grower has mostly frustrated this goal by removing the males and selectively breeding, but the plants will not know this and produce resins as fast as they can. You should stop feeding the plants nitrogen at this time and increase the ratio of phosphorus and potassium that the plants need for flowering.

During this phase, the careful grower spends quite a bit of time grooming the plants by removing yellowed leaves and clearing any plant debris that falls to the ground. This will decrease pest infestations and is essential in preventing different molds that effect cannabis plants (and particularly the flowers).

The End of the Cycle to Harvest

Different hybrids and even different plants within a strain will complete their flowering at different times. Some strains finish as early as early September, while others, typically sativa types, take weeks longer to maximize resin production and finish their cycle. Sometimes the outdoor grower is forced to compromise and take the late-finishers in to hang a little sooner than they would like. This is a trade-off: leaving the plants out can sometimes improve the quality of the finished product, but a rainy fall and late harvest leads to mold and the subsequent loss of ounces of bud.

Harvesting Outdoor Plants

If you love and grow cannabis, there is probably nothing more fun than harvesting a healthy, gorgeous outdoor plant. Not all of the plants will come in at once, and this is actually an advantage of the outdoor grow. Indoor growers generally take all of their plants at once and must therefore process them at once, too.

As the flowers mature, the grower should be watching the trichomes closely. Some growers like to take the plants while the trichomes are still clear since there is some indication that the clearer trichomes produce more of a psychoactive effect. Other growers wait until the trichomes are just starting to turn amber in color because they claim this produces more of a "stony" effect. A lot of the effects are due to genetics, but it is definitely important to not let the trichomes go dark amber; the plant resins are starting to deteriorate at this point and heading in the direction of diminishing returns.

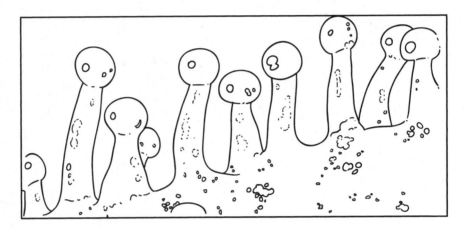

Enlarged image of trichomes (resin) on a cannabis flower.

Harvesting Essentials

Generally it is easier to have a helper when you harvest large outdoor plants. One person can hold and steady the plant while the other cuts the trunk. Have a clean tarp lying open to lay the plant on; you do not want any dirt in your lovely colas. If the plants have been rained on, shake as much moisture out as possible. Excess moisture adds weight, and you will be amazed at how much a good-sized fresh-cut cannabis plant can weigh.

Some plants are so large it makes sense to cut them in sections. This is fine as long as you have extra labels to keep track of which plant they actually are. Always remove the labeled seed branch and hang it in a special spot just for your seeders; this way you will not lose track of it, something that is easy to do with a largish crop.

Once your plants are safely indoors and hanging to dry, you still have to keep monitoring and acting decisively if you spot mold. Also be sure to keep your drying shed well locked and preferably monitored twenty-four hours a day until the harvest is dried and manicured. Rippers will be happy to relieve you of your entire crop if given the opportunity to do so!

After-Harvest Instructions

After the harvest is completed, the good outdoor grower goes out to the site and does some clean up and preparation for next year: removing old cannabis leaves that might encourage pests, pulling old root balls, and layering compost materials over the in-ground spots to mellow through the winter.

ALERT

Even if you grow legally, it is usually wise to take plants in at dusk or at some point when you will not be easily observed. It is very possible that someone, a ripper for example, has been watching you to see when the plants are ready. If you harvest one or two, that is a signal for the rippers to come in and clear your crop site. For a grower, nothing is more devastating; you have lost months of hard work, valuable genetics, and your cannabis supply for the next several months.

The outdoor grow has one more advantage: the growing period only happens once a year. The outdoor grower, like any farmer, gets a winter break.

CHAPTER 11

Growing Cannabis Indoors

Although some people in urban areas still grow a few cannabis plants in their vegetable gardens, generally the urban cannabis farmer is forced to grow inside. This is not because of law enforcement in medical use states, but because of thieves. Sadly, prohibition continues to make cannabis extremely expensive for those who must purchase it on the black market.

The Advantages of Growing Indoors

Indoor growing does have some advantages, especially if you live in a geographic area with very short growing seasons. You won't have to hover at the television watching the weather report and praying for warmth and sunshine; you can supply it by the flick of a switch.

Indoor growers are less tied to their crops; during the season, an outdoor grower must always be on site or risk losing their cannabis. Indoor growers can check the grow room in the morning and drive off to work. As long as they have been discreet about their growing activities, there is usually very little to alert thieves that valuable cannabis is inside.

ESSENTIAL

Protecting your indoor grow from animals includes pets. Do not take your cat or dog into the grow room with you; wagging tails can damage plants, cats may try to climb or eat young plants, and most importantly, animal hair will stick to the resiny plants, causing you to have an unclean end product.

Indoor growers are far less concerned about the accidental pollination of their prized female plants; unless they place a male in the grow room or carry pollen into the plants on their clothes, they are guaranteed pure sensemilla, or seedless, female plants. Outdoor growers, of course, must worry about wind-borne pollen that may have traveled silently and invisibly to the grow site. Although useable, seeded cannabis is not considered of high value and is usually harsher to smoke.

The indoor grower's crop is almost never bothered by wildlife bigger than a spider mite; deer, roving livestock, burrowing rodents, or wood rats cannot access your prized plants.

Another aspect of indoor growing is the ability to always have a crop in cycle; once the outdoor season is over, the outdoor grower has their harvest for the entire year. An indoor grower can produce a crop every ten to twelve weeks; crop failures or theft are still annoying and expensive, but the indoor grower has the option of starting again immediately.

Problems to Consider

One of the biggest problems with an indoor cannabis grow is the expense. The grow room, or rooms, must be constructed properly. Most indoor growers have a vegetative room and a flowering room so they can keep a crop in cycle at all times. The equipment for lights, ventilation, humidity- and odor-control requires an initial outlay of large amounts of cash. The power bills to keep the artificial environment running are also prohibitive. Without a doubt, a productive indoor grow is a costly investment.

FACT

Indoor growing technologies are constantly changing, both for improved product output and reduced energy expense. Keeping up is somewhat similar to a person with a fine recorded music collection. Do you stay with vinyl, or throw out the tapes and go to CDs? Each iteration and change to upgrade systems can be very expensive.

Another thing to consider is space. You will either lose personal space in your home after you designate an area for grow rooms or face the expense of building and maintaining a special building for your growing activities. This depends on each grower's personal situation, but many a marriage has suffered when the guest room is taken over for cannabis growing. This is less of a problem if you have a large basement in your house or unused outbuildings.

The other huge problem for indoor growers is keeping the grow rooms clean and uninfested with insect pests; spider mites are the number one enemy of the indoor cannabis grow. The artificial environment tends to preclude assistance from nature. Another downside to having your grow actually within your home is that you live there; if home invasion thieves come in for your cannabis, you are right there with it. Cannabis thieves can be armed and willing to kill for the financial value of your crop. The outdoor grower may lose their crop, but they have a choice to not confront thieves. In medical cannabis states, law enforcement is mandated to respond and protect the grower, so an outdoor grower can monitor a situation from inside their home and call the police for help.

What if you are not a licensed medical grower? If law enforcement gets a warrant to come in your home, you, your family, and your pets may be in great danger; not only of possible arrest and incarceration, but of being in the line of fire. This danger, plus the odds that your home will be trashed, greatly increases when the police perform a raid on an indoor grow.

FACT

Your grow rooms will ideally be located in a basement. There are some very good reasons to do so: a basement is not part of the general living area of a home and less likely to have visitors wonder about what you do there, and a basement is usually stable as far as temperature fluctuation. You can also block light loss more easily, and it is far more difficult for thieves to gain access since they can't simply smash their way in as they could with a greenhouse.

The final disadvantage of an indoor grow is that it is far less productive than an outdoor grow while using a great deal more diminishing world resources. Even if the financial expense is not an issue, the indoor cannabis grower must consider the immense use of fossil fuels necessary to produce a relatively small amount of cannabis.

Materials

The basic and essential materials you will need to grow cannabis indoors include:

- A prepared space to grow in, or grow room
- Lights
- Fans
- Odor control system, usually carbon-filtered
- Air intake and exhaust system
- Thermometer
- Hygrometer
- Pots or containers
- Soil or soil-less growing medium
- Cannabis cuttings, seeds, clones, or seedlings

The Grow Room

Most indoor growers start out with a single grow room; this makes sense until you decide whether indoor growing is for you. The high production approach uses two grow rooms: one for the vegetative stage of the cannabis life cycle and the other for a flowering room. This method lets the indoor grower continually cycle and harvest cannabis. Using only one room mimics the outdoor cycle, although on an immensely speeded up timeframe.

ESSENTIAL

Some cost conscious growers use fans from old computer cabinets, generally available from electronics liquidators for very little outlay. Dimmer switches can be used to regulate the speed and noise of the fans. Silicon should be used to secure the fans to PVC pipe run through floor and ceiling holes. Use more silicon to dampen the vibration of the fans, as the walls will resonate to the oscillations, alerting visitors or trespassers that something is going on in your basement.

Make certain the grow area has access to electrical outlets in good working condition. You will be placing a lot of power load on the electrical system, and many an indoor grow has gone up in flames when the electrical setup was done casually or too cheaply. Remember, this is usually also where you live, so you could lose far more than just your cannabis.

Venting

The space should be vented, as big lights generate a lot of heat. Separate exhaust and incoming air vents are best; one at the top of the room to release hot air into the attic or out through the roof, and one to bring in air from an outside wall or crawl space.

Odor Control

Cannabis plants emit a strong and distinctive odor during their reproductive phase. This can alert thieves or law enforcement that you are growing cannabis, as eventually this odor will need to be vented outside of your house. It can also permeate the inside of a home, again leading casual visitors to either wonder what the smell is or to know what the smell is. Depending on their views about cannabis, this could be problematic for you.

Most indoor growers eliminate the odor danger by forcing the grow room air through a carbon filter. Many home cultivators simply attach a large carbon filter to their air extraction system to remove any smell before the air is expelled from the grow room.

ESSENTIAL

If you are going to need any ducting or electrical work done by an outside repairman, plan ahead and get this done before your growing area looks like anything but a basement. You do not have to discuss anything with a contractor, but casual conversation about your new basement pottery studio can deflect any speculation you are setting up a cannabis grow.

Another way of eliminating odor is by installing an ozone generator in the extraction ducting. Air is forced past the ozone generator by the extraction fan, and the air is neutralized as it mixes with the ozone.

Room Prep

Once you select the location and have the electrical and exhaust systems figured out, you need to prepare the space. First, completely clean the room; floors need to be thoroughly cleaned, and the walls should also be sprayed with a light bleach solution and wiped down. Pretend you are going to be performing surgery in there, on your best friend, so the room starts out very, very clean.

Any windows in the grow area must be covered completely and checked from outside at night for light loss. Unless they are made of concrete, the floors should be covered in plastic tarps to prevent water damage. You will be gardening in this room, and water spills will inevitably happen. Whether the floor is yours or your landlord's, you do not want to create a mold-inducing environment, which wet wood, or soaked tile grout, can become.

Paint the walls flat white, choosing paint with high titanium dioxide content to maximize reflectivity. Some indoor growers cover the walls of their grow-room with some type of reflective material. The most common is 6 mil (150 µm) PVC plastic sheeting that is white on the room side and black to the wall. The white side reflects light, and the black side reduces mold growth. Another common covering is Mylar sheeting or Astrofoil, both of which reflect heat. There is also the option of Foylon, a foil-laminated, reinforced fabric that some growers have used successfully.

ALERT

Some indoor growers have experimented with using tin foil to intensify light, but this is not advised. The foil can actually focus light into hot beams and burn holes through the plants' leaves.

A broad, well-secured shelf above the main grow area can be used to root cuttings and germinate seedlings. The area will stay very warm, eliminating the need for a germination warming pad. If you are only using one grow room, hang a light-proof curtain to separate the shelf from the main area when the lights are on flowering cycle settings.

Lights

Lumen is a measurement of light output and refers to the amount of light emitted by one candle that falls on one square foot of surface located at a distance of one foot from the candle. Traditionally, lumens have been the benchmark of a lamp's ability to grow plants. In other words, the brighter the lamp, the better the plant performs. However, studies have shown that using a broader color spectrum lamp causes much better plant growth than a lamp with high lumen output.

High Intensity Discharge (HID) lighting is a special type of lighting that is intensely bright. An HID lighting system consists of a ballast, reflector, socket, and lamp (light bulb). The ballast acts like the engine, converting and driving energy to illuminate the lamp. HID lighting options for plant growth are typically Metal Halide (MH), or High Pressure Sodium (HPS) systems.

MH lamps provide more of the blue/green spectrum, which is ideal for plants in a vegetative stage. MH lamps provide a more natural appearance in color and are typically used for plants that have no natural light available. Cannabis can do very well grown full cycle under MH, but get daylight halide for best results.

HPS lamps provide more from the yellow/orange/red spectrum, perfect for plants that are actively flowering. Ideally, the indoor grower would use MH to grow their plants and HPS to flower their plants, but either choice is quite suitable for the entire cycle.

Traditionally, fluorescent lighting has been used for seedlings, cuttings, and plants with low light-level requirements, while HID has been used for established plants and plants with higher light-level requirements. These days, advances in fluorescent lighting technology have provided more options for indoor growers. T5 fluorescent lighting is the latest in plant growth lighting. T5's high light output, combined with low heat and energy consumption, makes it another light source choice for the indoor cannabis grower.

ESSENTIAL

An easy way to figure out your projected power bill for grow room lights is to multiply the grow room's total bulb wattage times the number of hours of operation and divide by 1000. This figure is the number of kilowatt-hours of electricity used. (Example: a 400-watt lamp running for 18 hours will use 7.2 kilowatt-hours.) Check your power bill for the cost of each kilowatt-hour. Then multiply the number of kilowatt-hours used by the cost of a kilowatt-hour (K/hr) to figure the cost of running your light for that many hours.

Your budget will decide how complex your initial lighting and ventilation setups can be; if you are growing medically, many compassion centers have used lighting setups available for reasonable prices. Always do your research by visiting indoor agricultural stores and asking questions; indoor growing technology is changing radically and rapidly.

Containers

Most indoor cannabis growers use containers that hold between two and five gallons of soil; a good compromise in terms of weight, space, and cost. They can be moved easily and hold an adequate reservoir of water and nutrients to support a large indoor plant.

You can calculate the right size containers to use by the amount of light per square foot. For a moderate light, or fifteen to twenty-five watts per square foot, you should use a minimum of one-gallon, but preferably three-gallon, containers. For plants receiving more light, or over twenty-five watts per square foot, use at least three-gallon, or preferably eight-gallon, containers. The containers must have several holes in the bottom to ensure drainage. Growers typically use black plastic nursery pots, but you can use flowerpots, plastic buckets, small trash cans, or plastic grow bags.

The Soil

Cannabis can grow an extensive root system in its natural state outdoors, especially in dry areas where the main taproot can grow more than six feet deep in its search for water. Cannabis also has a fibrous network of fine, lateral roots that branch off the main taproot. In moister environments with nutrient-rich soil, the lateral roots are able to supply water and nutritive needs and the taproot can remain small. Cannabis will adjust to the indoor grow site's space limitations as long as you feed and water properly.

Natural Soil

The growing medium is important: it serves as a source for water, air, and nutrients, and must also anchor the plant's roots. Cannabis has high water and nutritive needs and grows very fast, unlike most houseplants. The indoor grow room is also an unnatural environment; natural controls for harmful soil bacteria and insects must be replaced by the gardener's attention and care.

The texture of the medium determines how well it holds water and how well it drains. Cannabis requires a well-drained medium for healthy growth. Soils that hold too much water can drown the roots, leading to poor growth or even killing the plants. Well-drained soil allows roots access to air as well as water. Soils made of dense clay or are too rich in compost that holds too much water, will not have enough air. Soil-less media, like Perlite, usually drains almost too well but contains no nutrients.

The soil must be nutrient-rich to satisfy the heavy feeding needs of cannabis. To simplify, you may want to start out using really good bagged potting soil. The average size of a home indoor grow makes this a feasible expense most of the time. Some gardeners are adamant about using their own soil mixes because they have control over ingredients and amendments, but if you are just starting out you can take advantage of a good quality pre-mix. There are various kinds of bagged soils available at garden centers, but beware of cheap mixes that are fluffy in texture and heavy on the perlite. As previously stated, perlite isn't bad and, in fact is very good for drainage, but it contains no nutrients at all.

These mixes seldom contain enough nutrients to support healthy cannabis growth for long. Their nitrogen (N) is usually too low, phosphorus (P) level is adequate, and the potassium (K) level is usually very high.

It is far better to pay the higher price and use an organic bagged soil like Fox Farm's Ocean Forest Potting Soil. A mix of the Ocean Forest quality has the correct texture for good drainage and is already preloaded with ideal nutrients for the early vegetative phase cannabis plant, although the heavy feeding habits of cannabis will still require the grower to supplement as the plants grow. Black Gold makes an organic potting soil that is adequate, but for cannabis it needs to be adjusted with sandy loam; the texture is too fluffy and it contains less specialized organic nutrients than the more expensive mixes.

Soil-Less Soil

Some indoor growers prefer to use soil-less mediums and feed nutrients to their plants, or use a mix that includes real soil. These media can improve a natural soil that has troubling drainage characteristics.

Perlite, expanded sand or volcanic glass, is almost weightless, contains no nutrients, and is near neutral in pH. Perlite mixed with real soil can hold water, air, and nutrients from the soil, and is particularly good at aerating heavy soil.

Vermiculture is also near neutral in pH and holds water, air, and nutrients well while improving the texture of sandy or fast-draining soils. Jiffy Mix, Ortho Mix, and similar mixes are made of ground vermiculite and sphagnum moss and fortified with a small amount of nutrients.

Peat moss (also sometimes called sphagnum moss) is formerly living sphagnum moss from bogs that has partially decomposed. It is sometimes used by growers to improve water holding and texture. Used in excess, it tends to make the medium too acidic after a few months of watering. As a soil amendment, peat moss breaks down too fast, compressing the soil and creating an unhealthy lack of air for plant roots. It can be useful when lightened with perlite, but the mining of peat moss is an environmentally unsound practice. Environmentally conscious growers use alternative products or try to minimize the amount of peat moss they use.

The Best Strains for Growing Indoors

The modern indoor cannabis breeders have spent years modifying plant characteristics to optimize quality and adapt to the indoor methods of production. Cannabis competitions have created international arenas for breeders to compare accomplishments and to market their strains to the world.

Some strains remain "classics" and are available for years. Others are improved upon and become harder to find as growers continue to refine flavor, aroma, and psychoactive effects. Cannabis strain development and the ability to procure different recreational strains rise and fall with the fads and fashions in the industry. They are sometimes driven by clever marketing and publicity, so it's important you find the best product for you.

The best seed sites will list their strains like a good garden catalog; they list provenance, typical characteristics of the strain's appearance, preferred growing conditions, and the qualities of the end product, usually both for productivity and effects. This is very useful if you have limited space and need reliable information as to probable results for your grow.

Some well-known strains that grow easily and successfully for indoor growers include:

- The **Silver Haze** strain is a tall plant for indoors, due to a mainly sativa background. Silver Haze is a cross of a sativa, Purple Haze, to a non-dominant indica. The indoor breeder's goal was to minimize height and flowering time of the typical sativa, but still retain the unique sativa psychoactive effect.
- **Kush** is a pure Indica and a short compact plant. A two-time winner of the international Cannabis Cup, Kush is very popular among indica growers.

- **New York Diesel** is an Afghani/sativa hybrid. This strain is considered good for beginning growers because it is disease resistant and tends to grow uniformly.
- **Northern Lights** is another short, compact plant with big broad leaves and large flowers. This strain is considered a "classic" and is reputed to be easy to grow.
- **Big Bud** is also a "classic" and Cannabis Cup best strain winner in 1989. The yield is legendary and produces massive flowers.

These are only a few of the strains available to the indoor grower of cannabis; you may also start seedlings and produce your own unique individuals so you can start working on a strain of your own!

An Overview of the Indoor Growing Cycle

The cycle begins with procuring clones or starting your seeds. These little ones will need to be nurtured until they reach a big enough size to be transplanted to larger containers. The word "clone" can actually be a little vague; a clone does not have to be the size of a cutting, this is just when growers generally receive them from the propagator. Sometimes a clone arrives as a three or four foot tall plant, a happy bonus for the person receiving it. Or, perhaps you have to root some cuttings to get started. Plan on two to four weeks for the cuttings to root and become little plant clones.

ESSENTIAL

The soil mix for rooting cuttings is particularly important; make it light, well sifted, and well drained for best results and a quicker response from the cuttings.

Once you have little plants, you will want your grow room lights to cycle for the vegetative phase; make sure the plants get eighteen hour "days" and six hour "nights" for two full weeks.

The first transplant for seedlings is usually from their little four-inch starter pots to a three- or five-gallon container. This will allow enough room for the plants to grow while they make their sexual determination. Clones are known females, so the grower can put them right into their largest container.

The plants will be in what is called the vegetative phase of growth: they are working at growing roots and gaining size; building strong stems; and producing lots of healthy green leaves. Cannabis is light sensitive and requires a light trigger to begin the phase of flower development so desired by cannabis growers. During the vegetative phase, the plants will need plenty of water and more nitrogen than during the flowering phase.

If the grower plans to make clones from this crop, now is the time to take cuttings. It is possible to clone from a flowering plant, but this is not ideal since it takes the cutting far longer to root and the new little plant may try to flower right away. An eight-inch flowering plant is really not of much use or desirable in any way.

The plants will grow and grow until the seventh week when the indoor grower shortens their light cycle from eighteen-hour days and six-hour nights to symmetrical twelve hour cycles. This is the sign, or trigger, to the plants that the days remaining for reproduction are becoming fewer. The plants will begin flowering in an attempt to fulfill their natural goal of reproduction.. Some growers report that giving the plants an initial thirty-six hours of darkness before starting the twelve/twelve light cycle will shorten the time it takes for flowering to appear.

If the grower plans to breed for seed, they will have isolated one male or several males of preferred lineage and collected and labeled their pollens. As soon as the female plants show pistils, the grower can pollinate selected branches to create new hybrids and fresh seed.

As the plants grow flowers, their vegetative growth will slow and then stop. The plants are now concentrated on reproducing, and a large array of healthy, resin-covered flowers is their chance to catch pollen. The plants do not know they are in a grow room, and will produce resins as fast as they can. At this time the grower stops feeding them nitrogen and increases the ratio of phosphorus and potassium that the plants need for flowering.

During this phase, the careful grower spends quite a bit of time grooming the plants by removing yellowed leaves, clearing any plant debris that falls to the floor, and keeping a sharp eye out for mold on the flowers.

Different hybrids will complete their flowering at different times, but generally the end of the twelfth week in the cycle will be harvest time. As with outdoor cannabis, the indoor grower monitors trichomes to estimate the amount of finish on the harvest.

Harvesting Indoor Plants

Since indoor plants are much smaller than outdoor grown plants, one person can easily harvest them. Some indoor growers harvest in sections to give less finished parts of the plants a chance to produce more resins, or for their own convenience. As always, monitor the color of the trichomes to check for optimum harvest moment. Start using your oscillating fans as soon as your harvest comes into the drying area. The fans should be placed to maximize airflow around the hanging plants while avoiding a direct blast that continually blows on them. Avoid having the fans positioned too low as they may blow up dust from the shed floor. You can set your fan on high as the green (or "wet") plants are cut up and hung to dry.

As the plants dry out more, lower the fan settings to maintain a gentle, continual cycling of air. The dried flowers can be used within a few weeks, but really should be cured hanging for four to eight weeks (depending on moisture in the air, thickness of colas, and the temperature of your drying room). After the hanging plants are manicured, curing will continue for up to three or four months. It is important to monitor the bags or jars where the cannabis is stored. At least once a week, breathe the containers and test the taste. Do not seal uncured cannabis or you will ruin the taste and have a very harsh finish to your product.

CHAPTER 12

The Outdoor Growing Cycle

Outdoor growers tend to have a much longer relationship with individual plants, unlike the indoor grower who knows his plants only during a twelve-week cycle. This long term interaction often generates true affection for each plant as a living entity, especially if you are working with a small crop of ten to twenty plants. The first time you grow outdoor cannabis, you'll have a far greater chance of success if you do your homework first and are prepared for several months of activity; once the grow has begun you will need to perform for your plants if you want them to perform well for you. That being said, growing cannabis outdoors in a low-key, casual manner can result in a fairly bountiful crop. Nature is going to help you, and the characteristics of cannabis will help you, too. Cannabis is not called "weed" for nothing, and can be very tolerant of a lack of attention by the outdoor gardener.

The Importance of Sunlight

Cannabis is a plant that craves warmth. Depending on where you live, the return of sunlight and warm temperatures in the spring can come as early as the end of March or as late as mid-June. Trying to germinate seeds or transplanting your cannabis to the outdoors when the temperatures are still wintery is a waste of time and potential plants.

The best way for a first time outdoor grower to find out when to start is to contact the local Extension Service. These are usually state-funded agricultural information resources, but a quick look at your county government listings should supply a phone number or website address. Obviously, you will not ask about proper timing for planting cannabis, but inquiring about tomatoes is innocuous and will elicit the information you need. The Extension Service records information like local dates for the last and first frosts, as well as rainfall averages for different microclimates. This information will be very useful to you as you plan your schedule for the outdoor grow.

Many outdoor growers start their plants indoors and have them already well grown so they are ready for hardening off and outdoor transplant. This is a sensible practice, and is comparable to purchasing a well-grown tomato start from a garden center. The outdoor grower wants as much time for vegetative growth as possible; once the sunlight drops to twelve hours, your plants will slow and then stop increasing in size as they begin to concentrate on producing flowers. Unlike the indoor grower, you have no control over this timing. The female cannabis plant's hard-wired ultimate goal is to be pollinated so it can reproduce, so it will focus every bit of its energy on this very important activity. The grower benefits by frustrating the plant's desire by withholding access to male pollen.

When and How to Transplant on Schedule

Starting outdoor plants indoors can require very little other than a warm, clear, well-lighted workspace. Unless you are starting very early and will nurture the plants under grow lights for the first month or so, your plants are only going to stay inside for ten days at most. A seed-warming mat is useful, but not really essential. Grow lights can be help your plants along, but new, tender seedlings do fine with cool fluorescents and a side source for warmth. The grower needs seeds or clones; small starting pots; clean, lump-free soil; and clean water.

The outdoor grower who waits to ground plant will still need containers, especially if they grow from seed and must wait for sexual determination by the plants. It is far easier to control the male plants and pollen if you keep them in pots. When they start to flower you can simply pick up their container and move them into a closed environment away from your females.

Any seedling going in the ground should be strong and tall enough to do so safely. Until they are at least two to three feet in height, these young plants need the containers to protect them. This is also about the size at which cannabis normally shows its sexual identity. Until they sex, you should not plant undifferentiated seedlings in the ground or their final large container. It becomes too hard to move the males, and you'll be wasting all of the work and expensive materials needed to prepare a final plant site. The outdoor grower should plan on needing three-gallon sized and on to five-gallon sized containers for each of the seedlings' interim phase. The rooted cuttings, or clones, should also be allowed to reach the two to three foot size for ground planting. If you are growing them full cycle in a large container, go ahead and plant, or "bump," them right away; you know they are females and can therefore encourage vigorous vegetative growth right away. The clones will not have to experience more than one transplant shock; seedlings go through one or two. This shock can be so mild that the plants probably are not even aware that they have been replanted, but even the most careful grower can break a root ball.

Preparing to Transplant

When you get ready to transplant, always have your materials ready to go. It does not help the plant to be unpotted and then have to wait around because you forgot to get the bone meal out of your garden shed. The goal is to minimize any shock or damage to the plants; otherwise they lose valuable time recovering and adjusting themselves and this translates into lost size and productivity. You will need:

- The container, washed and clean, or the ground site prepared and lined with chicken wire for each plant to be transplanted
- Prepared soil, screened and amended with compost and minerals

- Bone meal
- Water
- Sharpie pen for writing on containers, or premade labels for each plant
- Young plant to be transplanted

Plan to transplant in the evening; this gives the plants a cool, dark period to adjust to their new homes. If you must transplant during the day, try to get it done in the early morning before the sun gets high and hot.

ESSENTIAL

Water the waiting soil, stir it to make certain it is uniformly dampened, and then check that the water is draining well from the container. Make a hole a few inches deeper and wider than the transplants' current containers, and scratch in a scant handful of bone meal. This will be easily accessible to the plant's roots and will aid in strong root production.

Transplant Assistants

One person can easily perform early transplants. Once the plants get three feet or more or are in heavy five-gallon containers, it is much easier and also safer for you to recruit a transplanting assistant. Remember that you are going to be turning the plant over and using gravity to slide the root ball out. If you are not particularly tall, finding a tall helper is essential. Root balls also do not always slide right out, and wrestling a heavy, earth-filled container while trying not to break the plant can get tricky.

If you are using a helper, always make certain that you both understand the plan: who is pulling the pot, and who is supporting and turning the plant. Skipping this discussion can lead to confusion and result in broken plants or root balls. This is always easier to work out before you are holding an extremely heavy container and are in mid-pull. As soon as the pot-puller frees the root ball, they can quickly set the pot down and help support the root ball until it is settled gently into its new container or the ground site. It is usually a good idea to bring the plants awaiting transplant to their ground site or the larger containers one at a time. Pot-pullers can get excited and fling an empty container as they jump forward to help support the root ball and a waiting plant can get broken if they fling blindly. This can lead to testy conversation between transplanter and assistant, so think ahead and keep the area clear.

Finalizing the Transplant

Once the transplant is settled gently in place, fill in with more of your prepared soil and gently press it flat around the plant's main stem with the palms of your hands. This will help bring the roots into contact with the soil. Gently water the plant and press again to settle it. Make certain the plant's identifying label or tag is secured or written on the side of the container with indelible pen. Your first plant is now finished, and you can start on the next one.

Companion Plantings and Plant Protection from Natural Pests

Cannabis is quite clever at producing its own insect-repelling qualities. Insects like leafhoppers usually only move in when the cannabis plants are stressed. It is thought that the stressed plant emits a pheromone that the insects pick up on as a signal to start attacking the weakened plant. The sudden appearance of insect pests can actually mean your plant is telling you that it is stressed for water or some other basic need.

Part of growing cannabis outdoors is working with nature, and using natural insect and pest controls is part of this program. You can create a balanced and healthy garden by interspersing what are called "companion" plants amongst the cannabis. These are plants that have many and varied benefits and attributes. Some of the plants attract beneficial insects or birds, some of these plants act as natural insect repellant, and some protect your plants from rippers by acting as contact irritants or poisons.

Some of the more common and useful companion plants available to American growers for pest control include:

- **Sunflowers** are thought to be the number one plant for trapping insects like grasshoppers, leafhoppers, and aphids. These pests seldom damage the sunflowers. It is amazing to see leafhoppers congregating on sunflowers only feet away from your cannabis plants; healthy and flowering cannabis is a far less attractive option for the leafhopper. Sunflowers are an annual and are very easy to grow; one small packet of seed will provide plenty of trap plants, as well as tall camouflage cover for your growing cannabis. You can harvest the sunflower seeds for birdseed as well as for planting sunflowers next spring. Sunflowers also attract hummingbirds, which eat ants, mosquitoes, aphids, gnats, midges, caterpillars, flying ants, weevils, small beetles, whitefly, and insect eggs in addition to feeding on flower nectars.

- **French marigold** (*T. patula*), is an annual that deters whiteflies and has roots that kill useless nematodes. You can ground plant these marigolds around outdoor cannabis, but marigolds in pots can be used in greenhouses as well. Make certain to get the specific T. patula variety, which is usually sold as French marigold.

- **Anise** is a tender annual herb that grows one to two feet in height. It is considered a good host for predatory wasps that prey on aphids, and is also said to repel aphids.

- **Chives** are perennials and keep aphids away. Chives are thought to repel Japanese beetles as well. A tea made from chives is sometimes used against downy and powdery mildews. A side benefit of growing chives as companion plantings is that they are a nice source for an excellent culinary herb.

- **Coriander**, also known as cilantro, is an annual culinary herb commonly used in Chinese and Mexican recipes. Coriander is known to repel aphids and spider mites. A tea made from coriander can be used as an organic spray for spider mites.

- **Yarrow** is an attractive flowering perennial herb that grows fairly tall; its feathery foliage can reach up to three feet or more. Yarrow has insect repelling qualities and is an excellent natural fertilizer.

- **Catnip** is a perennial member of the mint family. It deters flea beetles, aphids, Japanese beetles, squash bugs, ants, and weevils. Some growers report that it repels mice and voles as well. As with any mint, be careful it does not take over your garden; plant catnip in containers to keep it under control.
- **Clover** is useful as a green manure and fixes nitrogen into the soil. It attracts many beneficial insects like aphid predators.
- **Four O'Clocks**, or *nicotiana*, is a tall annual that is quite poisonous, so you should not plant it if your grow site is anywhere near small children. It will attract and kill Japanese beetles, which feed on the foliage and then die very rapidly. The flowers open in the evening (hence the common name of "Four O' Clocks") and have a strong scent reminiscent of the sun tan oils of the 1960s.
- **Geraniums** are an edible annual that will repel cabbageworms and Japanese beetles. They also are a trap plant for leafhoppers.
- **Gopher Purge**, or *Euphorbia lathyris*, is also sometime known as Mole Plant. It is a biennial plant (lives for two years) that contains milky sap in the roots, leaves, and flowers. This is a caustic substance that is not a repellant but rather a contact irritant; the animal must chew the roots to become ill or die. A thick stand of Euphorbia planted in the gopher's main tunnel is necessary to protect plants, as you want a preventative effect.
- **Horehound** (*Marrubium Vulgare*) is a sturdy perennial member of the mint family. Its many tiny flowers attract Braconid and Icheumonid wasps along with Tachnid and Syrid flies. The larval forms of these insects parasitize or otherwise consume many other insect pests. This plant blooms over a long season and continually attracts beneficial insects, an excellent attribute for a companion plant. It is said to stimulate and aid in fruiting in tomatoes and peppers.
- **Lavender** is a strongly scented, tall growing perennial herb. It comes in many varieties and colors and is known to repel whitefly, fleas, and codling moths. Lavender also nourishes many nectar feeding and beneficial insects. Lavender plants can be started in winter from cuttings, and planted out in spring.
- **Peppermint** is another perennial member of the mint family. Its high menthol content acts as a repellant for white cabbage moths, aphids,

and flea beetles. It also attracts bees and other beneficial insects. As with other mints, keep watch that it does not take over your entire garden. Peppermint will do fine in containers, which can be moved around as needed for aphid control.

- **Petunias** are an inexpensive and pretty flowering annual. They repel the asparagus beetle, leafhoppers, certain aphids, tomato worms, Mexican bean beetles, and other general garden pests. The leaves can also be used in a tea to make a potent bug spray.
- **Sweet Alyssum** is a self-seeding annual that is another natural control for aphids. Alyssum flowers attract hoverflies, whose larva devour aphids. They will reseed freely and make a beautiful groundcover every year.

Diatomaceous Earth (DE)

Diatomaceous earth is the finely ground fossils of prehistoric tiny, single-celled algae found in fresh water plankton called diatoms. Diatomaceous earth is a fine, white, crystalline powder that is perfectly safe for humans and other mammals, but deadly for garden pests. The abrasive quality of DE scrapes the protective outer shell off of insects. Without this protective layer, insects die very rapidly, usually within forty-eight hours of contact. A protective dusting of DE around plants will kill many insects, including slugs and fungus gnats. The use of DE is considered a good organic gardening practice and you can find it at most garden centers. You should use it to deplete pest populations, but still protect plants from slugs and snails by hand picking at night.

Wood Ash

Clean wood ash sprinkled around the perimeter area of a garden will deter slugs and snails, as well as supply beneficial potash to the soil. Always make certain the ash is from a clean burn, meaning no colored papers, plastics, or other household debris are in the ash. Dyes and plastics can add toxins to your soil.

Protection from Human Pests

Another use of companion plantings is to camouflage your cannabis. Tall annuals like dill, fennel, corn, and hops vines grow very rapidly and will help screen your plants from prying eyes.

Blackberry Maze

Some rural growers make tunnels through tall blackberry growth and create small clearings for their cannabis plants. This is quite labor-intensive, and frequently painful, as thorny blackberry does not give up without a fight. You will also have to pack all your soil and containers into each individual clearing, as well as plan a way to get water to the hidden plants. Hosing must be covered and hidden from aerial view; otherwise, you are creating virtual signposts right to where the plants are hidden. Unfortunately, this level of stealth is sometimes needed if the grower is to keep the crop from being stolen.

Fencing and Camouflage

Some outdoor growers fence their cannabis, while others hide it by camouflage plantings. Both of these systems have advantages and disadvantages. Fencing needs to be high and of stout materials. This can get expensive and can alert potential thieves that you have something of value enclosed. Using camouflage is generally less expensive, but can cost the grower their crop if casual trespassers, wildlife, or livestock come across the crop and steal it, or browse it to the ground.

Fencing has three functions: to screen your garden from casual observers, to keep out livestock and wild browsers like deer, and to keep out thieves. The thieves, or "rippers," are the most difficult to prevent reaching your crop. Heavy gauge wire can be breached with bolt cutters, they are intelligent enough to avoid or short out electric fencing, and have no problem climbing over a board fence once they know there is something to steal on the other side.

Timing Is Important

Even if you grow legally, it is usually wise to take plants in when it is dusk or at some point when you will not be easily observed. It is very possible that someone, like a ripper, has been watching you to see when the plants are ready. If you harvest one or two, that is a signal to the rippers to come in and clear your crop site. Nothing is more devastating for a grower; you have lost months of hard work, valuable genetics, and your cannabis supply for the next several months.

When and How to Sex Male and Female Plants

Cannabis from seed starts out with no visible sexual differentiation at all. The main concern is to provide them with light, water, and plenty of food for strong roots and healthy vegetative growth until they sex or "declare." At this point, all your seedlings can stay together, although you need to think through which genetics are the most important to you, how many males you want, and where to put them once they declare. They will have to be moved quickly once they provide proof of their sexual determination.

FACT

The males are not fed for vegetative growth, barely need watering, and can stay in small containers. A tiny male can produce more than enough pollen for breeding purposes and will require less space if you keep them small.

Male and female cannabis plants have very different looking different flowers that develop from a tiny nub known as the "primordia," located initially on the main stems.

The best place to check for flowering is at the top of the plant at the nodes (or intersections) where the plant develops a small leaf spur. The initial primordia will appear behind this spur and will start out looking like a tiny rounded pod. (See "Checking primordia" image in Chapter 7.)

Eventually the primordia will either elongate into a tubular looking female calyx or will become the more rounded nubbin of the developing male flower. The easiest way to sex cannabis plants is to wait for two white hairs or "pistils" that will appear from the end of the female calyx. These pistils can also appear pinkish or yellowish, but are very clear declarations of the plant's feminine nature. If you're a novice grower, you can save yourself some anxiety by asking an experienced grower to show you first pistils, but don't worry if this resource not available to you. You know what you are waiting for and it will be obvious to you when you see it for the first time. Also, remember that the plants will spend a fair amount of time going through this process; it is not something where you need to identify sexual determination and act within hours. You can keep watching for days until there is a clear and unambiguous display of the pistils. (See "Female calyx with pistils showing," "Early female declaration," "Early female flower beginning development," and "Cutting male flowers for pollen collection" images in Chapter 7.)

Moving Male Plants

Once your plants have declared, you must remove the males to their isolated, enclosed space to wait for pollen production. Make certain the males will be indoors where they can be completely segregated; absolutely no random pollen transfer should be possible.

As soon as you have collected pollen, you can breed selected branches on the females. There is no reason to wait until the female makes flowers; pollination and fertilization can take place as soon as the pistils are displayed. Breeding early on also allows time for seed to mature; breeding later in the season can result in immature seeds that are pale, whitish-green, and not likely to be viable.

Fertilizing for Vegetative Growth

Different organic soil amendments are usually needed when you start a grow site. Testing your soil and understanding the different properties of different organic amendments can, along with your budget, help you choose wisely. Packaged amendments generally list the Big Three of plant needs as follows: nitrogen coming first, phosphorus second, and potassium coming last. Always check, as extremely high nitrogen can burn plants.

Blood meal applications last up to four months, and should be used with caution; use no more than four ounces per square yard during the growing or vegetative phase. Growers sometimes use it as an element in tea for their plants; dilution with water makes it less likely to burn tender young plants.

As long as your plants are in a vegetative phase of growth, they will use a lot of nitrogen and push to grow big and leafy. Watch each plant as an individual, particularly if ground planted, but a normally feed a "power drink" of special compost or manure tea once a week. This can coincide with the plants' watering schedule for convenience.

Fertilizing for Flowering

You should stop any foliar feeding once cannabis begins its flowering phase. Flowering cannabis plants secrete resins for more than one reason, but one of the most important is that resins are a natural insulation from the elements. Foliar feeding in the flowering phase cools the plants and causes less resin secretion so your plants won't be as protected. The outdoor grower may also have to deal with rain near the end of the growing cycle, so adding moisture to finishing flowers is a good way to encourage molds. Foliar feeding should only be done in the vegetative phase and should be stopped within two weeks after flowering begins.

ALERT

Stop all feedings for two weeks before harvesting your plants, giving only water if needed. In many areas the grower will already be struggling with the beginning of fall rains, and probably will not need to water at all.

As cannabis begins flowering, the plants will need more phosphorus and more potassium than during the vegetative phase of growth. They will still need some nitrogen, but not as much as they did during vegetative growth. They also need calcium, which you can supply by scratching finely powdered organic eggshells into the soil around the main stem. If you are using pre-made organic supplements, look for 15-30-30 ratio, or close to it, for flowering.

Compost and Manure Teas

Organic fertilizers will help any soil; they build up the organic content of the soil, which improves its drainage and structure. By improving soil structure, you increase its ability to hold and release nutrients. The natural breakdown of the organic material by beneficial soil organisms can provide almost all the nutrients a plant requires during the vegetative and flowering phases.

The Importance of Compost Tea

Then why make a compost tea rather than just working compost into the soil? It seems like a lot of extra work, but there are several reasons. First, compost tea will make the benefits of compost go farther. Although it should only be used as a foliar spray (or, in other words, sprayed on leaves) during the vegetative phase of cannabis, compost tea helps suppress foliar diseases, increases the amount of nutrients available to the plant, and speeds the breakdown of toxins. If you only apply compost to your soil in the traditional way, you can miss out on additional benefits from compost.

FACT

Compost extract is a watery substance made from compost that is soaked in an old pillowcase or burlap sack and suspended in a barrel of water for no more than one hour before use. The result yields a supply of soluble nutrients that can be used as a gentle liquid fertilizer. This method is good for a quick mix, but lacks sufficient holding time for beneficial microorganisms to multiply and grow significantly.

Compost teas are different from compost extracts—they are brewed much longer with microbial food and catalyst sources added to the solution and, ideally, a bubbler aerating the solution with oxygen. The aim of the brewing process is to extract beneficial microbes from the compost itself, followed by growing these populations of microbes during the twenty-four to thirty-six hour brewing period. The compost provides the source of microbes, and the microbial food and catalyst amendments promote the growth and multiplication of microbes in the tea. Microbial food sources can include molasses, kelp powder, and fish powder. Some examples of microbial catalysts are humic acid, yucca extract, and rock dust.

Manure Teas

Manure tea is a term used almost interchangeably with compost tea, and it is made and used in the same way. It is still required that the manure by composted, but it is pure composted manure. Some people like manure from different sources. Manure from chickens steer, horses and even exotic animals found in the local zoo have all been used at some point. Generally, poultry manure is highest in nitrogen content, followed by hog, steer, sheep, dairy cow, and horse manure.

Bat guano is expensive manure, but it contains so many necessary macro- and micro-nutrients, as well as beneficial micro-organisms, that it is highly prized by cannabis gardeners. Guano from insect-eating bats is very high in nitrogen while fruit-eating bats produce guano that is higher in phosphorus. Commercially available bat guanos are generally labeled as to the type of bat and the N-P-K content.

Guano generally consists of ammonia, along with uric, phosphoric, oxalic, and carbonic acids. It also contains some earth salts and a high concentration of nitrates. The Big Three nutrients are supplied in these approximate amounts: nine percent nitrogen, six percent phosphorus, and two percent potassium. All manures used in making manure tea should be well composted. The heat generated by composting will kill unwanted seeds and possible pathogens.

Water Requirements (or How to Listen to Your Plant)

Watering outdoor cannabis, particularly plants grown in containers, can be a little tricky. You must learn to observe the plants closely since you are working with individuals, as well as the weather variations that are part of an outdoor grow. Although large outdoor cannabis plants prefer a deep, once a week soaking, high temperatures and drying winds can speed up their need for water. Do not feel like you must stick to a rigid watering schedule; if the plants are thirsty and stressed two days before their scheduled watering, the attentive cannabis gardener will water right away.

As a general rule, let the plants dry out slightly between waterings; you want their roots to reach or stretch a little bit. Cannabis is also very resentful of soggy soil; it can create a very unhealthy environment that is too full of ammonia and that lacks air, something essential for healthy roots and good plant growth.

If your plants are in large containers, the soil should be dry enough to just be starting to pull away from the edge of the container before you water again. The best way for you to check on the moisture level in your plants' soil is to put your finger down in the soil and feel around. Dew can make the top layer of soil look quite moist, but the finger test can show if soil is bone dry a few inches below, and if the plants need water.

ESSENTIAL

Always give cannabis a deep, long drink. Sprinkling a scant inch or so of water to the top layer of soil will leave the plants thirsty and unhappy, even though the soil looks moist to you.

Ground planted cannabis needs a slow drip that, depending on your soil, can be left on for hours; when water starts to pool around the plant's base, move the drip to the next plant. Plants in large containers should also have slow watering; this gives the water a chance to soak down through all of the soil. Trying to water quickly will just create channels of least resistance and possibly damage side roots. As a general rule of green thumb, water container plants so that the liquid pools and drains three times in the session. This will give the plants a complete deep drink.

How to Field Groom and Identify Harvest Time

Once the plants start into their flowering phase, there will be a natural yellowing and dropping of fan leaves. The cannabis gardener has cause for concern if this occurs before flowering begins; it usually means a lack of nitrogen or another soil imbalance and the grower should immediately test their soil for pH and N-P-K. Sometimes, excessive yellowing indicates that the plants have too much nitrogen, especially if they have been overfed. It is always important to test before trying to adjust soil values.

The natural yellowing and leaf dropping is a good sign that things are proceeding as nature intended, but you need to start grooming your plants. Clumps of dead leaves that catch in the plant stems or surround the main stem on the ground are breeding areas for molds and pests. The flowers need all the air circulation they can get, so you must help your plants by removing dying fan leaves on a daily basis. This is actually a very pleasant activity and has the added benefit of requiring the grower to closely examine each plant every day. This close contact will ensure that you spot any pest problems or developing molds right away, not later on when they have become a huge glaring problem you cannot help noticing.

Gently flex yellowed leaves near the stem; they will pop right off if they are ready. Do not tear or pull hard on the leaves. Some plants will drop far more leaves than other types; this has to do with their individual natures.

FACT

It is not uncommon to see plants that are almost completely naked of fan leaves from natural drop while others cling to their leaves pretty much all the way into harvest. The grower should note this characteristic in their grow book; leaves that do not fall will have to be clipped later on, making more work during the processing phase of cannabis production.

Always take leaf debris away from the grow site; this keeps the garden area cleaner and less likely to provide breeding areas for pests.

Once the plants are dropping leaves and the flowers are producing trichomes as fast as they can, the grower must monitor each plant daily for the best harvest timing. Growers generally take their plants when the trichomes are just starting to turn amber. Another way to estimate the length of time to harvest is to note the pistil "sets." The flower, or cola, will push out a first set of pistils that will brown. This is normal. It then produces a second set, it browns, and then the plant moves on to the third set. A ripe cannabis flower will generally have both white and brown pistils showing from the third set as the trichomes are starting to turn from clear to amber. This is the ideal time to harvest.

CHAPTER 13

The Indoor Growing Cycle

There are a large number of cannabis growers who grow their plants indoors. Many, if not most, grow indoors because they are forced to do so by the prohibition of cannabis for recreational use, and they cannot risk exposing their plants to potential thieves. Some indoor growers prefer the control they have over the plants' environment. Licensed cannabis growers in medical states are also frequently forced indoors; they, too, cannot risk losing their crop to thieves, especially because the cannabis is medicine patients rely on receiving regularly. There are many indoor growers who are not really gardeners, but can be considered producers of a product by artificial methods. Sometimes this lack of understanding of the plants' natural life cycle leads to using chemicals for a quick fix. The best indoor growers have adapted outdoor gardening knowledge and skills to an indoor environment and use only organic methods.

Light and Space Requirements

Currently, the most commonly used lighting for indoor grow rooms is HID lighting, which stands for High Intensity Discharge. An HID lighting system consists of a ballast, reflector, socket, and lamp (light bulb), and is intensely bright. The ballast acts like the engine, converting and driving energy to illuminate the lamp. HID lighting options for plant growth are typically Metal Halide (MH), or High Pressure Sodium (HPS) systems. It is important to get an air-cooled system; the lights will last longer and will not heat the grow room as much.

FACT

Some indoor growers with smaller grow rooms like the HPS 600 watt systems best, as they produce less heat than a 1,000 watt system and can be hung closer to the plants.

The basic rule of thumb on lighting is 50 watts of HPS or MH light per square foot. You need to measure your total growing space and do a few calculations. Reflectors are popular for getting the most out of your lights, and many are designed for smaller growing areas. A completely self-contained design will be lightweight and usually includes hangers. Many are lined with a high performance specular aluminum and come completely prewired. All you have to do is screw in the bulb.

To get a good idea for how many plants you can comfortably and healthily put into your space, measure the size of your final size containers, or better yet, lay the empty containers out in the grow room. Many growers use drip pans under the containers to catch any water spillage, so allow space for drip pans if you plan to use them. You'll also need to allow room for moving around and working on the plants.

Actually laying out the grow space with empty containers can save you a lot of work later on; it lets you walk through and revise your work flow requirements, and you can be realistic about how many plants can actually fit in your available grow room space.

You will also have to study how your fans and lights will be placed: do you have heavy ceiling beams to work with, or will you need to plan for and purchase light stands? Plan where to run venting, as well as any refits needed to prevent light leakage to outdoors.

Always be extremely careful to install and use lighting systems properly; grow rooms can get too hot very quickly, and you risk drying out or burning plants, not to mention the danger of fire from poorly installed or maintained equipment. Never have cords or outlets where water and electricity can mix.

ALERT

Another Best Practice advised by experienced indoor growers is to always have a spare bulb on hand at all times; the plants are very sensitive to changes in the light phases or photoperiods, and keeping them in darkness while you order another bulb is not good for your plants' well-being.

Growing indoors is a far more technical experience than doing so outdoors. Current technologies are rapidly changing in response a widespread movement to cut power costs and reduce light heat, while improving indoor plant performance. Many indoor growers are working with LEDs and T5 fluorescents for both these reasons. The best plan for an indoor grower just starting out is to know your space parameters, prepare the grow room properly, and do your research; today's state-of-the-art indoor lighting system will date almost as rapidly as a new computer.

Ventilation and Odor Control

Before the indoor grower even starts a crop, a ventilation system should be already in place. Controlling humidity in a cannabis grow room requires a constant supply of fresh air in and old air out. Remember that too much humidity will cause plants to stop growing. Cannabis plants in the reproductive phase also emit a strong and distinctive odor that is eventually vented to the outside of your house or whatever building you use to grow your crop. This can alert thieves or law enforcement that you are growing cannabis, or lead casual visitors to either wonder what the smell is, or to clue in to what you are growing.

Most indoor growers eliminate the odor danger by forcing the grow room air through a carbon filter. Many home cultivators simply attach a large carbon filter to their air extraction system and filter out any smell before the air is expelled from the grow room.

Another way of eliminating odor is by installing an ozone generator in the extraction ducting. Air is forced past the ozone generator by the extraction fan, and the air is neutralized as it mixes with the ozone, which in and of itself has a fairly distinctive smell.

When and How to Transplant Your Indoor Plants

The first thing that will determine your schedule is to know what you are starting with. Some propagators provide what is essentially a largish plant, two to three feet in height. Some provide a rooted clone, a tiny thing a few inches in size. You may be starting seedlings, or rooting cuttings of your own.

FACT

Seedlings create a space issue, so they end up being transplanted more than young plants already known to be female; it is completely impractical to commit the largest size containers and grow room space to speculation. This is also true in outdoor grows, but for indoor grows, warm, ventilated, sufficiently lighted space is a premium commodity.

If you are starting with a well-grown young female plant a few feet in height, transplant it at once into its largest, final container. You might as well get to work at turning expensive soil and light into strong roots and healthy vegetative growth. Indoor plants rarely grow a long or large central taproot; they instead rely on a fine mass of almost hair-like side roots to pull in water and nutrients. A ground planted cannabis plant can grow its central taproot as long as six feet, so this is a good example of how adaptable cannabis can be.

If you have a healthy clone with strong roots that are well started, again, go ahead and plant it in the final container for the same reasons as above; it will only go through any possible transplant shock one time and then should surge along nicely.

You should plan on two to four weeks for cuttings to root and become actual little plant clones. Until then, keep their light relatively cool; fluorescent light is suitable. They need warmth, but not hot, bright light just yet.

If you have started from seed and are not using feminized seed, you will be dealing with twice the amount of little plants that you want to end up with in your flowering phase. This is because cannabis is dioecious, and must declare for the grower to know if the plant is male or female.

The first transplant for seedlings is usually from their little four-inch starter pots to a three- or five-gallon container. This will allow enough room for the plants to grow while they make their sexual determination. Unsexed seedlings can also be allotted a two-gallon pot until they declare their sexual identities; this will not hurt them, though it may limit their final size. This is not necessarily a bad thing in an enclosed and finite space, and it has the added benefit of making it easier to move the males once you know which ones they are.

How to Transplant

Have the next size containers ready to go, filled partly with your prepared soil. Leave a hole a few inches deeper and wider than the transplants' current containers. You can check how much initial soil to put in the container by setting the plant in its existing pot inside the container and checking that you have left enough room for the incoming root ball.

Water the waiting soil and stir to make certain it is uniformly dampened; check that the water is draining from the container well. Scratch in a scant handful of bone meal so it is easily accessible to the plants' roots and will aid in strong root production.

Let the soil of the plants waiting for transplant get slightly dry; soil that is too wet will be heavy and has the potential to fall apart, breaking the root ball.

One person can easily perform early transplants. When the plants are taller and in heavy larger containers, it is far safer for the plants to have a transplanting assistant help you pull the pots. It will also be easier on you, and your back in particular, to have a transplant pal. Remember, to get the plant out of the pot, you are going to be turning it over and using gravity to slide the root ball out. If you are not particularly strong or tall, a helper is essential. Root balls also do not always slide right out, and wrestling a heavy, earth filled container while trying not to break the plant can get tricky and tiring.

ALERT

If you are using a helper, always make certain that you both understand the plan—who is pulling the pot, and who is supporting and turning the plant. Not getting these details straight before you start working can cause confusion that leads to broken plants or root balls. This is far easier to work out before you are holding an extremely heavy container with a root ball halfway falling out. As soon as the pot-puller frees the root ball, they can quickly set the pot down and help support the root ball until it is settled gently into its new container.

Sometimes, despite your best efforts, a root ball will break. While this event is not ideal, do not panic; cannabis is a very strong plant. The plant will spend a little time adjusting its root growth, and will eventually get back to strong vegetative growth; the root damage just puts it a little behind the schedule of its sisters.

Once the transplant is settled gently in place, fill in with your prepared soil and gently press around the plant's main stem with the palms of your hands flat to help bring the roots in contact with the soil. Water gently and press again to settle the plant. Make certain the plant's identifying label or tag is secured or written on the side of the container with indelible pen.

Lights and Your Transplants

Once you have your little plants transplanted, you will want your grow room lights to cycle for the vegetative phase; make certain the plants get eighteen hour "days" and six hour "nights" for two full weeks. If you are using HID, place the young plants so they are twenty-four to thirty-six inches under the light source. If you have concerns about burning the plants, hold your own hand under the light where the tops of your plants will be; if it feels like it's burning you, it will burn them. You may need to adjust the light height up or down as you observe the plants; if they are getting "leggy," or stretching too hard toward their light source, they are reaching too much, and the lights need to be lowered. Keep an eye on your lights; the plants are growing rapidly, so be alert and prepared to adjust the height as often as needed.

If you are working with clones, they should be one to two feet tall by the seventh week of the vegetative phase. At this time, you can change your light cycle to a twelve hour day and twelve hour night to induce flowering, or move the clones to a separate flowering room with the light cycle run on timers. This is the time to switch amendments with lower nitrogen content and to feed at appropriate levels for bloom.

Rotating Vegetative and Flowering Cycles

If you are working with seedlings, allow an extra four weeks of growth in the vegetative phase before inducing flowering. This is where having separate vegetative and flowering rooms can give you more options; the set up also allows for continual cycling of vegetative and flowering plants. As soon as one crop is harvested and the flowering room deep cleaned, another group of vegetative plants can be installed and induced to flower. The vegetative room can also be cleaned and ready to begin another cycle of young plants so the grower can keep up a perpetual growing cycle.

Protection from Spider Mites

Almost nothing is more destructive to an indoor grow than a spider mite infestation; the crop and grower are both in for a bad time. You must act quickly to protect your plants if you even suspect you have spider mites in your grow room.

Spider mites cause damage by sucking cell contents from the plant's leaves. The first visible signs of infestation generally show up as a stippling of light dots on the leaves. In more advanced infestations the leaves can take on a sickly gray or bronze color. As the infestation continues, the plant's leaves turn yellow and drop off. Your plant is signaling in every way it can that it is under attack and needs help. Leaves, twigs, and flowers become covered with large amounts of webbing, and the plants will appear sickly and stunted. As your plant's foliage declines in food value, female spider mites hitchhike onwards to other plants, and the cycle continues.

Spider Mite Features

Spider mites develop from eggs, which are usually laid near the veins of leaves during the growing season. After the eggs hatch, the old egg shells remain and can be useful in diagnosing spider mite problems. Check the underside of leaves for spider mites, their eggs, old eggshells, and the distinctive spider mite webbing. To the naked eye, spider mites look like tiny moving dots on the plant leaves. For a clear look at suspicious dots, examine your plants with a hand held lens with at least ten times magnification. The undersides of leaves are typically where spider mites start out living in webbed colonies containing hundreds of individual mites. Lightly misting your plants before spider mite inspections will make the webs much easier for you to see.

Preventative Measures

The very first preventative is to make certain you do not unknowingly bring infested plants, or carry mites on your clothes, into contact with your grow room or any cannabis plant, whether indoor or outdoor.

FACT

Spider mites, particularly the twospotted spider mite variety (*Tetranychus urticae*), are especially feared by the indoor cannabis grower. Although they are related to insects, spider mites are actually arachnids. The spider mite is the most common and destructive mite pest, and will reproduce rapidly in hot conditions like a cannabis grow room; a generation can be completed in less than a week. Mature female spider mites may produce a dozen eggs daily for a couple of weeks, so populations can increase with frightening rapidity. Plants under water stress are highly susceptible to spider mite attacks.

Spider mites can live on plants other than cannabis, so any plants you handle or purchase should be inspected for spider mites, not just your cannabis. Never put new clones or plants in your main grow room without a period of isolation. Inspect them closely under magnification, and give them a preventative bath with an organic insecticidal soap. The insecticidal soap kills the spider mites by compromising their cellular integrity; the spider mites are dissolved from the inside out.

Removing Spider Mites

Spider mites are happiest in hot, dryish conditions, with approximately twenty to thirty percent humidity. In temperatures above 80°F, spider mites can reproduce in as little as five days. To prevent an infestation during the vegetative phase of cannabis growth, periodic blasts with clean water can physically remove and kill many mites, as well as destroy the webbing where they lay their eggs. It is thought that spider mites may delay laying eggs until new webbing is produced. Spraying flowering plants with water is not advised; foliar drinking can slow resin production during the flowering phase, and too much moisture on colas can create an environment for mold.

QUESTION

What is the best way to make an environmentally safe insecticidal soap?
Use two to three drops of a soft, biodegradable soap like Murphy's Oil Soap, Castile, or Ivory liquid soap per quart of water; more is not better, as too much soap can stress the plant further. Apply by using a clean spray mister bottle, or, with small seedlings, cuttings, or clones, simply dip them into a wide mouthed jar of the solution. If you are dealing with larger plants, make certain to cover every inch of leaf, especially the undersides where spider mites prefer to live. You may have to repeat this every other day; the soap only stays effective for about a day.

Another alternative is using a horticultural oil, like neem oil, which is an extract from the neem tree. This is an excellent alternative to nonorganic compounds for controlling spider mites. Neem oil should be applied during the day to ensure quicker evaporation; this will reduce your chances of damaging the plants. Neem oil should always be used at the manufacturer's recommended strength; doubling up on the amount of oil may injure your plants.

Keep new plants in your isolation ward for at least a week, checking carefully under magnification for any sign of spider mites. If they pass as clean, give them one more treatment with the organic insecticidal bath before transferring the plants to your grow room.

FACT

Some growers recommend spraying infested plants with a 1:1 mixture of alcohol and water to kill spider mites on contact. Rubbing alcohol evaporates quickly and should do little damage to the plant; however, test the spray on a few leaves first and check the plant's reaction. Other growers prefer a gentler 1:3 mixture of rubbing alcohol to water. As with the soap solution, make sure to cover the entire plant, especially the undersides of the leaves.

If you have found spider mites on new plants or clones, you should realize that you are a vector, meaning now you can carry the spider mites along to your healthy plants. Treat the infested plants, remove all of your clothing, bag it in plastic for removal to a washing machine, and immediately shower or bathe yourself. Do not forget to wash your hair. Many growers actually work naked in their grow rooms to avoid an accidental introduction of spider mites from their outdoor clothing.

Chemical Treatments

Some growers think that chemical solutions to the spider mite problem are the only effective choice. For health considerations alone, especially when growing for medical patients, the grower needs to understand spider mite control. Just because a chemical manufacturer advertises that a product kills spider mites does not mean this is a real solution.

First of all, very few insecticides are effective for spider mites. Chemical controls for spider mites are usually miticides or acaricides. Miticides don't affect the spider mite eggs, so repeat applications at ten to fourteen day intervals are required to control hatching eggs. The frequency of application creates resistant strains of spider mites, and kills natural enemies like predatory mites, making long-term indoor control even more difficult for the grower.

For example, using Sevin, otherwise known as carbaryl, devastates most spider mite natural enemies and will actually contribute to spider mite outbreaks. Malathion, Marathon, and Merit are all commercial products that encourage spider mite outbreaks by eradicating all natural predators.

Spider Mite Predators

The most useful predators of spider mites are mites in the family *Phytoseiidae*. These mites are actually produced commercially for release as biological controls. The Cornell University Extension office refers to *Phytoseiulus persimilis* as "one of the mainstays of greenhouse integrated pest management." Once the spider mites are gone, these predators feed on each other and eliminate their own populations.

ESSENTIAL

Create sticky traps by smearing a resin like Tanglefoot on pot edges or cardboard that is an attractant color; spider mites appear to like yellow. Cardboard panels can be coated with Tanglefoot and placed on the walls. After you've applied your resin, periodically run your fans on high for about ten minutes. Users of this technique report the spider mites are blown off and stick on the Tanglefoot panel. You can also put Tanglefoot around air intakes; this can help trap incoming spider mites looking for a home. You will still need to treat the plants for eggs, but reducing the adult population will help you gain control.

When you are ordering mail order predators, generally figure that predatory mites should be placed out at a count of at least twenty per plant. The predators will not usually move from plant to plant, so they need to be placed in an even distribution by hand. Estimate how many to use based on the general idea that one predator mite can eat twenty spider mite eggs or five adult spider mites per day.

Other Treatments

Moisture management is also an important cultural control for spider mites. Plants stressed by lack of water can produce changes in their chemistry that make them more appealing to spider mites. The indoor grower of cannabis also has more control over how humid the grow environment is kept; and should remember that spider mites need a fairly low humidity level to thrive.

Bottom line, the best treatment for spider mites is extreme caution, close observation of the plants and the grow environment, and prevention before infestation.

Protection from Other Natural Pests

Here you'll find information on several common cannabis predators, and how to properly remove each pest.

Whitefly

Whitefly are quite small, approximately one-sixteenth of an inch long, and completely white. If you lightly shake the plant, they flutter around and then settle back. Whitefly suck on the juices in leaves, weakening plants and transferring disease from plant to plant.

French marigold (*T. patula*) is an annual that deters whiteflies and has roots that kill nonbeneficial nematodes. Marigolds in pots can be moved around the greenhouse or grow room. Make certain to get the specific variety *T. patula*, which is usually sold as French marigold.

Fungus Gnats

Fungus gnats can be problematic once they get a foothold in your grow room. They are spindly flies that look like tiny mosquitoes, with bodies about one-eighth of an inch long. The larvae that live in the soil are what actually cause the damage to plants, not the adult fungus gnats. Larvae are translucent gray to white, about one-quarter inch long, worm-like insects with no legs and shiny black heads. They can infest a crop from soil or algae under benches, from contaminated potting soil, or by adults flying short distances into the production area.

Larvae feed on decaying matter and on healthy and diseased roots in the soil medium; they are particularly damaging to seedlings or small clones. Fungus gnat problems result from overly wet conditions and diseased roots; the alert grower will make haste to amend poor cultural conditions. Soils should be stored dry, and pots and production areas must be well drained. Fungus gnats need soil fungi, algae under benches, or a damp mossy place to get established. None of these should be in a clean, well managed grow room.

Sometimes naturally occurring parasites can regulate fungus gnat populations, especially when broad-spectrum pesticides are not used in the production area. Fungus gnat parasites are much smaller than fungus gnats and look like fragile tiny wasps.

Adult fungus gnats are attracted to yellow sticky traps. Some growers also report using diatomaceious earth on the topsoil of the pots has good effect in killing fungus gnat larvae.

Molds

Botrytis is the most commonly seen mold in an indoor grow. It requires high humidity conditions (50 percent or higher), and some type of initial food source before it invades a healthy plant. Any debris from old leaves or bruised, broken plant parts can be enough to provide a food base; eventually, the fungus will invade healthy plant tissue, and you will lose some, if not all, of your harvest.

Botrytis can initially be mistaken for a dusting of trichomes, but once in full bloom it presents as gray, almost hair-like spots on the cola or flower, continuing rapidly to slimy, dark gray goo.

Prevention is the best cure; sanitation and good air circulation are the best weapons the grower has to prevent major botrytis or other mold outbreaks. Remove dead leaves or damaged tissue from the plants and keep the indoor grow room extremely clean. Do not throw dead leaves to the base of your plants; you will be creating a food source for botrytis and other pests.

Protection from Human Pests

Absolutely the most important thing you can do to protect your cannabis from theft is to not talk about it. This can be difficult, especially if your crop is beautiful, bountiful, and delicious. It is human nature to want to take credit for or to brag a little about your successful crop. You may be tempted to show your gorgeous grow to a trusted friend. If they don't need to know, don't burden them with the responsibility of knowing about your crop.

If someone asks where you got your wonderful cannabis, do not tell them. This can be someone you know well and trust implicitly; they may well be trustworthy and would never mean harm to you, but again, there is human nature and the desire to talk. Bragging about knowing a really great grower is something that people sometimes do. They feel there is no harm in it because they are not giving your name.

Growers have a saying: "loose lips cause rips." The value of cannabis makes it well worth a thief's efforts; they will spend hours and hours following your friend to find you, then observing you and studying how and when to steal your crop. They may just steal your crop, but there are additional possibilities like trashing your house, and possibly even harming or killing you, another household member, or your pets.

The Impact of Law Enforcement

Another threat to consider is law enforcement—this depends on where you live and your legal status as a grower. In the right state, and the right county within that state, law enforcement is not allowed to discriminate against licensed medical growers. It is sensible and right that a law abiding citizen can call the police for help and get the same response as, for example, a cultivator of expensive Bonsai who is being robbed would receive.

If you are growing indoors illicitly, your risk is doubled; the more people who know about your grow increases the chance that information about you will be traded to law enforcement by someone looking to improve their own legal situation.

Think ahead to any sort of reason a stranger might need to access your house or the building where your indoor grow is located. If you need any ducting or electrical work, get that work done before your growing area looks like anything but a basement, wood shop, or art room. You do not have to discuss anything with a contractor, but casual conversation about a wood shop or pottery studio can help deflect any speculations as to what you may be planning to do in the space.

Landlords

If you rent your home, remember that there is one person who does have a right to access it: your landlord. A landlord must give advance notice of a pending need to enter your home, either for a normal look around or to make some needed repairs. How you handle this depends on your own ethics, but in general, if you plan to grow anything larger than a closet grow, it is better to seek out a cannabis-friendly landlord and ask permission. Trying to dismantle a full sized grow room in seventy-two hours (a typical advance notice time frame in most states) is tricky at best, and of course raises the question of where to move it to.

Fertilizing for Vegetative Growth

Once your cuttings or seedlings are well started, the plants will be in what is called the vegetative phase of growth; they are working at growing roots and gaining size and building strong stems and lots of healthy green leaves. During this phase the plants will need plenty of water and a great deal more nitrogen than during the flowering phase.

ESSENTIAL

Your overall outcome will be much more superior if you pay attention to soil quality in your initial setup as opposed to trying to amend the soil mix later by top feeding. Strong vegetative growth will support large colas and healthy flowers. Spindly, poorly fed plants will produce smaller flowers or sometimes even droop over from the weight of flowering.

Organics are typically safer than chemical fertilizers because rarely burn plants, but testing your soil and understanding the different properties of different organic amendments can, along with your budget, help you choose wisely. Packaged amendments generally list the Big Three of plant needs as follows: nitrogen (N) first, phosphorus (P) second, and potassium (K) coming last.

Blood meal applications last up to four months and should be used with caution; outdoor growers use no more than four ounces per square yard during the growing or vegetative phase. Indoor growers are more likely to use it as an element in tea for their plants; dilution with water makes it less likely to burn tender young plants, and it is a good source of nitrogen.

Plants in a vegetative phase of growth will use a lot of nitrogen, and will push to grow big and leafy. Watch each plant as an individual, but you should normally feed your crop a "power drink" of special compost or manure tea once a week. This can coincide with the plants watering schedule for convenience.

Fertilizing for Flowering

As the plants start to flower, their vegetative growth will slow and then stop. The grower should stop feeding high nitrogen; the plants will need more phosphorus (P) and more potassium (K) for flowering. If you are using pre-made organic supplements, look for 15–30–30 ratio, or as close to these ratios as you can get, for flowering.

FACT

A good time to feed a liquid food (like compost tea) is immediately after watering. The liquid will be less likely to run straight through dry soil and out the drainage holes.

The plants will also need calcium, which you can supply by scratching finely ground organic eggshells into the soil around the main stem. An electric coffee grinder is a great tool to use when preparing the eggshells; wear a mask as the fine powder is easy to inhale.

Water Requirements for Indoor Plants

Every indoor grow room should have a thermometer and a hygrometer installed; accurate measurements are essential for maintaining a healthy plant environment. Ideally, you will use a thermometer that not only shows current temperature, but records the high and low measurements for each day. This will give you valuable information as to how well your cooling and venting systems are working. The ideal temperature for an indoor grow room is 72 to 76°F. The best range in relative humidity is from 60 to 70 percent for vegetative plants, dropping to 40 to 60 percent during the flowering phase.

The plants' water intake should be monitored daily; especially when they get bigger and use more water and have less room in their containers. If soil in the container is pulling away from the edge of the pot, it is time to water. The best time to water is when the soil is just starting to separate from the pot wall; otherwise you will waste a lot of water that will run down between the pot and the root ball, and the plant might not get much liquid at all.

Cannabis plants that are stressed for water will signal to you with drooping leaves and a wilted look. They can bounce back very quickly, but stressing the plant over and over will take its toll. Do not let the plants dry out and beg for water, but ideally water deeply once a week.

Identifying the Peak Harvest Moment

At the end of the twelfth week in the indoor cycle, the plants should be ready, or nearly ready, for harvest. The grower must monitor trichomes at least daily for the best harvest timing. Indoor growers, like outdoor growers, generally harvest their plants when the trichomes are just starting to turn amber.

The indoor grower has an advantage here in that they have a controlled growing environment. If they are working with a late maturing strain or feel the flowering plants need another week of finish, they can choose to do so without worrying about the weather and potential crop loss due to molds. A ripe cannabis flower will generally have both white and brown pistils showing from the third set as the trichomes are starting to turn from clear to amber. This is the ideal time to harvest.

CHAPTER 14

Dealing with Mold

Next to cannabis thieves, nothing else is as detrimental to a crop as mold. Different types attack at the new seedling stage (damp off), at the vegetative stage (the powdery type mildews), at full flowering (grey mold, or botrytis), and of course the cannabis stays vulnerable during the hanging, curing, and storage phases of production. The wise grower will maximize their chances of a bountiful harvest by following some simple steps to prevent molds.

What Is Mold?

Healthy plants require the presence of beneficial fungi and bacteria; however, there are some harmful versions of both that are massively destructive to your goal of successfully raising and harvesting high quality cannabis.

FACT

California's most respected cannabis testing location, Steep Hill Lab, says 3 percent of the cannabis it tests has unsafe mold levels under general guidelines for herbal products. Eighty-five percent showed traces of mold in 2010. Many California dispensaries contract with private laboratories such as Steep Hill to check medical cannabis for not only molds, but also toxic insecticides like bifenthrin.

One of the worst molds to attack cannabis is botrytis, a pathogenic fungus commonly known as gray mold or blight. In Webster's New Collegiate Dictionary, the second definition of blight is "something that frustrates one's plans or withers one's hopes." This sums up perfectly the cannabis grower's situation if they experience a rampant botrytis outbreak.

Botrytis is found virtually everywhere plants grow and attacks many different types of crops, not just cannabis and hemp. Hemp is a scientifically studied commercial crop in Canada, where it is farmed for food, fuel, and fiber. The single greatest threat to commercial hemp production has been botrytis mold; acres and acres of infected crops can be completely destroyed within three days from initial indications.

This observation is not meant to discourage, but rather to emphasize how vigilant you must be in observing your plants, and how important it is to take immediate steps to prevent and/or eradicate botrytis. As a small-time grower, you will have the ability to monitor all your plants very closely and provide individualized care for each of them.

How Does Mold Start Growing?

Botrytis, the most destructive mold to cannabis, must have high humidity levels (50 percent or higher) along with nutrients or a food source before it invades the plant. This is why good garden practices are important; any debris from old leaves or bruised, broken plant parts can be enough to provide a food base. This mold is frequently found in greenhouses or indoor grow rooms, though rainy conditions near harvest can provide perfect conditions for a botrytis outbreak in outdoor crops. If ignored and left unchecked, eventually the fungus will invade healthy plant tissue and you will lose a significant portion of, or even all of, your harvest.

To help prevent infection, monitor each plant on a daily basis for the following problems, and remove or repair the issue as soon as you can:

- Fallen leaves at base of plant, or hanging on axials
- Injured leaves
- Broken stems
- Cuttings from botrytis infected plants
- Wounded tissue from taking cuttings

Botrytis is spread by the wind or in water, or on your hands or clothing. Almost any activity can result in a release of spores and the subsequent transfer to the crop. Botrytis initially forms two types of resting structures on or in infected plant tissue: very dark brown or black multi-celled structures called sclerotia, or single-celled, thick, dark walled chlamydospores. The fungus then waits for the right humidity conditions to erupt into destruction mode.

What Does Mold Look Like?

Botrytis appears sometimes within hours from your last plant inspection. The reason for the common name "gray mold" becomes apparent when you first see the gray, smoke-like eruptions of spores appear on the flowers of your prized plants. Unfortunately, the mold starts from within the flower, so your first indication of botrytis can be only the tip of the iceberg. The mold can initially be mistaken for a dusting of trichomes, but once in full bloom it presents as gray, almost hair-like spots on the cola or flower, and rapidly devolves to a slimy, dark gray mess. Picture your cannabis flowers melting into gray goo.

Botrytis starting on a flower. (Notice the mold spot.)

Full blown botrytis.

Mold Prevention while Growing

Sanitation and good air circulation are the best weapons the grower has to prevent major botrytis or other mold outbreaks. Remove dead leaves or damaged tissue from the plants and keep the garden area extremely clean. Do not throw dead leaves to the base of your plants; you are only creating a food source for botrytis and other molds. If you have plant breakage or cut tissues (from an accident, high winds, or taking cuttings for propagation), repair immediately.

You will note that cannabis stalks and stems appear hollow inside. Water can collect where the plant has been injured or cut and provide a nice damp spot for mold to start. It is worth your while to seek out some pure beeswax to help you make repairs (for the best price, check online for local beekeepers to buy from, or you can purchase it at health food stores or candle making shops).

Remove any darkened or bruised looking plant tissue with a clean, sharp knife or pruning shears, warm the beeswax in your hands to soften, and make a little plug. The warmed wax will be pliable and easy to shape. Smooth the top into a little cap so that all cut plant tissue is covered with wax. Some growers use chewing gum for the same purpose, but beeswax, due to its purity and waterproof properties, is preferred. Be sure to thoroughly clean your knife or shears in between cuts. If you don't, you could be spreading what you are trying to prevent. Dip the shears in a one part bleach, four parts water solution to ensure sterilization.

Ventilate indoor grows to prevent high humidity conditions. A hygrometer that measures humidity is a must for the indoor grower. These frequently come paired with a thermometer and provide digital readings on both temperature and humidity levels in the greenhouse or grow room. The indoor grower has the advantage of control; they can increase venting and air circulation to reduce humidity levels below 50 percent. Keeping the grow room at a lower humidity will have a significant effect in inhibiting mold activity.

ALERT

Some growers use fungicides for mold prevention. This is not considered a Best Practice and in fact should not be an option. Molds develop a resistance to chemicals, and ingesting chemically treated cannabis can cause serious health problems. Control molds with vigilance and good garden practices, not poisons.

The outdoor grower must rely on existing weather and humidity conditions over which she has no control. Planting for good air circulation and constantly monitoring your crop for the early stages of outbreaks will go a long way in determining how much of your harvest can or will be damaged by mold. Bushier plants and very thick, dense colas need to be gently inspected on a daily basis, preferably twice a day. Part the branches (being gentle to avoid breaking) and examine the inner parts of the plant; air circulation is the worst at the center of dense vegetative growth.

You must react immediately once you spot botrytis. If you have outdoor plants and they are almost ready for harvest, remove any infected parts, bag them in plastic, and then harvest the plant. Shower and change your clothes after handling infected plants; never go directly from handling botrytis to a clean plant or you will spread the spores.

Powdery Mildew and Downy Mildew

Both these mildews present in a similar manner, and the treatments are virtually the same. Affected leaves typically display blotchy spots in yellow or bronze, and an overlying white, powdery fungal growth. These mildews are favored by high humidity, but not necessarily free water on leaves. Warm temperatures and shady conditions encourage these mildews to grow and spread. Luckily, the spores and mycelium are sensitive to extreme heat and direct sunlight.

ESSENTIAL

Certain types of cannabis will be more susceptible to mold, so each plant must be assessed individually if you are trying for more finish. It is better to harvest a little early than to lose an entire crop by waiting for an ideal moment that may not come.

The optimum temperature for infection is between 68 to 77°F and relative humidity between 40 to 100 percent is sufficient for the spores to germinate. Low, diffuse light also seems to favor the development of powdery mildew.

In general, healthy, vigorous leaves and stems are less prone to infection. Plants under nutritional stress will, in most cases, develop mildews much sooner than plants the same age grown under a good nutritional program.

Outdoors, plant in uncrowded conditions in full sunlight in a well-drained area to prevent mildew. Indoor growers should use dehumidifiers and maintain good air circulation and ventilation. Ideally, always water your crop in the morning.

Sulfur is highly effective against powdery mildew if used in a protectant program with a minimum of seven to fourteen days between applications. Garlic naturally contains high levels of sulfur, and a few cloves crushed in water can be used to make a homemade spray.

Another organic option is to spray once a week with a solution of baking soda. Do not spray more often than once per week, as added frequency may add too much sodium, something your plants will resent. Baking soda increases the surface pH, making it more alkaline and unsuitable for the growth of mildew spores. Spray the undersides of leaves as well as the upper surfaces when using any sprays.

BAKING SODA SPRAY
- 1 tablespoon baking soda
- 1 gallon water (alkaline water with a pH of just below 8 is best)
- A few drops of liquid soap (to help the solution stick)

Neem Oil (available at garden stores) is an organic solution used to combat both molds and mites. Always use sparingly and follow directions; more is not always better, and can in fact be harmful!

ESSENTIAL

If you must spray, either make your own organic sprays, or only use products approved by the nonprofit Organic Materials Review Institute (OMRI). Established in 1997, OMRI provides an independent review of products intended for use in certified organic production, handling, and processing. Upon request, OMRI will review a company's products against the National Organic Standards. Acceptable products are OMRI Listed® and appear on the OMRI Products List.

Damp Off or Pythium Wilt

Damp off is primarily a problem with young seedlings. You can prevent this malady by starting out with sterilized soil, avoiding heavy watering, and providing adequate ventilation. If your previously vigorous little seed starts to suddenly lose momentum, there's a good chance you are over watering. Also be sure to check the humidity levels and make sure you have adequate air circulation.

Mold Prevention while Drying

While your harvested crop is hanging, drying, and curing, you must continue with close inspections on a twice-daily basis, especially if you brought the plants in due to the onset of mold. Keep the humidity level as low as possible. Purchase a dehumidifier if the need arises, and of course maintain constant gentle air circulation.

How to Check Drying Plants for Mold

Examine each plant from top to bottom under good light. You will have already removed the fan leaves (see Chapter 16), so check each cola for any signs of mold. Remove any cola that shows mold, and dispose of it carefully. Clean your tools and hands, and change clothes after handling moldy plant materials to reduce the danger of spreading spores to clean plants.

ESSENTIAL

> Some growers use flat basket trays set on racks for drying. These can work very well, but can take up a lot of space unless your rack system is tall. If you do use baskets, make certain that they have airspace underneath to facilitate air circulation.

At-risk plants (those with very dense, bushy colas) may need to be taken apart wet and dried in parts. The thicker colas may show no sign of mold until you expose the inner parts of the flowers. Some indica crosses can have massive central top colas that are very prone to mold. Botrytis in particular starts growing within the flower, so the onset is hard to spot.

Sometimes a plant needs to be removed from the drying area and broken up for salvage. It depends on how far gone the mold outbreak is, and the act of breaking apart the colas can spread spores. If you have thick, dense colas and see botrytis outbreaks all over the hanging plant, odds are good that the insides of the colas are going to look scary. Do not hesitate to take all the colas apart and be ruthless in deciding what to dispose of. There is no "sort of okay" area. If it is moldy, get rid of it!

Mold Prevention During Storage

Once your crop has finished hanging and drying, you will manicure the flowers for storage and store them for the longer curing process. Manicuring the flowers allows you to closely scrutinize each flower for mold. Make certain you have good, bright light to work under; a dusting of mold can sometimes look like trichomes in dim light. You don't want to store moldy flowers with clean ones.

Some growers use an interim step of storing the manicured flowers in brown paper grocery bags because the paper breathes well. The flowers should be gently stirred every one to two days. You can go straight to plastic zip-top bags or, preferably, glass jars with sealable tops (like Mason jars). Whether you use bags or glass, make certain to "breathe" the cannabis by unsealing and resealing once per week. Smell the cannabis as you unseal it; you will notice the difference as soon as the plant material stops gassing.

The breathing of the cannabis is also very important for the end goal of a pleasant-tasting, smooth finish to the curing. Cannabis continues to gas, or release chlorophylls, for a few months until finish. Locking the gases in with the unfinished cannabis will result in unpleasant-tasting, harsh smoke. Mark your calendar for breathing, and stay on schedule for the next six to eight weeks of curing; otherwise you will ruin your harvest. Molds need moisture, so, as with any herb, store your cannabis in a cool, dark, dry place.

CHAPTER 15

Dealing with Mites

Outdoor growers may deal with many more variables than the indoor growers who, after all, can control light, water, wind, and humidity levels. One advantage the outdoors growers do enjoy is that, generally speaking, they do not have to battle spider mites. Nothing strikes greater terror in the indoor grower than a spider mite infestation because their entire crop is under great danger of destruction.

What Are Mites?

Spider mites, particularly the two-spotted spider mite (*Tetranychus urticae*) variety, are extremely destructive pests that mostly attack indoor cannabis grows. Although they are related to insects, spider mites are members of the arachnid class along with spiders and ticks. The spider mites are sometimes called web-spinning mites, and are the most common and destructive of mite pests. You must act quickly to protect your plants if you even suspect you have spider mites in your grow room.

FACT

Nothing is a sadder sight than a cannabis crop engulfed in spider mite webbing. The plants look like they are suffocating and there is nothing appealing about the thought of using the flowers that the suffering plants may produce. Some lazy or desperate growers will actually use the product, but the quality is severely impaired.

Spider mites reproduce rapidly in hot conditions like those found in a cannabis grow room. After mating, mature females may produce a dozen eggs daily for a couple of weeks, leading to extremely rapid increases in spider mite populations; a generation can be completed in less than a week. Plants under water stress are highly susceptible. As the food quality of your plant's foliage declines, female spider mites hitchhike onwards to other plants, and the cycle continues.

What Do Spider Mites Look Like?

Depending on your age and vision quality, spider mites look to the naked eye like tiny moving dots on the plant leaves. They are so tiny that an initial infestation is easy to miss until you start seeing damage to the plants. For a clear look at suspicious dots, it is more efficient to examine your plants with a hand held lens with at least ten times magnification.

Spider mite.

You are looking for adults and eggs. The adult spider mites have eight legs and an oval body, with two red eyespots near the head end of the body. Adult females, which are larger, are less than a twentieth of an inch long. Females usually have a large, dark blotch on each side of the body and numerous bristles covering the legs and body. The immature spider mites resemble the adults, except the newly hatched larvae have only six legs. If you spot what you think are spider mites, shake a few off the leaf onto a white sheet of paper. Once you disturb them, they will move around rapidly.

Spider mites develop from eggs usually laid near the veins of leaves during the growing season. Most spider mite eggs are round and extremely large in proportion to the size of the mother. Spider mite eggs are spherical and translucent; they look like tiny droplets of water that become cream colored just before hatching. After the eggs hatch, the old egg shells remain and can be useful in diagnosing spider mite problems. Check the underside of leaves for spider mites, their eggs, old eggshells, and the distinctive spider mite webbing.

Spider mites live in colonies frequently containing hundreds of individual mites, and these colonies generally appear on the under-surfaces of leaves. The name "spider mite" probably comes from the silk webbing typically produced on infested leaves. The presence of this webbing is the easiest way to distinguish them from other types of mites. Lightly misting your plants before inspecting them will make the webs much easier for you to see because they glisten like a regular spider web when wet.

An infested plant. Note that webs are like what a spider makes, but these are mites.

Remember, you are looking for a very tiny spider-like creature, usually appearing in colonies; make sure that you do not destroy beneficial small garden spiders, usually those operating as helpful individuals, as it is sometimes easy to confuse their small useful webs with spider mite webbing.

Plant Indicators of Infestation

Spider mites cause damage by sucking cell contents from the plant's leaves, injuring them as they feed and bruising the cells with their small, whiplike mouthparts. Spider mites are after the plant's sap. An infestation level high enough to show visible damage to leaves can be very destructive. The first visible signs of infestation show up as a stippling of light dots on the leaves; sometimes the leaves take on a sickly gray or bronze color. As the infestation continues, the plant's leaves turn yellow and drop off. Your plant is signaling in every way it can that it is under attack and needs help. Leaves, twigs, and flowers become covered with large amounts of webbing, a most depressing and unpleasant sight.

Mites on a leaf.

This is where your careful inspections and notes about your plants will pay off. You are much more likely to notice the very beginning of a spider mite infestation because you will have trained yourself to observe every detail of the plants' appearance. It is far better for the plants and your eventual harvest success if you spot the initial infestation and act quickly before it gets out of control. If you wait to notice anything until your plants are covered with spider mite webbing, it is probably too late to save the plants.

What to Do If You Have Mites

Spider mites are happiest in dryish conditions, approximately 20 to 30 percent humidity. They also crave warmth. In temperatures above 80°F, spider mites can reproduce in as little as five days. The indoor cannabis grower has to walk a fine line between humidity levels that are unattractive to spider mites, and the higher humidity desired by destructive molds, like botrytis or powdery mildew, that also plague cannabis.

During the vegetative stage of cannabis growth, periodic blasts with a forceful jet of water can physically remove and kill many mites, as well as destroy the webbing. It is thought that spider mites may delay laying eggs until new webbing is produced.

Treatment in an Isolation Ward

The very first preventative is to make certain you do not unknowingly bring infested plants in contact with your grow room or any cannabis plant, whether indoor or outdoor.

Spider mites can live on plants other than cannabis, so any plants you handle or purchase should be inspected for spider mites, not just your cannabis.

ALERT

Neem oil should always be used in strengths recommended by the supplier; doubling up on the amount of oil may injure your plants. Neem oil should be applied during the day to ensure quicker evaporation, which will reduce your chances of damaging the plants. Plants that are noticeably under water stress should not be sprayed with oils.

Since the initial indications of spider mites are so tiny, it is possible that, even with nothing but good intentions, another grower can provide you infested clones. Never put new clones or plants in with your existing crop without a period of isolation where you inspect them closely under magnification, and give them a preventative bath with an organic insecticidal soap. The insecticidal soap kills the spider mites by compromising their cellular integrity; the spider mites dissolve from the inside out. You only need to use about two to three drops of a soft, biodegradable soap like Murphy's Oil Soap, Castille, or Ivory liquid soap per quart of water; more is not better since too much soap can stress the plant further. Apply the bath by using a clean spray mister bottle or, with small clones, simply dip them into a wide mouthed jar of the solution. If you are dealing with larger plants, make certain to cover every inch of leaf, especially the undersides where spider mites prefer to live. You may have to repeat this every other day; the soap only stays effective for about a day.

If you find a really nasty infestation, but still want to salvage the plants, you can use something a little stronger. Some growers recommend spraying plants with a 1:1 mixture of alcohol and water to kill spider mites on contact. Rubbing alcohol evaporates quickly and should do little damage to the plant, although it is advisable to test the spray on a few leaves first and check the plant's reaction. Other growers prefer a 1:3 mixture of rubbing alcohol to water to make the spray gentler to the plants. As with the soap solution, make sure to cover the entire plant, especially the undersides of the leaves.

Another alternative is horticultural oil, like Neem Oil, an extract from the neem tree. This is an excellent alternative to nonorganic compounds for controlling spider mites.

Observe the new plants for at least a week, checking carefully under magnification for any sign of spider mites. If they pass as clean, give them one more treatment with the organic insecticidal bath and transfer the plants out of isolation.

If you have found spider mites on new plants or clones, you should realize that you are now a medium for the spider mites to travel to your healthy crop. The best thing is to treat the infested plants, remove all your clothing and bag it for removal to a washing machine, and immediately shower or bathe yourself. Some growers actually work naked in their grow rooms; it is certainly warm enough, and helpful in avoiding an accidental introduction of spider mites carried by their clothing.

Although all of the above may seem like a lot of trouble, it is nothing compared to what you are faced with if you get spider mites established in your grow rooms.

Organic Solutions

Some growers think that chemical solutions to the spider mite problem are acceptable to use as long as they are used early on in the vegetative phase of the cannabis grow. Putting aside the human health implications of using chemicals on a consumable, the grower needs to understand spider mite control and not just blindly spray poisons.

First of all, very few insecticides are effective for killing spider mites. Chemical control of spider mites generally involves pesticides that are specifically developed for spider mite control: miticides or acaricides. Because most miticides do not affect the spider mite eggs, a repeat application at ten to fourteen day intervals is needed to control the hatching of eggs. Frequent applications of miticides help create resistant strains of spider mites, making their control even more difficult.

Natural Enemies

Natural and extremely effective enemies of spider mites include small lady beetles, predatory mites, minute pirate bugs, big-eyed bugs, and predatory thrips. Spider mites, especially in an outdoor grow, usually only become problems when the use of insecticides destroys their natural enemies.

For example, carbaryl, commercially known as Sevin, devastates most spider mite natural enemies and can greatly contribute to spider mite outbreaks. Malathion, despite being advertised frequently as effective for mite control, can actually aggravate spider mite problems instead of preventing them. Systemic, or soil applied insecticides like Marathon or Merit, both of which contain the chemical imidacloprid, have also caused spider mite outbreaks by eradicating all their natural predators.

FACT

The predatory mites most frequently available by mail order are *Galendromus occidentalis*, *Phytoseiulus persimilis*, *Mesoseiulus longipes*, and *Neoseiulus californicus*. These are quite successful in controlling spider mites in indoor cannabis grows; predatory mites often like the higher humidity of a cannabis grow room, which is helpful as spider mites do not tolerate humidity very well.

Spider mites have many natural enemies that limit their numbers in gardens, especially when unaffected by pesticide sprays. The most useful are mites in the *Phytoseiidae* family, which are predators of spider mites. In addition to naturally occurring predatory mites, some are produced commercially for release as biological controls.

Phytoseiulus persimilis is referred to by the Cornell University Extension office as "one of the mainstays of greenhouse integrated pest management." This species of mite cleans up after itself. Once the spider mite population is gone, they feed on each other, decimating their own populations.

Metaseiulus occidentalis is another common predatory mite used to kill spider mites. It is an effective biological control only if temperatures average between 44 and 89°F.

Phytoseiulus longipes is a variant of the *Phytoseiulus persimilis* mite brought over from Africa. It can stand warmer ambient temperatures than its North American cousins. Longipes has quickly become the most popular biological spider mite control agent used by gardeners.

Most suppliers provide information regarding use of the predator mites that they carry, but as a general rule of thumb, predatory mites should be placed out at a count of at least twenty per plant. The predators have difficulty moving from plant to plant, so they need to be placed on each individual plant. You can place more if you like, depending on the state of your spider mite infestation. It is estimated that one predator mite can eat twenty spider mite eggs, or five adult spider mites per day. Like many super specialized biological controls, most of these predators will die once the food source (in this instance the spider mite colony) is fully depleted.

ESSENTIAL

For information on where to buy these predators, write or call the California Department of Pesticide Regulation, P.O. Box 942871, Sacramento, CA 94271-0001, (916) 324-4100, and ask for a free copy of their leaflet "Suppliers of Beneficial Organisms in North America," or view the leaflet online at *www.cdpr.ca.gov/docs/ipminov/bensuppl .htm*.

Other insects feed on spider mites and provide high levels of natural control. One group of small, dark-colored lady beetles (also called ladybugs) from the *Stethorus* species, are known as the spider mite destroyers; they are extremely specialized predators of spider mites. Additionally, minute pirate bugs, big-eyed bugs (*Geocoris* species), and predatory thrips are important natural enemies that can help the outdoor cannabis grower should you accidently bring spider mites to your grow site.

Other Prevention Techniques

Another nontoxic weapon in the battle against spider mites is the use of sticky traps. You can create them by smearing a sticky resin, like Tanglefoot, on pot edges or cardboard that is an attractant color like yellow. Some indoor growers have had success with this trapping strategy: smear cardboard panels with Tanglefoot, being careful not to touch it with your hands, or to the plants. As your fans rotate, the spider mites are blown off and stick on the Tanglefoot panel. You can also put Tanglefoot around air intakes; this can help trap incoming spider mites looking for a home. Of course you will still need to treat the plants for spider mite eggs, but reducing the adult population will help you gain control.

ALERT

Misting the plants two or three times a day with very cold water will help bring moisture levels up to an unhealthy environment for spider mites. Some growers set up timers and do this automatically during the plants' vegetative stage of growth.

Moisture management is also an important cultural control for spider mites. Plants stressed by lack of water can experience changes in their chemistry that make them more nutritious to spider mites. The dry conditions around these water stressed plants are preferred by all spider mites, and this is one reason they are so prevalent in the more arid areas of the United States. Spider mites also feed more under dry conditions, as the lower humidity allows them to evaporate excess water they excrete. The indoor grower of cannabis has more control over how humid the grow environment is kept; and should provide a less hospitable environment at all times.

Overall, the best treatment is extreme caution, close observation of the plants and the grow environment, and prevention before infestation.

CHAPTER 16

Proper Curing and Storage of Your Harvest

Harvest is a very exciting time of year, especially on the outdoor grower's annual cycle. The indoor grower has the option of several harvests throughout the year, but of course looks forward to safely curing, storing, and sampling each one. How you handle the plants now will have great effect on the quality of the harvest; inattention can result in molds, over drying, or improper curing that can destroy the aroma and taste. For many health and aesthetic reasons, moldy cannabis should never be used.

How to Prepare Plants for Hanging

There are a few different thoughts on how to properly hang cannabis for curing. Some growers prefer to hang the entire plants. This requires a fair amount of height in your drying shed, as well as more space in between plants. Since the first time grower is unlikely possess an empty barn, it is probable that the first crop will be cut into branches and dried in sections. Some growers even hang each cola to dry but, due to space requirements, this is only advisable with small harvests.

Plants almost ready to harvest.

Start prepping your drying area well before harvest time. Not being ready takes a lot of the fun out of the process, and being disorganized can cause you to lose track of which plants are which, especially if you cut the plants into branches for hanging. You will need:

- Heavy duty eye bolts
- Heavy gauge wire (size 17 gauge or larger)
- Wire cutters
- Step ladder

- Drill
- Screwdriver
- Paper grocery bags
- Electricity
- Multiple oscillating fans
- Good light

Setting up your drying shed will require a little visualization and measuring. You will be amazed at how large the plants appear when you bring them indoors. This is just the visual contrast created by enclosing them. This volume will only last a few days; much of it is water contained in the plants, plus you will be trimming the remaining fan leaves as you hang the plants. Remember that you most likely will be bringing the outdoor plants in a few at a time, as each individual plant should be harvested as near to peak maturity as possible.

Note that proper drying requires a cool, dry place with no direct sunlight. If there are windows in your shed, make sure to cover them with curtains or shutters. A good overhead electric light is important so that you can closely examine the plants daily for mold, but direct sunlight will degrade the quality of your harvest.

FACT

Depending on genetics and placement in the garden, different plants will be ready to harvest within a few weeks. This gradual harvesting is helpful as you will have plants that have been hanging and drying and already using less space. These can be moved closer to each other as the newly harvested, bulkier plants come in.

Preparing Your Drying Space

To prepare your drying shed, first make certain cobwebs and other dust and debris have been vacuumed out with a Shop-Vac (ideally) or swept out via vigorous work with a broom. Wash the flooring and make the shed as clean as possible. You may occasionally drop a branch or even an entire plant, and avoiding contamination and dirt are the name of the game.

You will be placing your eyebolts to support long runs of the taut hanging wires. Do not try to use heavy-duty fishing line or rope; these will bow in the middle of your run and cause the hanging plants to slide together. Until the plants shed their water weight, the hanging lines will be supporting an enormous amount of poundage. There is no horrified thrill quite like walking into your drying shed and finding collapsed lines and then having to repair the lines and rehang the plants. Start out right and avoid the problem.

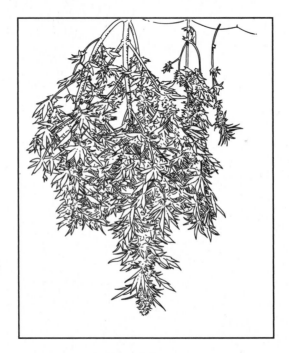

Preparing the plants for hanging.

Because an average axial branch can easily reach five to six feet in length, estimate the height needed to have the branch tips clear your floor by at least a foot, or two feet if possible. This is where your stepladder comes into play; you will need it for set up and for attending to the hanging plants. Of course, if your shed has more length than height available, it is perfectly fine to cut the longer branches in half and to hang them lower.

Allow enough space to move in between the rows, as you will be checking the plants for mold from all angles at least once per day, as well as continuing to trim fan leaves.

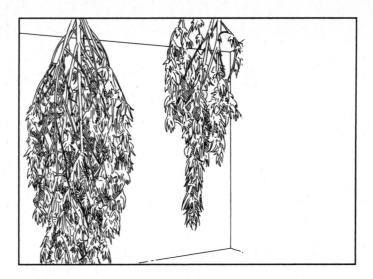

Hanging plants.

Air Flow Requirement

As soon as your first plant comes into the drying shed, the oscillating fans come into play. The fans should be placed to maximize air flow around the hanging plants, while avoiding a direct blast continually blowing on them. Avoid having the fans positioned too low as they may blow up dust from the shed floor. The fans can be set on high early on as the wet plants come in. Lower the fan settings to maintain a gentle continual cycling of air as the plants dry out.

ESSENTIAL

Always hang plants or branches top down. Never hang with the roots still attached; retaining the roots will not improve the quality of the harvest, and may add dirt to your flowers.

Ideally you will have harvested outdoor plants under clear skies, but frequently plants are brought in based on the weather and the ongoing forecast. If it has been raining for a week and the plants are close to or completely finished, you will most likely bring them in to dry. The chance of a few extra days of finishing is offset by the threat of mold.

As noted above, wet plants are very, very heavy. Before bringing them into the drying shed, give the plant a good shaking to shed as much external moisture as possible. If the plants are truly rain-soaked, be prepared to cut them in pieces for hanging. At this time you will start stripping the fan leaves that remain; this will help reduce weight and keep the large, wet fan leaves from touching the flowers and inducing mold. The big paper grocery bags on your list are for these leaves. Removing the fan leaves also makes it much easier to quickly check the flowers for molding; otherwise, you will need to lift the leaves to examine the flowers.

FACT

New growers should not worry about shaking the newly harvested plants; the resins are super-sticky and cannot be shaken off at this stage.

Drying Fan Leaves

Many growers do not bother with fan leaves; in part this depends on the size of the harvest. If your harvest is small you will want to use every part of the plants, and the fan leaves can be useful for producing bubble hash. Even if you do not plan to use them, check with your local compassion group to see if they want the leaves for making hashish. If you decide to use them, dry the fan leaves in large paper grocery bags.

If you plan on using the leaves, stir the bags daily to help them dry. Otherwise, remove the bags as they fill up and destroy the fan leaves. This will speed drying, as the fan leaves will not be releasing additional moisture into the air of the drying shed. You can either feed them to goats (they love cannabis leaves) or burn them. Composting the leaves is not advised, as again, these can be seized by law enforcement as supposedly useable cannabis.

The Importance of Good Handling Practices

Always remember that you are producing a product that will be ingested by humans, either through smoking or eating the cannabis. Cannabis should never be allowed to mold, especially when it's being grown for medical cannabis patients (whose health is often greatly impaired). Even with the best practices, hanging cannabis is very, very vulnerable to molds. Great care must be taken to identify and remove problem spots immediately.

ALERT

Keep in mind that law enforcement views large fan leaves as cannabis and will count them for weight should they try to enforce some sort of legal limit or prosecute you for growing cannabis. Having something that is of no use to you can have grave implications should you get busted. So stay tidy, keep track, and either process these leaves to hash, destroy them, or donate the leaves to someone who can use them immediately.

Molds can also greatly reduce your harvest's yield; it is not uncommon to have a pound and a half of superb bud reduced to a few ounces or completely destroyed within forty-eight hours. As with most of the other stages of cannabis production, vigilance by the grower is imperative for a successful harvest.

When and How to Clip the Crop

How long the harvest hangs has many variables: weather, moisture levels, plant size, and plant type. Expect a minimum of two weeks hanging, with a good possibility that you will wait six to eight. The easiest way to tell if your cannabis is ready to clip is to check smaller branches for "snap." A branch that is gently bent between two hands should break, not bend. It does not have to snap in half (this would be too dry), but there should be a definite break. Again, as with harvest, the plants will be ready to clip at different times, so each plant must be checked individually for finish.

FACT

If you estimate a general yield of a pound per outdoor plant, just one plant is going to take approximately sixteen hours to clip. Multiply that by your plant numbers and you should have a fairly good estimate of how much time to plan for clipping activities.

Clipping Tools

Preparing to clip means having the right space and tools readily available. Clipping a large crop is fun, but it can be a laborious process. You want to have a big table and chairs at a height that will be comfortable for long periods of sitting and working with your hands. You also need good light so you can examine the buds closely as you clip. Common sense dictates that the clipping room is not exposed to casual visitors, either by viewing through porch windows or folks stopping by to visit. Music and friends to help with the clipping are always welcome additions. You will need:

- A pair of pruning shears
- Large sheets of clean glass (framed picture glass is good)
- A pair of small sharp scissors for each clipper
- Gallon zip-top bags
- A Sharpie or other indelible pen
- Large brown paper grocery bags

A Best Practice is to clip one plant entirely before starting another; there's less chance of mislabeling product this way. Besides, the way the plants are hanging make this a logical progression as you work your way through the drying shed.

Allow approximately one hour to clip one ounce. This is only a general rule of thumb; some plants' structural characteristics make them an "easy clipper" while other types have lots of extraneous sugar leaf and require more finicky scissor work.

The Clipping Process

Now that your clipping table is set up, you are ready to go. Decide on your first plant and pick up your pruning shears. Cut enough axial branches to make a nice bundle; your table size will dictate how much to start with. Place a paper grocery bag to the left and right of each chair; one will be for the bigger remaining fan leaves, and the other for the sugar leaf. You might as well separate the two at this point, as excessive handling can knock the crystals off the dried sugar leaf.

Start stripping fan leaves off the larger branches. It's a good idea to do this with your hands as your fingers are going to get very tired of feeling scissors (blisters are common when clipping big harvests). Cut the smaller branches off the bigger axial and place over your glass (the glass will catch large amounts of kief which is then made into the delightful finger hash).

ALERT

As you process plants, keep an eye out for your marked seeder branch(es), unless you have already put the seeder branches in a separate area for drying. These should be set aside for careful examination during a seed session.

Take your scissors and cut the colas off the branch right at the nodes. The colas are the flowers and can vary from little "popcorn" buds to thick, dense, almost club-like structures, depending on the plant's genetics and its development during flowering. When you finish the branch, you have the option of trimming another one and stockpiling colas to fine clip, or fine clipping as you go. Each person clipping will find a rhythm and process that fits their style; there is no one correct way.

As you fine clip the colas, the goal is to remove the small sugar leaves. Keep moving the sugar leaves to one side of your glass and the finished colas to the other. Periodically put the sugar leaf into your other grocery bag. The colas will go into the zip-tops bags.

Storage

When your pile of colas is big enough, use the Sharpie to label a zip-top bag with the plant's information and set them in, leaving the tops unzipped so the colas can continue to breathe. Depending on the flower characteristics, a gallon bag should comfortably hold a quarter pound of colas. You do not want to pack the bags tightly, as you want to avoid crushing and packing down the flowers. If your harvest is small, clean and dry Mason jars are wonderful for storage even though they require a great deal more space than the plastic bags.

ALERT

Never seal your dried harvest in plastic or glass during the curing period without periodically breathing the containers to release gases that the plant matter continues to emit. If you fail to vent these gases, the bad taste is trapped and you will end up with some fairly nasty tasting cannabis.

Making Finger Hash

After a clipping session, you will notice that your fingers and hands are black and sticky with pungent cannabis resins. Now is the time to make finger hash; the resins will need to come off anyway, so see Chapter 17, "How to Make Finger Hash," to complete this process.

"Breathing" Stored Cannabis

As your cannabis flowers hang and dry, they will end up at about 25 percent of their fresh weight. At this point they are dry enough to store, but they will continue to cure. Drying and curing cannabis actually takes a fairly long time. Depending on the amount of humidity in the drying room, just drying hanging cannabis can take up to eight weeks. Curing continues as the chlorophylls and other pigments in the flowers start to break down. This is what will remove the "green" taste that is associated with uncured cannabis.

ESSENTIAL

Another common problem is finding animal hair stuck to the flower resins. This usually happens during the drying phase when cats or other household pets are allowed in the drying room. Always make certain the room has been well vacuumed before hanging your plants, and keep your pets outside.

Many growers find it helpful to mark their calendars, breathe the bags or jars once a week, and continue to sample the plant. Usually the curing process takes two to four months, so keep evaluating for progress. You will also notice that opening a sealed container releases the sweet aroma of properly cured cannabis, and no longer puts forth a rush of chlorophyll smell. Once curing is completed, you can seal your containers until you want to use the cannabis. Never freeze cannabis; this will have harmful effects to the resins you worked so hard to produce. Store your cannabis in a cool, dark place.

Common Problems and Solutions

The biggest problem outdoor cultivators can hope to experience is suddenly realizing that they have far more green plant material to hang up than they had planned for. This can be dealt with, as the plants are going to lose a lot of their bulk and water weight very quickly. Sometimes a spare room has to be put into use for a day or two, but do not panic; you will be able to move the hanging plants quite a bit closer to each other very soon. A shower rail can make an excellent temporary hanging spot for a large plant, or even the top rails of a canopy bed. You can use these temporary spots while you continue to clip off fan leaves, which is another quick way to make the plants less bulky.

Sometimes plants will be showing the first signs of mold issues when you cut and hang them; this is fairly common and simply requires a few days of close attention to air circulation and the removal of any mold outbreaks immediately. Always wash your hands and any cutting tools in alcohol, and be very careful to not spread mold by carrying it from plant to plant. Larger colas may need to be taken apart; if they are extremely dense and have a lot of moisture content you want to increase the air circulation immediately or risk losing a lot of good flowers to mold.

Do not run heaters to try to speed dry your crop since drying too fast will ruin the taste and texture of the flowers. Cannabis needs a cool, dry, dimly lit, and low humidity environment to dry at the proper rate. Direct sunlight can bleach and dry plant material too quickly and again affect the quality of your end result.

Sometimes trying to hang entire plants just does not work. Either the height of your space is lower than optimal, or the plants themselves are of a type that their branches fold together and create lack of air circulation. It is perfectly fine to cut the plants apart, just make certain that you keep the branches labeled or you will never figure out which plant is which. Their appearance will change radically as they dry and an old friend of several months will suddenly look very different hanging with several other cut up plants.

FACT

Some growers who hang only a few plants, and want to hang them in their entirety, will patiently brace the recalcitrant branches apart with chopsticks. This works fairly well, but is too time-consuming to use if you are hanging more than three or four good-sized plants.

Most problems with drying and curing can be avoided by paying close attention to the plants, checking for mold at least twice a day, adjusting the fans to ensure even air circulation, and keeping temperatures cool. If your drying room is in your home you will have to either not turn on your heat or make certain that the drying room remains unheated until the plants are finished hanging. Always remember to breathe the bags regularly once the plants are safely manicured and placed into containers, and you will end up with well-dried and cured cannabis.

CHAPTER 17

Hashish

Cannabis growers and users are continually looking for ways to use all of the beneficial parts of the plant. One of the most popular methods is to make hashish, a cannabis byproduct that produces similar effects, but is generally much stronger. Like cannabis, hashish is usually smoked or eaten.

What Is Hashish?

Hashish is obtained by collecting the trichomes from the flower tops of female cannabis plants, and by eliminating low-THC content plant materials. In older and time-honored methods, the trichomes are then usually pressed or forced into hashish. More recent methods use the nonwater soluble properties of THC to make hashish by the water method, commonly known as making "bubble hash." The bubble comes from how frothy and bubbly the process is while you mix the plant materials with ice.

ESSENTIAL

There is a theory that pressing the hash makes it more palatable than bubble hash, and possibly more potent. Many bubble hash makers will go one step further and press their bubble hash after extraction.

Hashish is an illegal substance on the federal level in the United States. It is designated as a Schedule 1 substance, meaning there is "no accepted medical use." In medical use states it is generally accepted as a preparation of cannabis. Be certain to check the laws in your particular state if you plan to make and store hashish. As with cannabis, the primary active ingredient in hashish is delta-9-tetrahydrocannabinol (THC).

Different Methods of Preparation

There are more than a few different methods of collecting and processing the THC-rich resins or trichomes. Some of these are centuries old; some are more recent and less labor-intensive than the older ways of making hash.

Sieving

Sieved hashish is made by using dried cured cannabis plants. The most efficient way is to clip or manicure your flowers over a fine silkscreen (stretched on a frame and set over clean glass). The silk screen should be fine, at least 65–125 microns (120–230 lines per inch). It is helpful to chill the flowers in the freezer for a few hours; this will help the resin glands break off easily. Ideally, lowering the flowers to 40°F will achieve this goal. Do not try to force the fine powder through the screen; you will only rupture the resin and it will stick in your screen. This powder can be smoked as it is, but taste and effects change when it is pressed. The quality of hashish depends on the quality of the plants you use.

ESSENTIAL

Many thrifty cannabis users build themselves a rolling box that has the silkscreen and glass already in place. As they prepare the cannabis for smoking, resins fall through the screen and are collected on the glass below. Once enough has collected to make a ball of hash, rescreen the powder a few times to make certain all plant debris has been removed. This powder can either be added to regular bud to enhance the smoke or hand pressed into hashish. Lately, these boxes have become commercially available at some smoke shops as well.

Pressing

Trichome resin (the hashish powder) is ideally pressed into a solid mass called hashish. Pressing alters the chemistry and taste of the powder and helps the produced hashish burn more evenly when smoked.

It also makes the powder easier to transport and allows the hashish to be stored for longer periods with less danger of mold. Properly made, hashish can last for several years if the maker stores it carefully in a dark, cold, airtight environment. Pressing ruptures the resin glands and enhances the distinctive taste of quality hashish. If you go through the trouble of collecting hashish powder, you should press it.

Shoe–Pressed Hash

This is a very simple and low labor method for making small amounts of pressed hashish. Place three or four grams of hashish powder in a plastic bag and seal. Put the bag in your shoe and applying pressure by walking. You will walk more evenly and process more if you put a package in each shoe. Walk for at least an hour and then check and see if the powder is changing color and sticking together. Keep walking until you have shoe-pressed hash.

Rolled Pressed Hash

If you are only processing a small amount you can, as with the shoe-pressed hashish, easily place the hashish powder in a zip-top bag and use a rolling pin to press and roll it. If you do not have a rolling pin, use a wine bottle filled with warm water for the same effect.

How to Make Finger Hash

After a clipping freshly cured cannabis, your fingers and hands will be black and sticky with pungent cannabis resins. The resins will need to come off anyway, so use this cream of your crop to make finger hash.

Use a credit card or similar scraping device to bring together the kief, or powder, your clipping activities has left on the clean glass. Discard leaf pieces or other plant materials. At this point you can store the kief in a clean, dry jar, or use it to add to the resins on your hands. It is preferable to screen the kief through a fine grade silk screen before making into hash, so just work with the hand resins on your first try.

Start by working the resin and warming it, using your right hand thumb on your left hand as though you are working to take off tight gloves. As the resin darkens and starts to pull together, pinch off a tiny ball and work it in circles in the very center of your two palms. Periodically rub your thumbs and fingers, and add the extra resin to the ball you are making between your palms.

It's a good idea to set the ball down on your clean glass while you roll more resin off your fingers and thumbs. Then press your new small ball into the existing one and keep rolling. When you are finished rolling, the outer surface of the hash will have a shiny and finished appearance and won't be sticky at all. You will end up with clean hands and a lovely black pearl of excellent hashish. Let the pearls sit out in a safe place to dry overnight, then wrap them up and store in a cool dry place. If you are making the finger hash plant by plant, be sure to label it with the plant of origin. If not, just label for the year made; properly made and stored, the hash will last for years.

How to Make Bubble Hash

Bubble hash is a very good way to extract all you can from your harvest. You want all the trichomes you can get. THC is nonwater soluble, which is an advantage in this process. You'll be chilling the plant materials and using ice water to crystallize the trichomes, allowing them to break off from the green plant materials. A vigorous mixing of plant material and ice water causes trichomes to separate from the plant; then the water is sifted through fine mesh bags to extract the hash.

ALERT

Making bubble hash can be quite messy, so be sure to process it in a basement or garage, or somewhere the floor can tolerate spilled water. The bubble hash bags can be purchased online, although for your first experience you might want to borrow a set if you can. You might find that making bubble hash is more trouble than you want to deal with, and purchasing the bags is quite expensive ($400 to $500).

You will need the following supplies:

- 5 Bubble Hash Bags, from fine (48 micrometer) to coarse (200 micrometer) mesh.
- The bags should be 16 to 18 inches deep with a 12-inch diameter to fit a five gallon bucket
- Two five-gallon plastic buckets with one secure lid
- One power drill, preferably with locking action
- One long paint-mixing attachment for drill
- Mixing handle for drill
- Bagged ice, seven to fourteen pounds
- Paper plates
- Paper towels
- Cheesecloth
- Two old credit cards for scraping
- Cold water
- A sink, preferably a laundry type
- 16 ounces of leaves, stems, shake, and buds, mixed

Prepping the Cannabis

Put the cannabis to be processed in a plastic bag in your freezer to chill. This will help the trichomes separate from the plant materials. A few hours will be sufficient.

Line your first five-gallon bucket with the finest-meshed (lowest numbered) hash bag, folding the excess over the rim to hold the bag securely. Then line the next finest-mesh hash bag inside the previous bag, and so on until all the bags are lined within each other inside the bucket. You want the bags to go in sequence of how fine the mesh is, so your last bag to go in will be the coarsest mesh (i.e., 48, 80, 120, 160, and 200).

You will need to cut a hole in the center of the second bucket's lid; this is so the paint stirrer can connect to the drill, while minimizing the amount of water that can splash out during mixing. Usually, a one-inch hole is sufficient.

Place the chilled plant material into stirrer-prepped bucket, and add one bag of ice to the plant material. Fill the bucket with very cold water, up to four to six inches from the top.

Blending

Place the lid with drill onto the ice and plant filled bucket. Make sure that the lid is on very tightly, as you do not want the drill to send it flying. Place the bucket between your feet to keep it steady, turn on the drill and blend the mix thoroughly for five minutes.

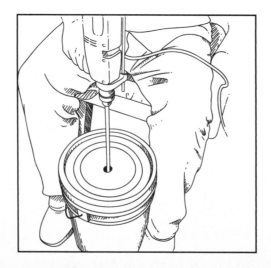

Blending the mixture.

Take a fifteen minute break to let the plant material soak and separate, then blend again for five minutes. Take another fifteen minute break, and then blend one last time for five minutes.

Mixture after blending. Notice the bubbly nature of the contents.

Transferring

Carefully pour the contents of the ice and plant bucket into the hash bag bucket; be careful, it is heavy! Remove the first bag and slowly lift it up. This bag will contain the plant material, and a greenish brown water that will drain from the mesh at the bottom. You can dip the bag a few times to clear the foam from the outside. Twist and squeeze the bag to get as much foam as possible from the mix, being careful not to rip the very expensive bag. You can now dump the plant material back into the other bucket.

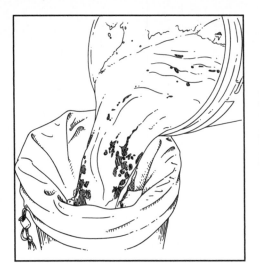

Pouring the mixture into the hash bag bucket.   Straining out water.

Pull the next bag, which will be almost all water so you may need to shake this bag vigorously to get the water to drain. Dip the empty bag to clear the foam. What remains in the bottom of the bag will be your first bit of hash.

Stretch out the mesh of the bag onto a flat surface, and carefully use a card to scrape up the hash. Transfer this to the cheesecloth that you have placed onto a paper towel on top of a paper plate. Scrape the hash onto the cheesecloth, and fold the cheesecloth over on top of the hash to enclose it. Pat gently with more paper towels to remove excess moisture. The hash will not be completely dry yet, but will be formed into a little thin brick. Take this hash off the cheesecloth and let it dry further on a paper towel.

ESSENTIAL

When you finish a bubble hash session, be certain to clean the bags extremely well. Thoroughly wash with clean water and then clean the screens with 96 percent alcohol to remove all the oil-based resins. Hang the bags in a well-ventilated area and let them dry completely before storing.

Wash the now-empty hash bag and hang it to dry. It is important to keep your bags clean and to take good care of them; they will last longer this way.

Pull the next bag and repeat the drain-dip-scrape-dry process. As the mesh gets finer and finer, each bag will be successively harder to drain.

Each successive bag will yield a finer, more potent hash. The first bag will generally give you dark green, coarse-looking, and grainy hash. The second bag should produce a medium green, less-coarse-looking hash. The third bag will produce the most hash, which will be a smoother-looking, blonder hash. Your last bag will produce the smoothest hash, but not as much as the third bag. Remember to wash and hang each bag as you empty it.

Finalizing the Process

The entire process may be repeated one more time. Take the water from the hash bucket and pour it back into the other bucket containing the plant material. Add more ice to keep the mixture very cold. Put your hash bags back onto the now-empty bucket, put the lid back on, follow the mixing schedule, and pull and drain the bags as before.

After pulling and scraping all the bags for the second time, go ahead and dump the remaining water and plant material (or compost it or save it for mulch). Some hash makers repeat the cycle three times, but two cycles will get you about as much hash as you are going to get. Let your hash dry for a day before trying to use it.

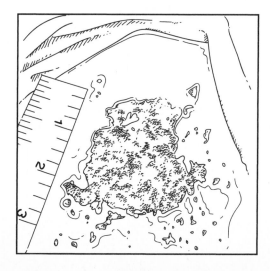

Hash.

Butane Extraction

Butane hash oil is made by passing butane gas through cannabis in a process that dissolves the THC. This method is not recommended as the process is quite dangerous to the processor. The fumes are extremely toxic as well as being volatile and explosive.

Proper Curing

Moisture needs to be removed from the hashish to prevent molding. Hand pressed or finger hash has had the moisture removed and usually stores well. The bubble hash extraction method involves water, so take care to remove all of the moisture.

Some bubble hash makers crumble the hash onto a screen and press any moisture out with paper towels. Others press and press the hashish to remove as much water as possible, and then flatten the hash into a flat cookie. This cookie is put into a freezer overnight so the water expands and appears on the surface area of the hashish. You can then wipe or scrape off the ice, pat dry again with paper towel, and wrap the hash for storage.

Proper Storage

Hashish needs to be stored in a cool, dark, dry place. It can be stored in a freezer if you plan on keeping it for a long time, but hash kept in airtight glass containers is fairly stable.

ESSENTIAL

Many hash makers recommend using an inexpensive kitchen device that sucks all the air out of plastic containers and seals them. Once the air is removed you can place the hashish in a refrigerator for long-term storage.

The only danger is mold, and removing excess moisture is essential. Some growers put a small packet of silica crystals in with the hash to absorb any humidity.

CHAPTER 18

Other Preparations for Cannabis (Capsules and Tinctures)

For both the recreational user and medical cannabis patient, the primary health hazard of cannabis is respiratory damage from smoke. Do not assume that a water pipe (commonly known as a bong) will protect your lungs from tars and toxins; recent studies have shown that both water pipes and solid filters are ineffectual at best, and the health hazards of using an unclean bong can be serious.

A Brief Description of Harm-Reduction Methods

Oral ingestion of cannabis has been a healthy delivery method for centuries, and is commonly combined with a palatable food (like brownies in our modern times). Alternatively, tinctures and capsules provide a method of oral ingestion that is more easily measurable (measured droppers or capsules), and removes the need to consume noncannabis extra calories that might not be in your diet.

As with any other cannabis "medibles," tinctures and capsules should be labeled "Contains THC" and kept well out of reach of children and animals.

Talk to your doctor about dosage, but as a general rule, start low and go slow. The ideal dose will depend on the patient and the condition. One can easily decrease a dose by dumping out, not tamping, or using smaller capsules.

FACT

Herbal capsules may have less adverse effects than synthetic THC capsules (like dronabinol or Marinol). Otherwise, adverse reactions are similar to those listed at *www.marinol.com.*

For Marinol or cannabis-experienced patients, an average starting dose might be one double 0 (00) size capsules every four to six hours as needed for pain or spasm. They work faster (thirty to sixty minutes) and work better if taken on an empty stomach (meaning one hour before eating or two hours after eating). With a big glass of water and empty stomach, any capsule gets absorbed faster with less risk of belching, heartburn, or bad aftertaste problems.

Activated Cannabis

Both of the following recipes contain activated cannabis. Ten minutes at 210°F to 220°F will decarboxylate (remove the carbon dioxide or -COOH or -CO2) the raw cannabis and make it more potent.

RECIPE FOR ACTIVATED CANNABIS CAPSULES

Prep time: 30 minutes before cooking | **Cooking time:** 60 minutes total | **Difficulty:** Easy

YOU WILL NEED:
Shake (leaf, trimmings, or immature/harsh/low-grade bud)
An oven with a reliable oven thermometer, preheated to 225°F
Food processor
Coffee grinder
A glass casserole dish
A capsule rack
Vegetarian 00 capsules (empty)
A big bowl

WARNING

Be certain the oven works so it is at the proper temperature before adding cannabis. Test the temperature for accuracy by putting an oven thermometer in an empty dish. You will vaporize your cannabis if the oven gets too hot, and this will remove the medicine. Cannabis ignites at 446°F, so keep the temperature below 250°F always.

1. For economy, separate leaf/trim/shake or immature/harsh/low-grade bud for making dried activated capsules. Dry the low-grade cannabis until very dry. You can cure your high-grade smoothest tasting bud and save it for your vaporizer.
2. Preheat oven to 225°F.
3. Using the very dry shake, conduct a primary grind in a food processor. Take this rougher grind out of the food processor and do a secondary grind in a coffee bean grinder for about 15–30 seconds. The fine grind allows for about 0.4 grams of cannabis per double 0 (00) capsule with a tamping tool that will experience less capsule breakage and possibly better absorption of the very fine grind or dust.
4. Transfer the cannabis dust to an ovenproof dish (like a casserole dish with or without cover). Rake the cannabis dust with a fork to get it evenly distributed on the bottom of the dish and remove stems and fibers. Cover the dish only to eliminate any mild terpene smell, or if using a convection oven,

to prevent blowing cannabis dust. Otherwise, there is little cannabis smell in the kitchen.

5. Place the cannabis filled dish in the preheated oven (never get above 250°F) for 20–60 minutes or longer. The extra time is so all the cannabis, including the middle part, gets evenly hot.

6. While the cannabis is activating, set up your capsule rack. You can find one from *www.cap-m-quik.com* or at most health food stores. A capsule rack for 50 double-0 (00) capsules works well, but you can use smaller capsules like a single 0 (0) to make pills easier to swallow or deliver a smaller dose, especially if using more potent cannabis (like high grade bud instead of shake). Vegetarian capsules work fine because there is no oil in this recipe. Oil will dissolve a vegetarian capsule.

7. Remove the hot dish with the now-activated cannabis from the oven and pour or spoon it into a room temperature dish; a glass serving dish or big bowl is fine. Let cool.

8. Make the capsules from the dried, activated, and finely ground cannabis just like you would from any dried ground herb. The instructions for legal herbs are at *www.cap-m-quik.com*. With the tamping tool, you can raise the amount of cannabis contained in one 00 capsule from about 0.2 grams to about 0.4 grams, or roughly double the dose per capsule.

RECIPE FOR "GREEN DRAGON" ALCOHOL-BASED TINCTURE

Prep time: 15 minutes before cooking, 30 minutes following | **Cooking time:** 50–60 minutes total | **Difficulty:** Easy

YOU WILL NEED:
⅛ ounce high quality cannabis bud, destemmed
A clean coffee grinder
Baking sheet or metal pie pan
2 wide mouth Mason jars
2 ounces Bacardi Rum, 151 proof (or use 2 ounces Everclear)
Water, as needed
A large deep heavy cooking pot (the enameled kinds are good for this process)
A candy thermometer
Cheesecloth

Mixing bowl
Dark brown glass tincture bottle with dropper top

ALCOHOL SAFETY
Run your kitchen fan on high to vent any alcohol fumes. Do not boil.

1. Preheat oven to 225°F. Grind cannabis very finely.
2. Place cannabis in a shallow pan or pie pan and bake at 225°F for 25–30 minutes.
3. Remove the pan from the oven and place cannabis in wide mouth Mason jar. Add alcohol to baked cannabis and place jar in approximately 1"–2" of water in a heavy cooking pot; bring water to simmer. Do not cover the jar.
4. Simmer in a hot water bath for 20 minutes. Maintain the temperature of the rum/cannabis mixture between 150°F–165°F. Place the candy thermometer in the mixture to monitor temperature.
5. Cool the mixture for safe handling. The liquid will be a dark green.
6. Strain the mixture through cheesecloth into a mixing bowl. You should have 1 ounce of product. Pour into a clean Mason jar and store. Transfer to dropper top bottle for more accurate dosing. 1/8 ounce of good cannabis yields approximately 30–34 doses of tincture (1 gram of liquid per dropperful).
7. One dropperful should have an effect in 1.5 hours and last 5 hours. Two droppers last approximately 7–8 hours.
8. Store tincture well sealed in a cool, dark, dry place.

RECIPE FOR GLYCERINE-BASED TINCTURE

Prep time: 15 minutes before cooking, 45 minutes following | **Cooking time:** 18–24 hours total | **Difficulty:** Easy

YOU WILL NEED:
A clean coffee grinder
4–6 ounces high quality cannabis bud, destemmed
1 gallon food grade USP glycerine
A slow cooker
A large fine-holed strainer or colander
Cheesecloth
Mixing bowl(s)

A soup ladle
A funnel
Amber or brown glass bottles (sufficient to hold a gallon when combined), usu-
ally found at home brewing supply stores
Dark brown glass tincture bottle with dropper top
A candy thermometer (optional)

IMPORTANT TIPS

Boiling the glycerine tincture will destroy the very properties you are
working to extract. Don't get impatient, and don't let it boil! Also, if
you have sturdy upper cabinet door handles above your kitchen counter, tie your cheesecloth shut with strong string and hang the bag from
the handles to drip over the bowl. Then you can go away and do other
things while gravity helps you glean more tincture.

1. Use the grinder to process the cannabis bud to a fine grind.
2. Mix with glycerine and cook in the slow cooker on the lowest setting for
    18–24 hours. Monitor to avoid boiling, and stir occasionally and gently (the
    glycerine will be very hot, so avoid splashing yourself). If your slow cooker
    has the "Keep Warm" setting, use that for the long, slow cooking needed
    to extract the benefit from the cannabis and into your tincture.
3. After cooking, let the mixture cool enough to strain it without burning
    yourself. Line your colander or wide strainer with cheesecloth, and place
    over the large mixing bowl. Depending on the size of your bowl, you may
    end up having to use more than one.
4. Ladle the glycerine by spoonfuls, gently pressing down on the plant mate-
    rial with the ladle (to push the glycerine through faster). Compared to
    alcohol-based tinctures, glycerine will take much longer to drain through
    the cheesecloth.
5. When you are ready to bottle your tincture, squeeze the cheesecloth hard
    to extract everything you can. Dispose of the plant debris and wash the
    cheesecloth for reuse. Ladle the tincture into the funnel set into your large
    storage bottles. Make sure the tops seal tightly.
6. Glycerine tincture needs to be refrigerated because it lacks the preserva-
    tive nature of alcohol. Store the glycerine in large amber-colored sealed
    bottles. Use the small dropper bottle for dosing. Some people add organic
    honey for palatability, but the glycerine alone is slightly sweet. Vegetable
    glycerine has 4.3 calories per gram.

TINCTURE WITH HONEY AND VITAMIN E

Prep time: 30 minutes total | **Cooking time:** 40 days steeping, 1 hour cooking | **Difficulty:** Easy

YOU WILL NEED:
½ gallon 190-proof alcohol (Everclear)
A clean 1-gallon glass jar with lid
A clean coffee grinder
4 ounces high quality cannabis bud, dry, destemmed
Cheesecloth
A large, deep, heavy cooking pot (the enameled kinds are good for this process)
4 ounces organic, pure honey
8 capsules vitamin E oil
Pair of sharp scissors
Dark brown glass tincture bottle with dropper top

TINCTURE TIPS
This tincture is very palatable, which is helpful with patients who are experiencing nausea. Make sure to keep it out of the reach of children, just as you would liquor or prescription drugs.

1. Pour ½ gallon of Everclear into the gallon jar. Use the grinder to roughly grind the cannabis and add to jar. Shake well and refrigerate. Keep in the fridge for 30–45 days, remembering to shake the elixir every few days.
2. Strain through the cheesecloth, following the similar process in the two other tincture recipes above. At this point you can store the strained elixir in your refrigerator, or proceed to making the honey tincture.
3. To make the tincture, use eight ounces of the strained elixir, and bring to a low simmer on the stovetop. You want good ventilation, especially if you have a stove hood. Let this simmer until reduced by half. Add the honey, bring back to a slow simmer, and reduce by half again. Let cool, and add the vitamin E oil (cut the capsules with your scissors), stirring to combine. Store in glass in the refrigerator and use your dropper bottle for dosing.

Using More or Less Cannabis During Preparation

When lower grade cannabis has been activated and eaten, you might be surprised at how potent the effect can be. As you become more familiar with the processes, what they produce, and their effects, you may want to adjust the amounts of cannabis in your tinctures.

Remember, ingested as opposed to smoked, cannabis is much slower in onset and lasts longer. It is always better to start with lower doses and note the timing of onset and the duration of the tincture's or capsule's effects. This way, you can use cannabis medicines sensibly and for a maximum health benefit.

CHAPTER 19

Cooking with Cannabis and Using Vaporizers

Cooking with cannabis should be for pleasure and for healthful nourishment. In addition to the more typical sweet foods like brownies, try using infused oils for dips and spreads. These foods can be of great benefit, especially for patients who are in hospice or other environments where smoking cannabis is not an option, and who need a palatable, nutritious alternative.

Butters and Infused Oils

Two basics you need to learn are how to make cannabis butter, or "cannabutter" as it is commonly known, and how to infuse oils with cannabis (extra-virgin olive oil, grapeseed oil, canola oil, etc.). THC sticks to the fat cells in butter. Cannabutter or infused oils can be used in any recipe that calls for butter or oil.

Just as with growing, processing cannabis can produce a very strong odor, so be considerate and aware of your neighbors.

Be careful and remember that sometimes less is more. The effect from medibles comes on slower, lasts longer, and is often considered much more intense than inhaling. Until you have tested your response to eating cannabis foods, go slowly. Unlike inhaling, which has an almost immediate effect (helping you gauge your response and adjust ingestion), expect to wait 30–90 minutes to feel an effect. You can also expect the effects to last a lot longer.

Always keep medibles clearly labeled ("CONTAINS THC"). No one in recorded medical history has ever died from a cannabis overdose, but unknowingly eating medicated food can be a frightening and unpleasant experience. Always keep medibles secured from children and pets.

SIMPLE AND QUICK CANNABIS BUTTER

Prep time: 15 minutes | **Cooking time:** 30 minutes | **Difficulty:** Easy

YOU WILL NEED:
A double boiler
Water, as needed
2 pounds unsalted butter
1 ounce cannabis bud
A clean electric coffee grinder
A long-handled stirring spoon
Cheesecloth
A large mixing bowl

1. Partially fill lower pot of double boiler with water and bring to a gentle simmer. Set butter to melt at low heat in upper pot while you grind the bud

finely in the coffee grinder. Unplug the grinder to scrape out the ground bud. Add ground cannabis to melted butter, stir, and bring back to a simmer.

2. Simmer the mixture for 25–30 minutes, stirring frequently with the long-handled spoon.
3. Cool mixture for 30 minutes. Arrange cheesecloth in bowl and strain out the butter. Squeeze to separate all the butter out of the plant matter (which can now be discarded). The cheesecloth can be washed and reused.
4. Cool to room temperature, and then refrigerate to allow butter to solidify. Use in your favorite recipes as you would butter. May be stored frozen for up to 6 weeks.

ULTIMATE CANNABIS BUTTER

Prep time: 15 minutes before cooking, 15 minutes following | **Cooking time:** Approximately 3 hours (stove top) to 18 hours (in a slow cooker) | **Difficulty:** Easy

YOU WILL NEED:
A clean grinder (electric or manual, coarse grind is fine)
1 ounce cannabis bud (double this amount for more potent butter)
3–6 cups water
A large, deep, heavy cooking pot (the enameled kinds are best), or slow cooker
2 pounds unsalted butter
A long-handled stirring spoon
3 plastic containers (Tupperware-type or disposable with lids), approximately 4-cup size
3 pieces of cheesecloth
Large (produce-type) rubber bands

1. Coarsely grind or even chop the cannabis. Set aside.
2. Bring 3–4 cups of water to a boil in a large pot, and add butter to start melting. Turn heat to a medium setting and occasionally stir butter to avoid burning.
3. Once the butter has melted completely, reduce heat to low and add the cannabis, stirring frequently. The goal is to have the cannabis continually floating about 1½"–2" from the bottom of the pan.

4. Simmer uncovered for approximately 3 hours (or up to 18 hours in a covered slow cooker). When the top of the mixture turns from a watery consistency to glossy and thick, it's ready to cool.

5. While the mixture is simmering, prepare the containers. Fold each sheet of cheesecloth into two layers, place one over each open container (with the lid off), and secure the "ears" back with the large rubber bands.

6. Place the containers with the cheesecloth in the sink and slowly pour mixture to fill the containers. Allow plenty of room, as you will squeeze quite a bit more liquid out of the cannabis.

7. Once the pan is empty, pick up the cheesecloth from all four sides and squeeze all of the remaining butter into containers. At this point you can throw the cannabis away (or compost it). Leave the cheesecloth in the sink to be rinsed, then washed and reused.

8. Place the lids on your containers and refrigerate overnight. This step will separate the water from the butter. As the liquids cool, the butter will rise to the top and solidify, taking the THC with it.

9. Once you have solid butter on top, remove the container lid and place a clean plate in the sink (to catch any butter that falls). Gently squeeze two sides of the container as you tilt it over the sink to pour away all the water. You will now have a solid block of cannabis butter. Use in your favorite recipes as you would butter. Keep refrigerated. May be stored frozen for up to six weeks.

INFUSED EXTRA-VIRGIN OLIVE OIL

Prep time: 15 minutes before cooking, 15 minutes following | **Cooking time:** 3 hours (in a slow cooker) | **Difficulty:** Easy

YOU WILL NEED:
A clean grinder (electric or manual, coarse grind is fine)
2 ounces cannabis bud or bud and sugar leaf mix (double this amount for more potent oil)
5 cups organic extra-virgin olive oil
A slow cooker
A long-handled stirring spoon
Cheesecloth
A large mixing bowl
A clean jar or olive oil bottle with screw cap

1. Coarsely grind the cannabis. Set aside.
2. Add oil into slow cooker and slowly stir in cannabis. Set pot to high setting for 1 hour and cook covered, stirring occasionally. Turn pot to low for 2 additional hours, still stirring occasionally. Keep covered.
3. Cool mixture and strain through cheesecloth into bowl, squeezing to get as much oil as possible.
4. Store the oil in a screw cap jar or bottle in a refrigerator. Be sure to label it as "medicated." If oil looks coagulated in fridge, allow it to come to room temperature before using (this is normal). Shake well. Use in any recipe that requires olive oil.

INFUSED GRAPESEED OIL

Prep time: 15 minutes before cooking, 15 minutes following | **Cooking time:** 1½–3 hours (in a slow cooker) | **Difficulty:** Easy

YOU WILL NEED:
A clean grinder (electric or manual, coarse grind is fine)
1 ounce cannabis bud or bud and sugar leaf mix (double this amount for more potent oil)
4 cups organic grapeseed oil
A slow cooker
A long-handled stirring spoon
Cheesecloth
A large mixing bowl
A clean jar or bottle with screw cap

1. Follow olive oil infusion technique previously described in this chapter.
2. Store the oil in a screw cap jar or bottle in a refrigerator. Be sure to label it as "medicated." If oil looks coagulated in fridge allow to come to room temperature before using (this is normal). Use for dipping pita bread, lightly on salads.

INFUSED CANOLA OIL

Prep time: 15 minutes before cooking, 15 minutes following | **Cooking time:** 1½–3 hours (in a slow cooker) | **Difficulty:** Easy

YOU WILL NEED:
A clean grinder (electric or manual, coarse grind is fine)
1 ounce cannabis bud or bud and sugar leaf mix (you may double this amount for more potent oil)
1 48-ounce bottle canola cooking oil
A large deep heavy cooking pot or slow cooker (recommended)
A long-handled stirring spoon
Cheesecloth
A large mixing bowl
A funnel

1. Coarsely grind the cannabis. Set aside.
2. Pour all of the oil into the pot and bring to just below boiling. Do not let the oil boil. Add ground cannabis, stirring continually, and lower heat to a very low simmer. Stir every 10 minutes or so for the next 2 hours. Do not let the mixture boil or your oil will be burned.
3. After 2 hours, take pot from heat and let cool (approximately 30 minutes).
4. Strain oil with through the cheesecloth into a mixing bowl. Use a funnel to return the cool oil to the original bottle.
5. Store the oil in the refrigerator. Be sure to label it as "medicated." If oil looks coagulated in fridge, allow it to come to room temperature before using (this is normal). Shake before using. Use in any recipe that requires canola oil.

Dips, Spreads, and Sauces

Since many patients have a limited capacity for pleasurable eating, it is important that the food they can manage to ingest be healthier overall than just eating sweets. Cooking with cannabis has developed a long way from the Alice B. Toklas brownies craze of the 1970s. The sweet things can be a lot of fun for a party, but if you are cooking for someone with poor health and little appetite, it is far better to use foods that deliver better nourishment along with the pain relief from cannabis.

BABA GANOUJ

This is a healthy and tasty way to use infused olive oil. Note: this recipe only uses 2 tablespoons of oil, so the effect should be low-key and pleasant.

Prep time: 1 hour (for best flavor, prepare the day before use) | **Cooking time:** 45 minutes to 1 hour | **Difficulty:** Easy

YOU WILL NEED:
2 eggplants (2–3 pounds total)
1 tablespoon Tahini
Juice of 1 lemon
2 garlic cloves, finely minced
2 teaspoons fresh mint leaves, chopped
4 teaspoons flat-leaf Italian parsley, chopped
Sea salt and pepper, to taste
2 tablespoons Infused Extra-Virgin Olive Oil (see recipe in this chapter)

1. Preheat oven to 425°F.
2. Pierce the eggplants several times with the tip of a sharp knife. Wrap separately in aluminum foil and place on a baking sheet.
3. Bake for 45 minutes or until soft. Unwrap and cool eggplants. When cool enough to handle safely, remove the flesh, discarding the seeds and the skin, and chop coarsely.
4. In a medium bowl, mix Tahini, lemon juice, garlic, mint, 2 teaspoons parsley, salt, and pepper. Add eggplant and mix well.
5. Place the mixture in a serving bowl, drizzle Infused Extra-Virgin Olive Oil over the top, and sprinkle with the remaining parsley. Makes 2½ cups. Refrigerate until ready to serve. Bring to room temperature before serving.

BASIL PESTO

Use with pasta, or on grilled meats and vegetables. | **Prep time:** 15–20 minutes | **Difficulty:** Easy

YOU WILL NEED:
A blender or food processor
2 cloves garlic
4–5 tablespoons pine nuts
½ teaspoon sea salt
3 cups basil leaves, without stems and loosely packed
½ cup Infused Extra-Virgin Olive Oil (see recipe in this chapter)
½ cup freshly grated three cheese blend (Parmesan, Romano, and Asiago)

Process garlic, pine nuts, and salt until finely chopped. Add basil and chop. Slowly add oil and purée until smooth in texture. Add cheese and lightly process until just combined. Keep refrigerated until ready to use.

TAPENADE

Prep time: 15–20 minutes | **Difficulty:** Easy

YOU WILL NEED:
A blender or food processor
5 cloves garlic
4 tablespoons capers
½ cup black olives
2–3 anchovy fillets
½ cup Infused Extra-Virgin Olive Oil (see recipe in this chapter)

Blend all ingredients in a food processor, or chop coarsely. This is best prepared a few hours ahead of time so the flavors can marry. Use as a spread on good quality French bread.

ASIAGO HERBED DIPPING OIL

Prep time: 10 minutes | **Difficulty:** Easy

YOU WILL NEED:
A large jar with screw-on lid
½ cup Infused Extra-Virgin Olive Oil (see recipe in this chapter)
1 tablespoon balsamic vinegar
1 clove garlic, minced
A large pinch coarse sea salt
Freshly ground black pepper
¼ teaspoon chopped fresh rosemary (or experiment with different fresh herbs like dill)
Freshly grated Asiago cheese

Combine all ingredients except cheese in jar and screw lid on firmly. Shake well. To serve, pour into saucers and sprinkle with Asiago. Use as a dip for good quality French bread.

PESTO-FLAVORED DIPPING OIL

Prep time: 10 minutes | **Difficulty:** Easy

YOU WILL NEED:
2 cloves garlic
¼ teaspoon sea salt
3–4 tablespoons pine nuts
A blender or food processor
3 cups loosely packed basil leaves, stemmed
½ cup Infused Extra-Virgin Olive Oil (see recipe in this chapter)
½ cup freshly grated Parmesan or Romano cheese
½ cup noninfused extra-virgin olive oil
A large jar with screw-on lid

1. Process garlic, salt, and pine nuts in a blender or food processor until finely chopped. Add basil and Infused Extra-Virgin Olive Oil; purée until smooth. Add the cheese and process until just combined; taste and adjust seasonings.

2. Place 2 tablespoons prepared pesto and ½ cup noninfused extra-virgin olive oil in a jar with a lid. Shake well. Pour into saucers. Use as a dip for hot crusty French bread.

MUSHROOMS WITH FENNEL

Prep time: 15 minutes | **Difficulty:** Easy

YOU WILL NEED:
1 medium mixing bowl
1 pound fresh whole button or portobello mushrooms, sliced
1 small sweet white onion, thinly sliced and separated into rings
1 cup Infused Extra-Virgin Olive Oil (see recipe in this chapter)
¼ cup lemon juice
¼ cup apple cider vinegar
1 teaspoon sea salt
1 teaspoon fennel seed
1 teaspoon dried basil leaves
½ teaspoon minced garlic
¼ teaspoon finely ground white pepper
1 slotted spoon

1. Combine mushrooms and onion in a medium mixing bowl. Set aside.
2. Blend all other ingredients and toss with mushrooms and onions. Cover and refrigerate at least 12 hours, stirring occasionally. Remove mushrooms and onions with slotted spoon to serve.

INFUSED OIL AND RICE VINEGAR SALAD DRESSING

Prep time: 10 minutes | **Difficulty:** Easy

YOU WILL NEED:
1 small shallot, finely chopped
2 tablespoons rice vinegar
1 teaspoon Dijon mustard
½ teaspoon fine sea salt
½ teaspoon sugar

Freshly ground black pepper, to taste

½ cup Infused Extra-Virgin Olive Oil (see recipe in this chapter)

Whisk shallot, rice vinegar, Dijon mustard, salt, sugar, and pepper in a small bowl. Let sit for about 20 minutes. Whisk in olive oil, and season to taste with additional salt and pepper. Serve over fresh sliced tomatoes or mixed lettuce salads.

Sweets

Everyone is going to make traditional "pot brownies" at least once. They are a delicious cultural icon and quite fun, especially for a party. Make sure that partygoers are aware they are "medicated," and absolutely make certain they are not within reach of children! Cannabis-added cookies or brownies are also easy to take to events like concerts where you might want to enhance your experience, but public smoking of cannabis is frowned upon, and illegal.

BROWNIES

Prep time: 15–20 minutes | **Bake time:** 25 minutes | **Difficulty:** Easy

YOU WILL NEED:
8" square baking pan lined with foil
Nonstick spray, as needed
4 ounces bittersweet chocolate, chopped
⅓ cup Infused Extra-Virgin Olive Oil (see recipe in this chapter)
2 large eggs, at room temperature
¾ cup granulated sugar
An electric mixer
1 teaspoon vanilla extract
¼ teaspoon sea salt
½ cup all-purpose flour
⅔ cup unsalted chopped almonds or walnuts, roasted

1. Preheat the oven to 350°F.
2. Lightly coat foil with cooking spray or a small amount of infused oil. Melt the chocolate in a microwave or in a double-boiler on stovetop. Whisk in the infused olive oil and set aside to cool slightly.

3. Beat eggs and sugar in a mixing bowl at high speed 4–5 minutes. Beat in the vanilla and salt. Fold in the cooled chocolate mixture. Fold in the flour. Stir in the nuts and pour the batter into the pan. Bake for 20–25 minutes. Let cool completely. Cut into squares.

CHOCOLATE CHIP COOKIES

Prep time: 15–20 minutes | **Bake time:** 9–11 minutes | **Difficulty:** Easy

YOU WILL NEED:
2¼ cups flour
1 teaspoon salt
1 teaspoon baking soda
2 eggs
¼ cup Infused Extra-Virgin Olive Oil (see recipe in this chapter)
¾ cup granulated sugar
¾ cup brown sugar
1 teaspoon vanilla extract
1 cup chocolate chips
1 cup chopped walnuts

1. Preheat oven to 375°F.
2. In a medium bowl, mix flour, salt, and baking soda. In larger mixing bowl, beat eggs. Add Infused Extra-Virgin Olive Oil to eggs and beat until completely mixed. Add sugars and vanilla and beat in slowly. Fold in chocolate chips and walnuts.
3. Drop dough by rounded teaspoon onto ungreased baking sheets. Bake cookies 9–11 minutes. Remove from oven, and place on wire racks after 2 minutes to cool.

WHOLE WHEAT ZUCCHINI BREAD

Prep time: 20 minutes | **Bake time:** 50 minutes | **Difficulty:** Easy

YOU WILL NEED:

3 eggs
½ cup melted butter
½ cup Infused Extra-Virgin Olive Oil (see recipe in this chapter)
Zest and juice of 1 lemon
1¼ cups maple syrup
2½ cups whole wheat flour, or substitute half whole wheat with half all purpose
white flour
½ teaspoon regular salt, or ¼ teaspoon sea salt
1 teaspoon cinnamon
1 teaspoon baking soda
½ teaspoon baking powder
3 cups well-packed shredded zucchini (unpeeled)
2 9" greased loaf pans

1. Preheat oven to 325°F.
2. Beat eggs, butter, oil, lemon zest, lemon juice, and syrup together in a large mixing bowl. In a separate bowl, completely blend the flour, salt, cinnamon, baking soda, and baking powder. Mix the dry ingredients into the egg mixture and fold in the zucchini.
3. Pour batter into 2 greased 9" loaf pans. Bake 50 minutes or until a knife comes out clean. Let cool thoroughly before serving.

PUMPKIN, CARROT, AND ZUCCHINI BREAD

Prep time: 30 minutes | **Bake time:** 60 minutes | **Difficulty:** Easy

YOU WILL NEED:

4 large eggs
1 cup Infused Extra-Virgin Olive Oil (see recipe in this chapter)
½ cup water
2 cups puréed canned pumpkin, or 2 cups fresh puréed pumpkin (reduce water to ¼ cup if fresh is used)
2¼ cups sugar

1½ teaspoon salt
1 teaspoon freshly ground nutmeg
1 teaspoon ground cinnamon
1 teaspoon ground cloves
½ teaspoon ground ginger, or 1 teaspoon fresh grated ginger
2 teaspoons baking soda
3 ⅓ cups sifted all purpose flour
½ cup grated zucchini
¾ cup grated carrots
½ cup golden raisins
½ cup walnut (or pecan) pieces
3 small loaf pans, or 4 mini pans, greased with olive oil

1. Preheat the oven to 350°F.
2. Beat the eggs in a large mixing bowl. Add the Infused Extra-Virgin Olive Oil, water, pumpkin, and sugar and beat with an egg whisk or fork to combine thoroughly.
3. Add salt, nutmeg, cinnamon, cloves, ginger, and baking soda, and blend well. Add the flour and stir into egg mixture with a wooden spoon until just combined. Stir in zucchini, carrots, raisins, and nuts.
4. Pour into prepared loaf pans; not more than two-thirds full as batter will rise. Bake for 45 minutes to 1 hour, or until a knife inserted into the center comes out clean. Cool on a rack for 10 minutes before removing from pan, and finish cooling on a rack.

LEMON POUND CAKE WITH BLUEBERRIES

Prep time: 30 minutes | **Bake time:** 70 minutes | **Difficulty:** Easy

YOU WILL NEED:
2 cups granulated sugar
¾ cup Infused Extra-Virgin Olive Oil (see recipe in this chapter)
4 large eggs
2 tablespoons plus 3 cups all-purpose flour
2 cups fresh or frozen blueberries
1 teaspoon baking powder
½ teaspoon baking soda
½ teaspoon salt

1 cup sour cream
5 teaspoons lemon juice
1 teaspoon vanilla extract
10" Bundt pan lightly coated with olive oil
½ cup powdered sugar

1. Preheat oven to 350°F.
2. Beat sugar and oil at medium speed with a mixer until well blended. Add eggs and beat well. Combine 2 tablespoons reserved flour and blueberries in a small bowl and toss well to coat. Combine remaining flour, baking powder, baking soda, and salt. Add flour mixture to sugar mixture alternating with sour cream. Fold in blueberry mixture, 1 teaspoon lemon juice, and vanilla; pour cake batter into oiled pan. Bake for 1 hour and 10 minutes or until a toothpick or knife inserted in center comes out clean.
3. Cool cake in the pan for 10–20 minutes; remove from pan. Combine powdered sugar and remaining lemon juice in a small bowl and drizzle over warm cake. Yields 16 servings.

What Is a Cannabis Vaporizer?

Cannabis vaporization is a technology designed to deliver inhaled cannabinoids by heating cannabis to a temperature where therapeutically active cannabinoid vapors are produced, but that keeps the cannabis below the point of combustion where noxious byproducts are formed.

FACT

An upcoming trend in medical use states is the increase in members only "Vapor Bars" that provide a sociable atmosphere and access to using vaporizers. Many patients who could benefit from vaporizers just cannot afford them. Patients bring their own cannabis to use or the club supplies it for free to use on the premises.

The most commonly available high quality vaporizers consist of the heating base, the bag(s), and the delivery mouthpiece. The best one on the market today is made in Germany and recognized by the Dutch as an approved medical delivery device. In the United States, vaporizers are often used without the bag part by restaurants and shopping malls for mood enhancing aroma therapy, although of course no cannabis is heated in these particular usages!

Using Vaporizers

Why would you want to invest in something as expensive as a good quality cannabis vaporizer? The primary reason is health-related because reducing or completely eliminating smoke in the lungs is going to be better for you.

ESSENTIAL

Another benefit of vaporizers is that the patient can prepare a bag and the mouthpiece will keep all vapor inside until the user releases it by activating the mouthpiece and inhaling as much as they need. A prepared bag of vapor will stay useful for hours, allowing all of it to be used as needed and not wasted by going up in smoke.

Vaporizers let the user have the almost-immediate effect that comes with smoking cannabis, and users are therefore able to gauge their dosage very quickly and accurately. This is the best method for quick pain relief since eating cannabis food preparations can take too long for the effects to begin and therefore make it more difficult to easily figure optimum dosing.

Another reason people use vaporizers, or "vapes," is that many recreational or medical cannabis users cannot risk the pungent fragrance of cannabis wafting through their apartment building or out the window to the unsympathetic neighbors. The vaporized cannabis is completely contained in a bag and reduces tricky odor problems.

Why Are Vaporizers Healthier?

A feasibility study by NORML and MAPS has demonstrated that an electric vaporizer can successfully generate THC at 185°C while completely suppressing benzene, toluene, and naphthalene formation.

This study was designed to evaluate the efficacy of an herbal vaporizer known as the Volcano, produced by Storz & Bickel GmbH & Co.KG, Tuttlingen, Germany (*www.storz-bickel.com*). The analysis of the vapor found that the Volcano delivered 36 percent to 61 percent of the THC in the sample, a delivery efficiency that compares favorably to that of a rolled cannabis cigarette. The analysis showed that the gas phase of the vapor consisted overwhelmingly of cannabinoids, with trace amounts of three other compounds. In contrast, over 111 compounds were identified in analysis of combusted smoke. The results indicated that vaporization can deliver therapeutic doses of cannabinoids with a drastic reduction in harmful smoke compounds.

CHAPTER 20

General Troubleshooting: Common Problems/FAQs

Every gardener or grower of cannabis will have times when the plants are puzzling and things are not going right. These frustrating times can be the result of a new pest, like a gopher, suddenly appearing in your outdoor garden, or perhaps a donated clone has brought spider mites into the indoor grow. First you will notice that something seems a bit off; you suspect, you worry, you watch, and then, finally, you have confirmation that there is a problem. All growers go through these troubled times. This is actually farming, especially when you grow outdoors. Some garden problems, like rippers or hailstorms, can come up unexpectedly and devastate the crop's chances of success, but most plant problems can be prevented by focus, foresight, and proper garden practices.

Plants Are Yellow

Seedlings and young plants in the vegetative phase should have uniformly deep, healthy green leaves. Yellow leaves are your first warning sign that something is amiss and can indicate a variety of different problems. Your first response should be to test your soil for pH levels and for N-P-K. Plants that are nitrogen-starved will yellow, starting with the older leaves and continuing until the entire plant has yellowed. Cannabis uses nitrogen for stem and leaf growth; a nitrogen-starved plant will grow slowly and appear stunted.

Sometimes novice growers think if some is good, than more is better. Not so! Excessive fertilizing can burn the plants and cause yellowing as well.

Testing the pH is essential; if the soil is too acidic or too alkaline the plant will not be able to use the soil's available nutrients. If the soil's pH range is not between 6.5 to 7.5, the plant's food is locked up. Blindly adding more nitrogen to acidic soil will just compound the plant's problem, so it is very important to test the pH first.

Magnesium, manganese, sulfur, and boron deficiencies can all cause some type of yellowing; a magnesium deficiency shows initially in older leaf growth, while a lack of sulfur shows yellowing in the newer growth. Starting out with a well-balanced organic soil is the best preventative.

Yellowing leaves from nutritional problems should not be confused with the plant's natural cycle; as cannabis proceeds into and through the peak floral stage, the outer leaves will yellow, wilt, and drop. This is perfectly natural; the amount of yellowing and leaf drop depends in part on the genetics and phenotype of each plant. Avoid propagating mold during the peak floral phase by cleaning up dropped leaves and grooming the plants to remove loose, yellowed leaves on a daily basis.

Also note that cuttings in the process of rooting will show some yellowing at approximately one week, especially on the lower leaves; this is normal and will rectify itself once the root system has developed.

Plants Are Not Growing

There can be various reasons for stunted plant growth; poor soil, poor drainage, lack of nutrients, lack of light, temperatures too hot or too cold, or excessive humidity or dryness. Other reasons may be fungal root infections or pest infestations.

Poor performance by seedlings is an indication of damp off; you have used contaminated soil or the growing medium is too wet. Damp off thins the plump white root in sections, so gently dig up the most pitiful specimen and inspect its root. Generally you will have to start more seed, using clean soil and sterilized pots. Make sure not to over water young seedlings and inadvertently create a welcoming environment for damp off. Provide good air circulation and ventilation at all times.

Seedlings will also grow slowly if their environment is too cold; if you grow outdoors, make certain you are not trying to get too far ahead of your local growing season. If you want to get seedlings started early, you must provide enough light and warmth indoors, and plan for a period of hardening off when you transfer the plants to outdoors.

Cannabis growth is very rapid during the vegetative phase; if your plants are not transplanted to larger containers or fed for growth in smaller containers, they will eventually run out of room and food. As always, a quick check of pH and N-P-K levels will give you a great deal of information, and probably point you to the correction needed.

Next to unhealthy pH levels, bad drainage is probably the most common cause of stunted growth in cannabis. Cannabis hates soggy soil and responds by sulking and slowing its growth. Conversely, cannabis also has big water requirements and drinks deeply; you can expect poor growth performance if you consistently forget to water your plants.

If you are growing outdoors in the ground, and just one or two plants suddenly slow dramatically, look carefully around the grow site for telltale gopher mounds. Gophers throw up soil from their tunnels and can appear quite suddenly in outdoor gardens, partly because your good soil is full of earthworms and other tasty food for them. You do not have to see the gophers for them to be a problem. The mounds will let you know they have invaded.

Unfortunately, a gopher will power right through a cannabis root ball, severely impeding the plants support system. If you plant directly into the ground, make sure to line the planting holes with chicken wire. If gophers show up once your plants are already in the ground, there is no moving the plants without causing great stress and shock to the plants.

I Have Lots of Green Leaves but No Flowers

This could be for a number of reasons. The indoor grower must trigger flowering by cutting the light cycle to twelve hours. If the plants still make no move to begin flowering, check that the dark phase is truly dark. Light leakage can confuse plants. The outdoor grower must wait until the sun's cycle reaches this critical trigger point for cannabis. Make note of how many hours of sun the plants still receive, and check for light sources outdoors that may be disturbing the plants. Certain genotypes will flower later than others. Many outdoor cannabis breeders place a lot of emphasis on strains that flower earlier rather than later, particularly in areas that typically have heavy rains in the fall.

Check the N-P-K ratio of your plant's food. Another factor can be too much nitrogen (N) is being fed during the flowering phase. The plant needs lots of N, in a ratio of approximately 10:7:8 during the vegetative phase, but continuing to feed too much will delay flowering after the light changes. Flush the soil with plain water, and feed flowering plants more phosphorus, ideally in a 4:8:8 ratio. Plants should be allowed to become N-deficient late in flowering; some growers say this improves flavor.

Plants Are Wilting

Sometimes plants become overheated or their soil dries out. The obvious solution is to give them water, and water deeply so the plant gets a good drink. The plants should recover quickly if you carry out this simple step.

Sometimes, however, the problem can be damaged roots or a salt build up in the soil. Not much can be done after roots are damaged, but flushing the soil with clean water can help leach out excess salts.

I Have Mold

Different types of molds and mildews attack cannabis at all phases of growth and production. If you fail to recognize this and the mold's growth is left unchecked, eventually you will lose a significant portion of, or even all of, your harvest. When cannabis growers say they have mold, they generally mean they have an outbreak of the dreaded botrytis.

Botrytis, or "gray mold," is the most destructive to cannabis. It requires high humidity conditions (50 percent or higher), and debris from old leaves or bruised, broken plant parts to provide a food base before it invades the plant. Rainy conditions outdoors, high humidity indoors, and the natural leaf drop near harvest time can provide perfect conditions for a botrytis outbreak. To prevent infection, remove dead leaves or damaged tissue from the plants and keep the garden area clean as well. If you accidentally break a plant or take cuttings for propagation, repair the affected area immediately. Once you spot botrytis, remove any infected portion at once, adjust humidity levels, and monitor each plant on a daily basis for continued outbreaks.

Once the plants are hanging, make certain to check humidity levels and to provide excellent air circulation. Examine the plants carefully twice a day and remove any spots of mold as soon as they appear. Some growers take a lighter or barbecue starter and burn the area where they have removed botrytis; this may have the effect of completely drying out the wet, mold infected area and preventing further spread on the plant.

I Have Mites

Spider mites reproduce rapidly in hot conditions like a cannabis grow room; a generation can be completed in as little as five days. Females can produce a dozen eggs daily for at least two weeks, so spider mite populations grow rapidly if left unchecked. Plants under water stress are highly susceptible, so make certain to water on schedule.

Spider mites are so tiny that an initial infestation is easy to miss until you start seeing damage to the plants. Examine your plants closely with a hand-held lens with at least ten times magnification. Spider mite eggs are usually laid near the veins of leaves during the growing season; they look little drops of water until they become cream colored just before hatching. Check all over, but particularly on the undersides of leaves for old hatched egg shells as well as the adult spider mites, their eggs, and the distinctive spider mite webbing.

Adult spider mites have eight legs and an oval body, with two red eyespots near the head end of the body. The immature spider mites resemble the adults, except the newly hatched larvae have only six legs.

Spider mite colonies can contain hundreds of individual mites and produce very distinctive silk webbing on infested leaves. The presence of this webbing is the easiest way to distinguish them from other types of mites. Lightly misting your plants before inspecting them will make the webs much easier for you to see. Act quickly if you spot mites and bathe the plants with an organic insecticidal soap, or use organic Neem oil. Make certain to get the undersides of the leaves and the entire plant; leaving any spider mites behind will just start the cycle all over again.

Other than seeing the spider mites themselves, the first signs of an infestation show up as a scattering of light colored spots on the plant's leaves. The leaves take on a sickly gray or bronze color as the infestation continues, eventually turning yellow and dropping off. The entire plant can become engulfed in spider mite webbing; at that point, destroy the plants and clean and sterilize your grow rooms.

Always check new plants from outside sources very carefully for spider mites. Be especially wary if the plants were started indoors. Keep the new additions isolated from your other plants until you are certain they are not carrying spider mites. This little bit of extra care will pay off over and over.

Deer Are Eating My Plants

Cannabis eaten by deer is primarily a rural grower's problem, but not always. Outdoor growers in more urban areas know that deer are quite apt to move around at night, particularly in cities with large parks like Portland, Oregon, for example. There is usually so much green, well-watered food for deer in a city that the urban grower should worry more about human thieves, not Bambi and his pals.

The rural grower has more trouble if they live in a drought-prone area; all that well-watered, green, delicious cannabis looks worth a lot of risk to a hungry deer. They will jump very high if they need food, so the grower in this area needs to use at least ten-foot fencing—twelve is better and safer.

A grower who lives in a green belt should be less concerned; if you have rose bushes, the deer will prefer them, particularly after the cannabis starts producing resins heavily. A lower fence, even six feet, will suffice; rural deer do not like to jump into anything that could trap them if they have other food choices. It is only during droughts that they get desperate and take risks to eat fenced-in cannabis plants.

Urban deer in drought areas will frequently wander into enclosed areas; they are much less afraid of people, partly because no one can shoot at them. The rural deer are more easily spooked; they know that humans have guns and that they frequently use them.

Some growers save dog hair from clipping their dogs, or get some from a dog groomer friend to put in the brush around an unfenced grow to discourage deer. Other deterrents that sometimes work are sprinkling blood meal around the site or winding string around bushes. Again, the deer will not like how trap-like the string appears and feels.

Tarps or old metal roofing panels laid on the ground around the crop site will discourage deer as well as elk or sheep; the texture and sound make them unwilling to walk across either of these. Just bear in mind that goats have no trouble walking across almost anything, so do not confuse goats with sheep.

Gophers Are Eating the Roots

Many types of burrowing rodents can take up residence in a garden; gophers, pocket gophers, moles, and voles are some of the more common ones. Usually you will notice gophers as their tunnel digging creates mounds of fresh earth; these appear very suddenly and are quite large.

Gophers can be quite destructive to plants that are ground planted. They are not really after your cannabis, but will tunnel right through an unprotected root ball if it gets in their way. The best solution is to line your planting holes with chicken wire, leaving a standing rim of wire at least eight inches in height. This will keep the gophers from making the planting a point of entry, and the lower wire protects the plant's root ball. The exposed chicken wire will also alert you to remove it should you later till the planting area. Unwinding chicken wire from your tiller tines is time-consuming, and wastes chicken wire.

Moles tunnel along just under the surface, and are usually not harmful to cannabis plants, unless they get into a large raised bed and cannot figure out how to get out again. The chicken wire solution will work fine for voles, too.

Voles are small rodents, but they can sometimes girdle a cannabis plant by gnawing away the cambium around the plant's trunk or main stalk; this kills the plant by interrupting the circulation of water and nutrients. Protect the stalk with chicken wire.

All of these rodents can be eradicated by a good garden cat. Make certain you get a cat of proven hunting ability since not all cats are good hunters. Some growers use gopher traps; these can be effective, but always make sure to cover the set trap with a heavy bucket so other animals like pets do not get hurt. Never use poisons. Poisoned gophers suffer horribly and are often caught and eaten by cats, or sometimes the family dog, who are, in turn, poisoned.

Wood Rats Are Taking Branches

If you grow in a wooded area, you and your plants may encounter wood rats (genus *Neotoma*). These are also known as pack rats or trade rats, and are about the size of the common Norway rat that you might see in an alley or dumpsite. They are a very pretty rodent with a furry tail; soft, fine fur; large ears; and light-colored feet and bellies.

The first indication you will have of wood rats is that some of your cannabis will be missing branches. Then some more branches will be missing. Wood rats are mostly active at night, and feed primarily on green vegetation, twigs, and shoots. Most species of the wood rat family build a large stick den or house on the ground or in trees; some of these houses are as big as four feet in size. A nest, usually made of finely shredded plant material, is located within the larger house.

Wood rats show good taste and sense in choosing cannabis branches for building their houses, but as a grower, you must stop them or you will lose your entire crop.

First, locate their stick house nest. This is usually fairly easy as the structures are so large. It will not be too far away from your crop site, so search until you spot the nest. You will find your cannabis branches neatly woven into the structure. Then, sadly for the wood rats, you must destroy the nest. Sometimes this is enough to make the wood rats move on to more friendly territory. Sometimes it's not.

One grower reported success by setting her cannabis containers inside moated circles. The wood rats that tried to cross the water all drowned, probably because they could not climb out of the slippery plastic sides of the moats. Some growers scatter mothballs around the base of their plants; this has varied success, and is not ideal due to the chemical nature of mothballs.

If you must kill them, wood rats are easily trapped with standard rat-sized snap traps. Good baits include peanut butter and dried fruits. As with using any trap, cover or secure it so children or other animals cannot get hurt. Always wear gloves when emptying a trap, as wood rats are a vector for plague and other diseases.

Broken Branches

Although cannabis is usually very strong, a branch will break on occasion, either from accident, high winds, or from the weight of the colas pulling it down and tearing it from the trunk. If this happens, just take the branch in and hang it to dry and use. Fill the wound left on the trunk with some beeswax. Lower branches that start to pull away from the main stalk can be propped with five gallon plastic buckets laid on their sides; the weight of the branch holds it in place, and the bucket supports the too-heavy branch. Higher branches can be propped or tied, but this generally has limited success. You can try to see if the plant responds, but it is generally better to cut and treat with beeswax.

Corn Earworms

Some growers have never had to deal with these little pests while others have had episodes and then did not see them again for years. Corn earworms actually seem more common in outdoor urban grows, perhaps because backyard corn growers are sometimes untidy gardeners and create a habitat for corn earworm moths and their caterpillars. These small, smooth-skinned, green caterpillars generally have with a thin white horizontal racing stripe on their bodies. Their coloration is perfect camouflage for hiding on cannabis; the green is sativa-green, and the thin white stripe looks like a cannabis flower pistil.

The corn earworms love to bore into cannabis buds just as much as they love to bore into the tips of growing ears of corn (hence their name). Sometimes, the first indication that corn earworms are eating a cannabis crop is to actually see an apparently healthy large cola drop from the plant to the ground. Cannabis flowers are very firmly attached to the plant; so something has to eat through the stem to remove a flower.

A corn earworm is more likely to be seen where corn has been growing. An initial infestation starts because a corn earworm moth lays eggs in the soil; these hatch into the little green caterpillars that eat your cannabis, drop back into the soil to pupate, and then become the moth that will lay the eggs to perpetuate this elegant cycle. Unfortunately, this cycle does not suit the grower's purposes, so it must be interrupted.

As soon as you spot the earworms, pop them with your fingers and leave their little corpses on a larger older leaf of the plant. Groom every inch of your plants at least twice day, and pick off the earworms. They treat the cola, or flower, like an ear of tender young corn, so don't just focus your attention on the leaves. Since leaves are starting to fade as the plants produce flowers, you will be grooming the plants every day at this point anyway. Pay more attention to the colas if you have spotted earworms because they like to burrow to the inside of the flower.

If you notice earworms right before or at harvest, you will be able to perform a night capture of most of the earworms left on each plant. Hang the harvested plants as you normally would and put a few light colored tarps underneath. Periodically check the hangings, but the earworms should start to let down from the plant within a few hours in the dark, each on a long, silver, individual thread. Somehow changes in the plant's chemistry tell them the plant is dying (that it has been cut down) and they need to get to the ground to pupate so they can return as the moth in the spring. This is your chance and you must be ruthless about killing them all.

If you grow a well-balanced and organic garden with your cannabis interspersed, you will find that beneficial insects and birds are tremendously helpful. If you do find yourself with an earworm outbreak, birds are your cannabis's best friend.

Earwigs

Earwigs are generally not a problem after your cannabis grows beyond the seedling stage. They can snip off very young seedlings, however, so be careful when you put seedlings outside to harden off. Make sure the area is clean of debris; earwigs hide under bark, in old plant pots, or in any sort of dark hiding place convenient to the plants. A good earwig trap can be made by rolling up newspaper or using short lengths of small PVC pipe. Take a bucket of hot sudsy water with you and tap the traps into the bucket every morning. Some growers protect their seedlings during this phase by placing clean jars over them at night. This is a little time-consuming, depending on the size of your grow site, but only needs to be done for a week at most; the seedlings will get too big to be bothered by earwigs and your traps will have done their work.

Pill Bugs

Pill bugs are actually crustaceans. They are known for their ability to roll into a ball, and are sometimes called roly-polies. They are most active at night and are only really hazardous for cannabis during the short seedling stage of the plants. A very special treat for pill bugs are monocotyledonous leaves, which are first little leaves a seedling opens. Protect your seedlings from pill bugs as you would against earwigs; as soon as the plants are at least eight inches tall, the pill bugs will leave them alone. Pill bugs are generally useful in compost piles where they help break down dead plants and eat different fungi.

Oddly, pill bugs are monogamous. A pair will raise a family in a burrow together and gather food for the young pill bugs until they disperse to start their own families.

Aphids

Sometimes cannabis can be attacked by aphids, a sucking insect that stings the plants. As an aphids feed, they also exude a honeydew or sugary sap that attracts ants and can also make a good environment for black sooty mold. Aphids also spread disease from sick plants to healthy plants as they feed and migrate back and forth. The best solution is to wash the aphids off the plants and buy some ladybugs. Ladybugs come in bulk through mail order, and most garden centers carry them as well.

Slugs and Snails

Both slugs and snails can cut down seedlings and shred leaves of older plants. Protect your seedlings as you would for earwigs, and get rid of the pests by handpicking and destroying. This is best achieved at night when they come out to feed on your plants. Drop the slugs and/or snails into a bucket of soapy water as you pick them. A good dusting of diatomaceous earth around main plant stems is a good way to keep them from getting to larger plants. Diatomaceous earth is made from fossils of freshwater organisms that have been crushed to a fine powder. The powder particles resemble bits of broken glass when observed thru a microscope, and are very destructive to slugs and almost any insect, while remaining harmless to humans and animals. Diatomaceous earth can be found at almost any garden center.

Thrips

Thrips are small, flying, plant-sucking insects that are generally most damaging in greenhouses. Thrips have recently become a problem in soil-less greenhouses that use rockwool and hydroponics. A soil fungus could grow in old soil-floored greenhouses that infected and killed thrips when they dropped to the ground to pupate. Soil-less greenhouses have no damp soil and fungus for biocontrol.

Use sticky traps to catch them on the wing, and apply insecticidal soap spray until you get them under control.

Glossary of Terms

Acid soil
Soil with a pH value of below 7.0.

Acclimatize
The physiological adaptation of a plant to changes in climate or environment, such as light, temperature, or altitude.

Aerate
Loosening packed soil to allow water and air to penetrate.

Alkaline soil
Soil with a pH value above 7.0.

Asexual propagation
Directed reproduction of genetically identical plants, accomplished by taking cuttings.

Ballast
Regulates electrical flow; used in indoor grow systems.

Blood meal
Organic fertilizer containing high nitrogen; made from dried blood from slaughter houses.

Breathing
Term used in the cannabis curing process; opening stored dried cannabis to release chlorophylls.

Bud
Slang term for a cannabis flower.

Calyx
A small pod containing the male or female reproductive organs in cannabis.

Cannabinoid
A unique hydrocarbon in cannabis.

CBC
Cannabichromene, a cannabinoid.

CBD
Cannabidiol, considered to prolong cannabis' psychoactive effect.

Chromosome
Any of the organized components of each cell that carry the plant's individual hereditary material, or DNA.

Clipping
A term for manicuring, or removing the leaves from, dried cannabis flowers.

Clone
A rooted cutting from a plant, or when used as a verb, the asexual propagation of a plant.

Cola
Slang word used for the cannabis flower.

Cold frame
Unheated glass or plastic greenhouse for protection of young plants.

Compost
Fully decomposed organic matter. High in valuable bacteria and nitrogen.

Cotyledons
The rounded seed leaves that first appear on a plant.

Crossing

Creating a hybrid by breeding two unrelated individual plants.

Curing

A slow process where cannabis becomes more palatable and dry enough to store without breathing the containers.

Cutting

A slip taken from a parent plant for asexual propagation by cloning.

Damp off

A damp-loving fungus that attacks young seedlings' initial roots and young clones' stems. Also known as "wire-stem," or Pythium Wilt.

Dioecious

Sexually distinct; the male and female reproductive organs occur on different individual plants. Cannabis is dioecious.

Drill

A seed-planting hole, usually made using a pre-measured stick.

Fan leaves

The largest leaves on cannabis; primarily light gatherers.

Fertilization

To unite male pollen with the female plant ovary.

Fungus

Mold, mushrooms, and mildew are fungi.

Gene pool

Assembly of all gene combinations available in a population.

Genotype

The specific genetic makeup of an individual plant; a combination of genes inherited from the parent plants that is unique.

Germination
The seed sprouting process.

Hardening off
The process of gradually acclimating greenhouse plants to the outdoors.

Hashish
A strong psychoactive made from the compressed resins of the cannabis plant.

Hemp
Very fibrous cannabis with low THC content. Used for making textiles and fuel.

Hermaphrodite
A cannabis plant with flowers of both sexes appearing.

Hybrid
Offspring resulting from cross-breeding two different gene pools.

Indica
A species of cannabis; particularly found in medical cannabis strains.

Leach
Washing or flushing soil of soluble components, achieved by heavy watering.

Leafing
Removing yellowing or dead leaves from flowering plants; also known as grooming.

Marijuana
A common term for cannabis.

Mildew
A powdery mold found on leaves.

Mother plant
A female cannabis plant used as a source for clones by taking cuttings.

Mulch
Surface dressing, preferably used in conjunction with compost, to reduce water evaporation and to provide plant nutrients.

N-P-K
Nitrogen (N), phosphorus (P), and potassium (K); essential elements for plant life.

Organic gardening
Gardening by natural method, without synthetic chemicals.

Phenotype
The expression, or outward form of a plant, created by how the environment influences the genotype.

Photoperiod
Duration of daily exposure to light, whether artificial or natural sunlight.

Photosynthesis
The process in green plants by which carbohydrates are synthesized from carbon dioxide and water using light as an energy source. Plants then release oxygen as a byproduct.

Pistils
Fuzzy white hairs that appear at the tip of the female calyx in pairs. Used to catch male pollen.

Pollen
Microspores that contain the male plant genes.

Pollination
Transfer of male pollen to the female ovules for seed production.

Primordia
The earliest stage of both male and female cannabis flowers that first appear along the main stalk and limbs.

Root ball

The plant's roots and the soil contained by them.

Root bound

A condition where a plant's roots have filled its container.

Sativa

A species of cannabis known for strong psychoactive effect. Frequently crossed with the indica species.

Senescence

A natural phase of decline in a plant; from peak to death.

Sexual propagation

Reproducing plants by fertilization.

Shake

Slang term for lower grade cannabis, meaning mostly leaves.

Sinsemilla

A Spanish word meaning "without seeds," commonly used slang for the preferred state of recreational cannabis for consumption.

Soil-less medium

A mix made of vermiculate, perlite, sand and pumice that is sterile and contains no nutrients.

Sport

An individual or new genetic character, arising or resulting from mutation.

Stamen

The pollen-producing reproductive organ of a flower.

Sticky traps

Any number of organic pest solutions that involve a nontoxic, nondrying sticky substance spread on attractant colored sheets of cardboard.

Strain

A line of offspring from shared ancestors.

Terpene

A hydrocarbon found in resinous plants like cannabis or rosemary; the organic molecule of strong aroma.

THC

Tetrahydrocannabinol, one of the psychoactive chemicals found in cannabis.

Transplanting

The process of transferring plants to larger containers or into the ground.

Trichome

A plant hair that secretes resin.

Vegetative Phase

The growth phase of cannabis that precedes the flowering phase.

Vermiculite

A soil-less medium used by indoor growers for moisture retention.

Web Resources and Organizations

Americans for Safe Access
www.safeaccessnow.org

Students for Sensible Drug Policy
www.ssdp.org

National Organization for the Reform of Marijuana Laws (NORML)
www.norml.org

Marijuana Policy Project
www.mpp.org

Media Awareness Project (MAP Inc.)
www.mapinc.org

Drug Policy Alliance
www.drugpolicy.org

International Association for Cannabis as Medicine (IACM)
www.cannabis-med.org

Law Enforcement Against Prohibition (LEAP)
www.leap.cc

Patients Out of Time
www.MedicalCannabis.com

APPENDIX C

Helpful Books for Further Reading

McVay, Douglas A., Editor. *Drug War Facts*, compiled by Common Sense for Drug Policy, see *www.drugwarfacts.org* for regular updates.

Gray, Judge James P. *Why Our Drug Laws Have Failed and What We Can Do About It.* (Temple University Press: 2001).

Cervantes, Jorge. *Marijuana Horticulture: The Indoor/Outdoor Medical Grower's Bible.* (Van Patton Publishing: 2006, see *www.marijuanagrowing.com* for distributors).

Clarke, Robert Connell. *Marijuana Botany; An Advanced Study: The Propagation and Breeding of Distinctive Cannabis.* (And/Or Press, Berkeley, CA: 1981).

Rodale, J.I., Editor. *How to Grow Vegetables and Fruits by the Organic Method.* (Compiled by the staff of *Organic Gardening and Farming Magazine*, Rodale Press).

Pollan, Michael. *The Botany of Desire, A Plant's Eye View of the World.* (Random House, Inc., 2002).

Rosenthal, Ed and Steve Kubby with S. Newhart. *Why Marijuana Should Be Legal.* (Thunder's Mouth Press, An Imprint of Avalon Publishing Group, Inc.: 1996, 2003).

Miron, Jeffrey A. *The Budgetary Implications of Marijuana Prohibition.* (Harvard University: 2005).

Zimmerman, Bill, with Rick Bayer and Nancy Crumpacker. *Is Marijuana the Right Medicine for You? A Factual Guide to Medical Uses of Marijuana.* (Keats: 1998).

Russo, Ethan and Franjo Grotenhermen, Editors. *Handbook of Cannabis Therapeutics: From Bench to Bedside.* (Haworth Press: 2006).

Zimmer, Lynn, and John Morgan. *Marijuana Myths, Marijuana Facts: A Review of the Scientific Evidence.* (The Lindesmith Center: 1997). *www.marijuanafacts.org*

Grinspoon, Lester, and James Bakalar. *Marihuana: The Forbidden Medicine.* (Yale University Press: 1997).

Rosenthal, Ed, Dale Gieringer, and Tod Mikuriya. *Marijuana Medical Handbook: A Guide to Therapeutic Use.* (Quick American Archives: 1997).

Mikuriya, Tod, Editor. *Marijuana: Medical Papers 1839–1972.* (Medi-Comp Press: 1973). Online at *www.mikuriya.com/mmp.html* and *www.mikuriya.com/cannabis.html.*

Index

We Have EVERYTHING® on Anything!

With more than 19 million copies sold, **the Everything® series** has become one of America's favorite resources for solving problems, learning new skills, and organizing lives. Our brand is not only recognizable—it's also welcomed.

The series is a hand-in-hand partner for people who are ready to tackle new subjects—like you!

For more information on the Everything® series, please visit *www.adamsmedia.com*

The Everything® list spans a wide range of subjects, with more than 500 titles covering 25 different categories:

Business	History	Reference
Careers	Home Improvement	Religion
Children's Storybooks	Everything Kids	Self-Help
Computers	Languages	Sports & Fitness
Cooking	Music	Travel
Crafts and Hobbies	New Age	Wedding
Education/Schools	Parenting	Writing
Games and Puzzles	Personal Finance	
Health	Pets	